EDUCATIONAL JUSTICE

Educational Justice

Teaching and Organizing against
the Corporate Juggernaut

HOWARD RYAN

with Debra Goodman, Joel Jordan, *and* Joseph Zeccola

MONTHLY REVIEW PRESS
New York

Library of Congress Cataloging-in-Publication Data:

Names: Ryan, Howard, 1953– author.
Title: Educational justice : teaching and organizing against the corporate
  juggernaut / by Howard Ryan with Debra Goodman, Joel Jordan, and Joseph
  Zeccola.
Description: New York : Monthly Review Press, [2016] | Includes
  bibliographical references and index.
Identifiers: LCCN 2016039149 | ISBN 9781583676134 (pbk.) | ISBN
9781583676141 (hardcover)
Subjects: LCSH: Business and education—United States. | Privatization in
  education—United States. | Teachers' unions—United States.
Classification: LCC LC1085.2 .R93 2016 | DDC 379.1—dc23 LC record available
at https://lccn.loc.gov/2016039149

MONTHLY REVIEW PRESS, NEW YORK
www.monthlyreview.org

Typeset in Dante Monotype

5 4 3 2 1

Contents

Acknowledgements

A GREAT MANY PEOPLE—TEACHERS, PARENTS, students, union leaders, academics, activists from various fields—contributed to this project through interviews, consultations, and other supports. Several folks graciously housed me while I visited their cities; local teachers unions in Madison, Wisconsin; Washington, DC; New Orleans; and British Columbia extended office space to me.

I would like to thank the three contributing authors—Debra Goodman, Joel Jordan, and Joseph Zeccola—for bringing their expertise to the book. Each of them also gave very helpful feedback on my draft chapters. Others who read and critiqued various chapters include Bill Ayers, Kate Beaudet-Garcia, Alex Caputo-Pearl, Carole Edelsky, Cathy Garcia, Latina King, Sarah Knopp, Jackson Potter, Jim Randels, Jerry Skinner, Jane Slaughter, and Eric Wagner.

I am indebted to *Labor Notes*, which helped shape the vision of rank-and-file unionism that informs this book. *Labor Notes* also instilled in me a strong appreciation for on-the-job organizing stories, influencing my use of organizing case studies in the book. My study of corporate school reform as a global phenomenon, as reflected in chapter 1, was much aided by Yanina Norma Parada, an educator who speaks widely on public education and human rights issues in Honduras, and by Larry Kuehn, research director for the British Columbia Teachers' Federation. Both kindly arranged interviews for me and introduced me to lead activists and resource people in their respective locales.

Finally, I would like to thank the Monthly Review Press team for their faith in the project and Monthly Review Press editor Michael Yates for his fine guidance.

Introduction

July 1, 2005: A pro-corporate Department of Education Reform is established at the University of Arkansas, the state's flagship public university, aided by a $10 million gift from the Walton Foundation, owners of Walmart. The university would be a willing partner: it had previously received a record-breaking $300 million gift from the Waltons.[1]

ᴗer 2008: Microsoft founder Bill Gates is visited by a pair .ey seekers. One is director of a national group of state .1ool chiefs; the other runs an education think tank. The two ask Gates to back a privately run educational initiative. The billionaire agrees, and thus is born the Common Core State Standards that now drive the nation's public schools.[2]

July 25, 2009: President Obama launches Race to the Top, a program offering federal grants to states that adopt Common Core and other school reform measures favored by corporate interests. Hired to run the program at the Department of Education would be Joanne Weiss, an executive of NewSchools Venture Fund, a group that funnels venture capitalist money into pro-privatization school initiatives.[3]

RECENT STORIES OF PRIVATE AND CORPORATE takeover in education—with its regime of high-stakes tests, deskilled teaching, under-resourced public schools, and billionaire-backed charter school chains—could easily fill books, and the pages ahead contain many such stories. However, as this book's title— *Educational Justice: Teaching and Organizing against the Corporate Juggernaut*—makes clear, the authors support the democratic resistance. We offer theory, strategy, and organizing case studies to inform and inspire those who are working to rebuild public education and put an end to the corporate occupation of our schools. The book's particular focus is K–12 education in the United States, while it also addresses global education trends and connects these to broad economic forces.

When I embarked on this book project in summer 2011, I had minimal background in the K–12 field. I had taught college writing and worked for many years as a union organizer in higher education. But my interest in the plight of public schools had grown after my hire the previous fall as a journalist at *Labor Notes*, a media and resource center for labor activists. I would cover teachers and public sector labor for the center's magazine. My first story treated a contentious teachers union election in Washington. The D.C. public schools had, since 2007, been led by Michelle Rhee, a Teach for America (TFA) alumna who had become a media darling for her willingness to fire allegedly bad teachers. In summer 2010, Rhee had fired over two hundred teachers, many because of low student test scores. The fired teachers were overwhelmingly black and veteran, whereas many of their replacements were white rookies from TFA. The mass firing was aided by a recently settled union contract that had sharply reduced D.C. teachers' job security. To help swing the contract deal, Rhee had engaged billionaire school reform philanthropists including Eli Broad and the Waltons, whose donations funded a merit pay scheme. One of the story's central controversies was how the union, rather than fighting for a decent contract, had peacefully accepted terms that would prove injurious not only for the city's black teachers but also for its predominantly black and low-income students, who would increasingly be served by inexperienced teachers.[4]

My grasp of the K–12 field deepened that fall with the release of education historian Diane Ravitch's *The Death and Life of the Great American School System*, which placed the D.C. events in the context of a national assault on teachers and schools. That same fall saw release of *Waiting for Superman*, the documentary that glorified charter schools and the anti-teacher heroics of Michelle Rhee while it vilified teachers unions. I wrote a critical review of the film[5] and later learned that Bill Gates and Eli Broad had co-sponsored the project.[6] My education reporting also brought me into contact with teachers who were organizing rank-and-file caucuses inside their unions, challenging traditional leaderships that too often align themselves with corporate interests. The caucuses were building a new social-movement teacher unionism, the national exemplar of which would be the Chicago Teachers Union.[7]

By the time I left Labor Notes in order to focus on this book, I had become convinced that public schools had a particular importance in the lifeblood of communities, and that the fight to defend public schools had particular potential for energizing larger movements for democracy and social justice. But I had much to learn and explore. On the one hand, I wanted to better understand the corporate assault on schools: Who was really driving it? What were their motivations? Where was the project heading? On the other hand, I wanted a broader view of the resistance, its various trajectories and possibilities. I interviewed scores of teachers and teacher unionists, as well as parent and student activists, in a dozen U.S. cities. I also met with teacher activists in British Columbia and Honduras, and consulted with education professors in the United States and abroad—which helped me gain a more global view. Along the way, I secured the help of three talented writer-educators. Debra Goodman, a literacy professor at Hofstra University, and Joel Jordan, a retired Los Angeles teacher and now teachers union consultant, have each contributed a chapter to this book. Joseph Zeccola, a high school English teacher in Los Angeles, coauthored one of the book's organizing case studies and provided editorial assistance and guidance.

The book is composed of three parts. Part I, addressing the corporate assault on schools, begins with a chapter outlining corporate school reform and then inquiring into its underlying aims. The identified aims link school reform to wider corporate goals and strategies in the United States and globally. Chapter 2 examines a "partnership" strategy, or non-adversarial unionism, that has aligned the two major national teacher organizations with corporate interests. The chapter also points to an alternative *social-movement unionism*—democratic, militant, community-connected—that is breaking ground nationally and has won teachers union leadership in several U.S. locales.

Part II takes up resistance to the corporate assault. In chapter 3, a Chicago elementary school mobilizes full-bore—teachers, students, parents, religious and community leaders—to fend off a school district plan to hand the site to a charter high school. In chapter 4, teachers stand together to challenge a Chicago high school principal who undermines the school's mission through unilateral program cuts and a bullying predisposition. In the process, the teachers build a more participatory union and make common cause with students and parents. In chapter 5, Joel Jordan reflects on teachers union strategy for public education, addressing both the challenges and possibilities. The chapter includes an innovative statewide approach to fighting privatization, which is currently in development in California.

Part III turns to a different arena of education organizing that I call *democratic school transformation*. This begins with Debra Goodman, in chapter 6, who describes whole language as a theory of literacy and language learning, as a democratic pedagogy, and as a teachers' movement that blossomed in the 1980s and 90s and holds important lessons for today's public education fight. Chapter 7 turns to a group of elementary school teachers in Los Angeles who create a "professional learning community" and challenge a resistant principal as they shift their reading instruction from a rigid, scripted model to a more democratic and effective "balanced literacy" model. In chapter 8, which I coauthored with Joseph Zeccola, teachers and community partners at a historically neglected Los Angeles high school design and pilot a cross-disciplinary curriculum that connects classroom learning with community action.

An afterword concludes with general reflections on organizing strategy and next steps for the educational justice movement.

Resistance and Transformation

Education activists often describe our work in terms of *resistance*—and I do as well—since we are resisting the corporate education juggernaut. But all too often, when we are opting out of high-stakes tests, or marching against budget cuts, or protesting some other new blow dished out by corporate interests, we haven't had time to construct our positive alternatives to corporate schooling. My proposition is that the building of positive school models, living examples of educational justice, can be as strategically powerful as the resistance initiatives. In fact, the positive models may themselves be considered a kind of resistance; but I prefer to distinguish these with the term *democratic school transformation*. School transformational work can have its pitfalls: a project may come to be seen as an end in itself, or may operate in isolation from a larger educational justice movement that is challenging corporate power. On the other hand, transformational work that is consciously linked to the wider anti-corporate resistance can enrich the latter.

Though Part III's coverage of school transformation focuses on teaching and pedagogical/curricular change, the term *transformation* is defined here more broadly to encompass any project that effects change in a public school, or that establishes a new public school, based on models that strengthen democracy, such as:

- a shift in pedagogy from corporate-defined or scripted instruction to a locally defined model driven by students' own curiosity, interests, and purposes;
- a shift from a traditional punitive model of school discipline to a restorative justice model, whereby students learn problem-solving and conflict resolution skills;
- a parent engagement program that extends to parents an effective voice in school governance;
- a small learning academy—or "school within a school"— that personalizes learning and includes an effective voice for students and staff;
- a curriculum that gears classrooms toward study and action around community problems.

A transformational approach should not overlook the many obstacles to democratic schooling imposed by the corporate regime. Policies that starve schools of resources, or that reduce education to testing, require direct challenge and resistance. But the approach looks for spaces and opportunities for democratizing initiatives, or "contesting the terrain," which can and do arise within traditional institutions. If the project is done well, the transformation can serve the wider movement in a few ways. First, it can provide a living democratic model that gives a movement vision and hope, helping people believe that another world is possible. Second, it can develop teacher, parent, and student leaders at the school-site level, or in some cases in cross-school or citywide projects. And if those involved target achievable goals, the transformation can extend to participants the political confidence that comes with winning. Blocks Together, a community organization on Chicago's West Side, joins resistance with transformation in its work with youth to challenge criminalizing policies in the schools. On the one hand, the organization resists "zero tolerance" discipline that overuses suspension/expulsion and resists school safety models that emphasize policing, metal detectors, and surveillance cameras. On the other hand, its campaigns have in many cases won concrete improvements that push schools and the school district toward restorative justice. As a member of the Chicago Teachers Union (CTU) community board,[8] Blocks Together consciously links its school transformation work to the larger citywide battle against school closures and privatization, and its youth leaders engage in that battle. It also affiliates with Dignity in Schools, which "challenges the systemic problem of pushout in our nation's schools" and has member organizations and local chapters in several states.[9]

Another kind of transformational strategy is suggested in the "schools our students deserve" contract campaign model pioneered by CTU.[10] Incorporating a vision of authentic school reform into their contract platform helped Chicago teachers win parent and community support for their historic seven-day strike in September 2012. The contract settlement included several concrete gains for school quality, such as ensuring textbooks on day one of the school year; bettering working conditions for clinicians, counselors, and special education teachers; and committing the school district to add 512 art, music, and physical education teachers.[11] The "schools that students deserve" approach to teacher contract campaigns has since been applied in Portland, Oregon; St. Paul, Minnesota; and Los Angeles.[12]

Public Education and Democracy

Resistance and *transformation* are offered here as conceptual tools or paradigms to help us reflect upon the project of education organizing. A third such paradigm is *democracy*. Public education is fundamentally about democracy, equipping young people with skills for effective citizenship and participation. Official sources will sometimes allude to such aims. "Since our founding," remarks former U.S. education secretary Arne Duncan, "America's leaders have recognized that one of the most important purposes of educating the nation's citizens is to protect and strengthen democracy."[13] But his words ring hollow. If democracy were truly the official aim, then why aren't our schools and classrooms organized as rich laboratories for democratic innovation? Democracy, after all, is best learned through its practice.

Suppose, in building an education organizing strategy, we begin by assessing our school or school district along democratic lines, with questions such as these:

Student voice: Are the students situated as co-directors of their own learning and as members of a learning community practicing the arts of collaboration and citizenship? Or, conversely, are students following instructions and being groomed in the arts of obedience and compliance?

Teacher voice: Does the school or district regard teachers as empowered professionals? Or are teachers expected to implement prepackaged programs driven by standards and tests?

Parent/community voice: Does the school or district engage parents and community? Is it responsive to their needs and concerns?

Educational resources and equity: Which communities boast well-resourced and stable schools that empower students, teachers, and parents? Which communities do not?

System administration and education policymaking: Is the orientation democratic or autocratic?

We could then ask, Where do opportunities lay for engaging teachers, parents, and students in the quest for democracy? Each of the organizing case studies presented in this book (chapters 3, 4, 7, and 8) illustrate a school community that rallies together for democratic pedagogy or democratic policy. Likewise, in chapter 6, Debra Goodman describes a pedagogical movement that embraced democracy in fundamental and practical ways.

The success of an educational justice movement also depends intimately on another democratic quest—that of transforming the teachers unions into organizations that enfranchise and empower the members, that ally with communities, and that expose and confront corporate power in schools and beyond. That unionized teachers are now embracing this aim around the country, and vying for and sometimes winning union leadership, is one of today's greatest sources of hope for public education. The challenges and promises of teacher unionism at city and state levels are taken up in chapters 2 and 5. But equally critical is what happens at the individual school site, exemplified at Chicago's Kelvyn Park High School (chapter 4), where a shift in union culture opened the door to an effective schoolwide fight for quality instruction and programs. The Kelvyn Park story, focused here on the years 2009 and 2010, mirrored similar initiatives at other Chicago schools, all building toward a new kind of citywide union, as the feisty Caucus of Rank-and-File Educators took leadership of CTU in June 2010.

As asserted in chapter 1, a fundamental aim of corporate school reform is to squelch democracy by converting schools into centers of obedience training for working-class youth. For those who have a different vision for schools, we hope that this book may support and inspire your work.

Part 1

The
Problem

1

The Hidden Aims of School Reform

Howard Ryan

We can make market forces work better for the poor if we can
develop a more creative capitalism.
—BILL GATES, Harvard Commencement, 2007 [1]

IN 1983, A BLUE-RIBBON COMMISSION appointed by the Reagan
administration issued a report, *A Nation at Risk: The Imperative for
Educational Reform*, which attributed America's falling global economic competitiveness to mediocre teachers and schools. The
report received extensive media coverage, issuing similar harsh judg-
ments of the nation's public schools. *Fortune* magazine remarked
that the "open classrooms" of the 1970s had turned schools into
"dens of babble," and that school superintendents "hire the worst
of each new crop of graduating teachers."[2] *Newsweek* claimed that
the quality of education was in decline despite public school spending having more than doubled in the prior decade.[3] An educational
crisis had placed the nation's economy at risk, according to official
sources, and something needed to be done. Thus was born a school
reform movement that has sustained, intensified, and expanded
globally for more than three decades.

The school reformers have rarely proposed changes—such
as increased resources for high-poverty schools, or stronger
professional support for teachers—that might actually enhance
teaching and learning conditions. The argument, rather, is that

"great teachers" will succeed regardless of conditions. What schools needed, according to the reformers, were rigorous standards enforced by testing and accountability systems. Plus, school systems needed to shift from public to private control in order to engage the creativity of the market. "Institutions of democratic control are inherently destructive of school autonomy and inherently conducive to bureaucracy," theorized John Chubb and Terry Moe in their influential 1990 book, *Politics, Markets, and America's Schools*. Under a private system, by contrast, market forces would stir excellence and "weed out, through natural selection" the low-performing schools.[4]

Unacknowledged by Chubb and Moe, and by a large number of similar authors, is that the modern school reform movement is a project of corporate interests and a cohort that Diane Ravitch has named the Billionaire Boys' Club.[5] One need only glance at the contributors' list for Achieve, the lead think tank driving the Common Core State Standards. Besides the Gates Foundation, backers include AT&T, Boeing, DuPont, Exxon Mobil, General Electric, and IBM.[6] What motivates such companies and billionaire philanthropists such as Bill Gates? Is school reform, at least by intention, a rich people's movement to help poor kids?

Public education activism needs grounding in an analysis of the problems before us and, most immediately, of the corporate assault on schools. Here I approach the topic from a specific angle that I hope will prove useful to education activists: an inquiry into the underlying aims of corporate school reform. Given the lack of transparency in the reform movement and the corporate world generally, our task is necessarily speculative. From their public statements, we learn only that the reformers want to "prepare America's children for success in college and careers" (Barack Obama), "give low-income and minority students a world-class education" (Bill Gates), and help Americans "maintain our standard of living" (Eli Broad).[7] Speculation about hidden aims, and the marshalling of evidence and counter-evidence, is nevertheless worthwhile. It can help an educational justice movement make sense of complicated forces; it can inform our strategic planning and the setting of our own objectives. Although K–12 education is the particular focus of the present chapter and book, it should be noted that higher education is equally facing corporate takeover and with a similar agenda.[8]

Definitions

Certain terms need definition in this chapter. The terms *school reform* and *corporate school reform* are used here synonymously, referring to a package of public policies, private investments, and informal processes through which corporate and private actors are seizing control of education. Alternate terms such as *school corporatization, corporate schooling,* and the *corporate school agenda* refer to that same package, whose key components include:

- The setting of curricular standards, such as the Common Core State Standards, by national or state bodies with no effective voice for teachers, parents, or local schools and communities.
- High-stakes testing and so-called data-driven teaching.
- Sanctions against allegedly failing schools (as measured by test scores) leading to closure, or "turnaround" with mass firing of staff, or conversion to charter schools.
- School system restructuring that favors privatization or reduces levers of local and democratic control; the latter would include removing elected school boards and shifting to mayoral or direct state control of schools.
- Weakening teachers' job security, professional voice, and union organization. This includes the scripting of instruction, punitive teacher evaluation systems, capturing of university schools of education by corporate interests, and shifting away

from university-based teacher preparation toward minimal training through private agencies.

School privatization, a subset of corporate school reform, encompasses charter schools, which are publicly funded but privately operated; voucher programs, a form of public subsidy for private schools; and the outsourcing of public school management and services to private contractors. Other forms of privatization include the defunding and closing of public schools, and the introduction of public school fees and tuitions. Finally, though the school reform movement is top-down in character rather than grassroots, we will nonetheless identify it as a *movement*—a network of companies, entrepreneurs, foundations, advocacy groups, think tanks, policymakers, and education leaders who work together to enact policies and effect change.

Progressive Interpretations of Corporate Reform

Progressive educators and activists have challenged the official and elite rationales for corporate school reform. Yet progressives themselves have varied opinions about the corporate movement's aims and purposes. Three influential perspectives merit discussion. One very common analysis sees corporate reform as a scheme to turn schooling into profits. Referring to the charter school push, David Sirota sees "cutthroat businesspeople making shrewd financial investments" and wealthy CEOs "getting rich off of schoolchildren."[9] In a similar vein are Michelle Fine and Michael Fabricant, who observe that, with the American empire losing ground to global competitors, ruling groups have "opened a fire sale" on the public sector including schools: "We may be witnessing the cannibalization of our children's future as their public assets are being sold to private sector bidders."[10]

School-related profits clearly play large in the mix of reform objectives. Corporatization of schools means expanding markets for education companies, technology companies, real estate investors, and others. Yet school profiteering doesn't explain why an airplane manufacturer or an oil company backs Common Core. Or consider a philanthropy such as the Doris and Donald Fisher Fund, which has given more than $60 million to the KIPP (Knowledge Is Power Program) charter chain, $37 million to the Charter School Growth Fund, and over $12 million to Teach for America.[11] Barring some evidence to the contrary, it does not appear that the Fishers—founders of The Gap clothing stores—had a plan to cash in from their charity.

Another progressive interpretation is that of Elizabeth Bloom, co-editor of a recent book on resisting corporate reform, who highlights the role of neoliberal ideology. Rich corporate donors, she says, "are motivated by neoliberal political and economic ideology that favors marketing virtually all aspects of public life." The concept is that schools will improve if forced to compete. "These people believe that public education is bad, and in fact the whole public sector is bad, and it needs to be privatized and marketized in order to save it."[12] Neoliberalism (taken up in the next section) certainly plays an important role in corporate reform, although ideology alone doesn't provide a complete picture since, as already observed, some companies support school reform because of the profits to be made.

A third progressive stance likewise points to corporate reform's neoliberalism, but links it to an overarching aim of sustaining a system of racism and white supremacy. Such is the perspective of Bree Picower and Edwin Mayorga, core leaders of the New York Collective of Radical Educators and editors of a recent volume, *What's Race Got to Do With It?* With contributions from some of the most respected thinkers in the educational justice movement, *What's Race* documents how the corporate assault on U.S. public schools has particularly targeted students of color and communities of color. A chapter by Brian Jones, for example, points out how corporate reform, which claims the mantle of civil rights, has worked to undermine a historic civil rights victory: public sector unionization for African Americans. "Unions in general," Jones observes, "and public sector unions in particular have been central to wealth accumulation and social mobility for African Americans." Today, however, corporate reform has brought falling employment of black teachers in many large urban school districts, with deleterious impact on African-American prosperity.[13]

What's Race also places school racial inequities within a larger analytic framework, presented in Picower and Mayorga's introduction. Quoting educators Louise Derman-Sparks and Carol Brunson Phillips, the authors position school reform within "a web of economic, political, social, and cultural structures" that unequally distributes "privilege, resources and power in favor of the dominant racial group at the expense of all other racial groups." It is critical, the authors add, to "name this system and process of domination," that being "White supremacy."[14]

While their book offers compelling analyses of corporate reform's racist impact, Picower and Mayorga's "integrated racial and economic framework" has an important shortcoming: it does not clearly identify the powerholders who drive corporate school reform or who shape the larger political and social structures. Picower and Mayorga seem to point the finger at white people as a group—with school reform described as a system "set up" by whites, and white supremacy defined as "the way in which our society was founded and remains organized so that White people are at the top of the hierarchy of power."[15]

While whites as a group, without doubt, reap educational and other privileges relative to people of color,[16] most whites are far from being "at the top of the hierarchy of power" in a class society ruled by corporate elites. Moreover, some blacks (such as Obama) enjoy class power far beyond that of working-class whites. Any analysis of corporate reform, or of what Picower and Mayorga call "racial capitalism," would be woefully inadequate without addressing issues of class power and how that impacts education policymaking. Although the authors do make reference to class, and present their book's framework as a "race and class synthesis,"[17] their various other statements overlook class.

Very likely, Picower and Mayorga do recognize the powerful role of corporate elites in directing corporate school reform; the book's chapters mention various corporate players. What the authors do not do is spell out the specific role of corporate interests within their frameworks on school reform, white supremacy, or racial capitalism. Perhaps, for example, the authors would contend that the CEOs and billionaires who sponsor corporate reform are out to advance white supremacy as much as—or more than—advancing corporate and class interests. In any case, the perspective needs more fleshing out. Demonstrating corporate reform's wide racist impact, as the book does, is not the same as demonstrating who is running the show or toward what ends.

What's Race underscores a continuing debate—which bears on education and across the social sciences—about race, class, gender, other forms of stratification, and the relationship among these.[18] The present chapter adopts a class-based Marxian framework in which social power under capitalism grows out of the elite ownership of production and then moves out to impact every other social arena. A working assumption is that the corporate drivers of school reform are acting, first and foremost, out of corporate interests. These corporate actors share a common allegiance *as a class* toward aggrandizing wealth and power, and they engage institutional racism and other stratification systems that have wide support in mass consciousness to help them achieve their goals. Stratification and hierarchy benefit the corporate class by squelching democracy, silencing diverse voices, and facilitating control from above, which helps to explain the hierarchical character of corporate school reform, including its racism. The analysis below zeroes in on the corporate actors, situates their school reform project in a historic and global context, identifies distinct aims and interests among their ranks, and highlights a particular sector of the corporate class that appears to be globally dominant in the movement for corporate schooling.

Neoliberalism and a Bosses' Revolt

A historic perspective can shed light on the purposes of corporate school reform. The project grows out of a broader corporate movement, a hyper-capitalism that took root in the 1970s in the United States and Britain, and which came to dominate the globe from the 1980s forward. In prior decades, the economic model of John Maynard Keynes—which, in its progressive versions, emphasized full employment and a strong welfare state—had enjoyed global preeminence. The Keynesian approach was expressed in President Roosevelt's New Deal in the 1930s and President Johnson's War on Poverty, rolled out in 1964. But in the seventies, corporate leaders shifted away from the Keynesian framework in favor of Milton Friedman and Friedrich Hayek's neoliberalism, which professed faith in market forces.[19] Friedman, awarded the 1976 Nobel Prize in Economics, would serve as adviser for both Prime Minister Margaret Thatcher and President Ronald Reagan, under whom neoliberalism began its now global reign. While first postulated as an economic theory, neoliberalism also became a political ideology and policy paradigm that, as Peter Evans and William Sewell describe, extols the private sector and associates government programs with inefficiency, corruption, and incompetence. The policy paradigm includes lowering taxes, disempowering labor unions, and suppressing state regulation of business; globally, it supports free-trade agreements and the unrestricted movement of capital across borders. Neoliberal values emphasize entrepreneurship, self-reliance, and individualism, equating the "pursuit of self-interest and consumer satisfaction with human freedom."[20] Though proponents speak of the free market and limited government, neoliberal practice actually includes a strong role for the state when it serves corporate purposes—as in aggressive military policy, education "accountability," or bailing out Wall Street when the market crashes.

The corporate neoliberal movement emerged partly in response to intensified global economic competition and falling rates of profit, as Japan and West Germany came to challenge the U.S. reign in global markets in the mid-1960s and after.[21] But it was equally a response to democratic movements that were springing up around the world in the sixties and early seventies. In the United States, movements for civil rights, women's equality, student power on college campuses, and against the war in Vietnam were challenging social hierarchies and injustices of all kinds. The country saw a wave of strikes that included teachers who were unionizing nationally. These efforts won advances: civil rights and anti-poverty programs; union rights and workplace safety; environmental and consumer protection laws; free speech at the universities. The spirit of the sixties also spilled over into classrooms, in a movement of independent "free schools" that experimented with democratic teaching models,[22] and in public schools where some teachers were exploring multicultural and learner-centered pedagogies that empowered students, as opposed to drilling them with worksheets and the memorization of facts.

None of these developments were received well by the country's right wing or by corporate leaders, who pushed back with a reassertion of corporate power that continues to this day. A movement that one writer describes as a "revolt of the bosses"[23] and another as "the business rebellion"[24] was urged along by an August 1971 memo sent by corporate lawyer Lewis Powell to a friend at the U.S. Chamber of Commerce; after being leaked to the *Washington Post*, the memo was distributed widely. Powell warned that the attack on the "American free enterprise system" is "gaining momentum and converts." He singled out leftist college professors and especially consumer advocate Ralph Nader, who had become "a legend in his own time and an idol of millions" and, in the words of *Fortune* magazine, "aimed at smashing utterly the target of his hatred, which is corporate power." Powell's remedy was clear and urgent: "Independent and uncoordinated activity by individual corporations, as important as this is, will not be sufficient. Strength lies in organization, in careful long-range planning and implementation, in consistency of action over an indefinite period of years, in the scale of financing available only through joint effort."[25] Two months after his memo, Powell was appointed to the U.S. Supreme Court, where he would serve for fifteen years.

Business leaders answered Powell's call. In 1972, the heads of General Electric and Alcoa, an aluminum company, spearheaded formation of the Business Roundtable, an organization of two hundred big-company CEOs that collaborates with the U.S. Chamber of Commerce but with a more aggressive posture. The following year came two new right-wing think tanks—the American Legislative Exchange Council and the Heritage Foundation. By 1978, big business had built an army of two thousand trade associations operating in Washington with a combined staff of fifty thousand employees.[26] The number of corporate political action committees skyrocketed from 89 in 1974 to 1,467 in 1982.[27] By the end of Reagan's first term of office, the corporate sector had clearly swung national politics its way. Reagan dealt the labor movement a huge blow by firing eleven thousand striking air traffic controllers in 1981. He cut taxes for the rich, slashed services for the poor, and weakened enforcement of environmental and workplace safety laws. The bosses' revolt combined new government priorities (deregulation, tax shifts, weakening the social safety net) with new industrial priorities (cutting wages and

benefits, moving jobs abroad to access cheaper labor, deunioniza-
tion). All of this helped the richest Americans further concentrate
wealth. The top 1 percent doubled its share of national income
(including capital gains), from 9 percent in 1978 to 19.8 percent in
2010, according to data compiled by Emmanuel Saez, director of
the Center for Equitable Growth at UC Berkeley. In 2010 alone,
that increased share translated into a $434 billion expansion.[28]

The rightward tide swept into the schools as well. The 1983
Reagan commission report, *A Nation at Risk,* identified an "education crisis" and prescribed more rigor and testing.[29] States began
adopting high school exit exams and other standardized tests,
whose political significance was pinpointed by New York City
educator Ira Shor: "In the 1960s, masses of people confronted the
system together. Now, the system was confronting you, alone."[30] In
language arts, a promising movement of whole language teachers,
who shifted power to their students in reading/writing workshops, came to the fore in the eighties, only to be beaten back in
the late nineties and early 2000s by a coalition of conservatives and
textbook publishers touting "systematic phonics" and corporate-
scripted reading programs (see chapter 6). Teachers committed
to bringing multicultural and social justice perspectives to their
language arts and social studies classrooms found less space or support for such departures as school districts increasingly demanded
test-prep instruction.[31] Today, the resurgent conservatism in classrooms is epitomized by the KIPP charter schools' widely emulated
"no excuses" model, which imposes a militaristic discipline—"sit
up," "nod," "track the speaker with your eyes." Obedient students
are rewarded with privileges and "scholar dollars," while students
who break the stern rules face demerits, humiliations such as facing
the wall, or suspension/expulsion.[32]

When placed in its historic context, corporate school reform
becomes an extension of a neoliberal bosses' revolt, seek-
ing to grapple both with threats from afar in global economic

competition and threats at home in grassroots movements demanding democracy and equality.

Aims of Corporate Reform: Mythical and Real

Corporate school reformers have sterling intentions, according to their statements. They want to ensure college and career readiness, promote civil rights and educational equity, stir excellence by making schools compete for students, and foster economic prosperity. Their economic rationale figures especially large, as an Obama White House position statement declared: "America's ability to compete begins each day, in classrooms across the nation—and President Obama knows we must comprehensively strengthen and reform our education system in order to be successful in a 21st century economy."[33] Before theorizing as to the real aims of the corporate reformers, let's examine their oft-repeated economic case for school reform.

When the Reagan administration launched its campaign to remake schools, it needed a powerful rationale and sense of urgency. *Why Johnny Still Can't Read*, the cry of a 1981 pro-phonics book, wouldn't be enough. Instead, Reagan's education commission said that our nation was at risk. Others were "matching and surpassing" our educational attainments, and the educational crisis had created economic crisis: "Our once unchallenged preeminence in commerce, industry, science, and technological innovation is being overtaken by competitors throughout the world."[34] Here, a set of economic propositions was fashioned that would become a permanent fixture in corporate school reform messaging in the United States and globally.

One proposition points to education as the linchpin of economic growth. This makes use of a "human capital" theory pioneered by neoliberal theorists Gary Becker and Theodore Schultz at the University of Chicago in the 1950s and 60s. The theory holds that, by advancing your own education (that is, going to college), your economic productivity increases, and this, in turn, gives rise to higher income over the course of your life. Then, by extension, if many are better educated, an entire nation prospers through enhanced productivity.[35]

A second related proposition is that our nation suffers a "skills gap": employers are having difficulty filling skilled positions that are vital to company survival and national prosperity. Corporate reformers document the skills gap with regular reports. In a period when China doubled its yearly STEM (science / technology / engineering / math) graduates and India's tripled, U.S. STEM degrees grew by only 24 percent, warns one corporate-sponsored report.[36] Employers and business groups add testimonials. Young people "arrive at our doors unable to write a proper paragraph," says the Business Roundtable.[37] The same message echoes abroad: "Britain's skills levels are lower than those in most of its competitor countries and the gap is widening," remarks the Confederation of British Industry.[38] Thus, according to the narrative, better schooling and more college graduates—most vitally in the STEM fields—are critical to everyone's future.

But corporate reform then makes a third assertion, since a generic approach to better schooling won't do. Rather, our economic prosperity is only assured if we embrace an education model driven by standards, tests, and accountability. In fact, say reform theorists, we can project our nation's economic future based on student test scores. George Shultz and Eric Hanushek, in a 2012 Wall Street Journal commentary, claim that if America's students raise their international math test scores by forty points over the next twenty years—competing with Canadian scores— we can expect $70 trillion more in gross domestic product over the next eighty years. "That's equivalent to an average 20% boost in income for every U.S. worker each year over his or her entire career," contend the authors, both fellows of the conservative Hoover Institution at Stanford University.[39]

Corporate reform's economic claims and formulations are readily contested. Human capital theory's linkage between education and economic growth has been called reductionist by critics.[40] Its focus on the "supply side" of the job market (workers' skills) tends to leave the "demand side" (the actions of employers) underexamined. While many employers do need educated workers, an educated workforce does not create jobs: investment creates jobs. And job-creating investment has been in long decline. Economist Gerald Friedman points out that U.S. domestic private investment, net of depreciation, fell from roughly 10 percent of gross domestic product in the late 1970s to 2 percent in 2011.[41] This was during a period when the portion of twenty-five-year-olds in the United States with at least a bachelor's level education rose from 17 percent to 30 percent.[42] The country's falling investment owes in part to the growing global mobility of capital, including the outsourcing of jobs abroad to access cheaper labor. Other patterns that diminish job prospects include the cutting of workforces through labor-saving technology and speed-up; and an increasing "financialization" of the economy that shifts away from job-creating productive investment and toward non-job-creating financial investing and speculation.[43] Corporate reformers who leave such trends unaddressed while declaring that "education is key to the nation's prosperity and security"—as does a recent volume from the Brookings Institution—do not promote understanding of education *or* economics.[44]

The claimed skills gap likewise runs into contrary evidence, with U.S. educational achievement long outpacing the available skilled jobs. "The consensus among top economists," urban policy specialist Marc Levine found in a 2013 research review, "is that the skills gap is a myth."[45] Many college graduates are taking jobs that traditionally wouldn't require college degrees. Between 1970 and 2010, according to one study of U.S. labor statistics, the number of taxi drivers with at least a bachelor's degree climbed from 1 percent to 15 percent, and among retail salespersons, from 5 percent to nearly 25 percent.[46] The STEM skills shortage regularly cited by tech companies, media, and politicians is also an invention. "Nearly all of the independent scholars and analysts who have examined the claims of widespread shortages" in science and engineering "have found little or no evidence to support them," says Michael Teitelbaum of Harvard Law School's Labor and Worklife Program.[47] Ron Hira of the Rochester Institute of Technology observes that companies such as Microsoft advocate for more federal STEM education money and more visas for foreign information technology workers—even as they lay off thousands of American employees with comparable skills.[48] "This is all about industry wanting to lower wages," adds Norman Matloff, computer science professor at the University of California at Davis.[49]

Corporate reform's economic narrative is handy in multiple ways. It helps market particular education policies, while it also discourages the search for systemic solutions to unemployment and underemployment. The notion that "education drives economic growth" favors the individual route to success—study hard and great opportunities await you—and discourages the collective route of organizing for jobs and justice. But let's now turn to an alternative explanation of corporate school reform and its objectives.

Drivers and Sectors

Corporate school reform is a complex movement with varied aims; thus, we'll employ certain classifications to help us sort out the territory. The movement's *drivers* consist of its major funders along with key institutions they control. The movement's *implementers* are the politicians, think tank directors, school district superintendents, and other influential actors who carry out the drivers' wishes and may also provide them with strategic advice.

The drivers are of particular interest in this chapter's analysis; the implementers are less consequential, since their movement participation typically depends on the decisions and preferences of the drivers.

The drivers are divided into three sectors. *The organized business sector* consists of business federations such as the Business Roundtable, U.S. Chamber of Commerce, Confederation of British Industry, and BusinessEurope. It also includes certain quasi-governmental agencies that operate, in effect, as arms of business and that lead corporate school reform on a global scale; key among such agencies are the Organization for Economic Cooperation and Development (OECD) and the World Bank. The *edubusiness sector* encompasses large companies and investors with a direct financial stake in corporate reform; among these are publishing and testing companies; technology companies; and real estate and banking interests that feed off charter school expansion. The *philanthropic sector* consists primarily of foundations, with the "big three" foundations of Gates, real estate / insurance magnate Eli Broad, and the Walton family leading the field in the United States.

The drivers of corporate reform appear to have three overarching aims:

Aim #1: *Educate toward corporate hegemony* (i.e., corporate domination of society). This is the chief aim of the organized business sector.

Aim #2: *Educate toward the market-based world vision or ideology of the school reformer.* This aim is notable within the philanthropic sector, though the ideology is present among all the drivers.

Aim #3: *Make profits from schools or spin-off opportunities.* This is the chief aim of the edubusiness sector.

A fourth aim, which seems to be a variable priority, is the cutting of education budgets while routing the funds into private hands, such as through tax cuts for corporations and the wealthy. Here, education falls within a larger package of public provisions—including health services, welfare, unemployment benefits, and public employee pensions—that corporate actors widely demand curbing. Thatcher and Reagan set the mold for this kind of wealth transfer. More recent examples can be found in the fiscal policies of Michigan governor Rick Snyder and New Jersey governor Chris Christie, both of whom have coupled corporate tax reduction with social service and education cuts.[50] Such raiding of public budgets also finds a global corollary in policies affecting developing countries and, more recently, the struggling economies of Southern Europe. In order to obtain assistance from international lending agencies, borrower countries must accept loan conditions that typically include budget austerity. The austerity means cuts in education, health, and social services, with attendant social impact and job losses. Economically struggling countries get caught in cycles of debt, with local populations effectively held hostage by the lending agencies and the big investors who buy the World Bank's bonds.[51]

This fourth aim, however, is a variable priority insofar as corporate interests do continue to support public education finance—albeit at inadequate levels—in many countries and locales. As one indicator: public education funding shows slight growth over time in a majority of countries for which data is available. Table 1.1 (see page 38) provides a sampling, comparing public education spending (for all levels including higher education) in 1990 and 2010, expressed as a percent of gross domestic product.

In the sections that follow, we'll take a closer look at each of the driving sectors, with particular attention to the three chief aims outlined above.

TABLE 1.1: Public Education Spending for Selected Countries in 1990 and 2010, as a Percent of Gross Domestic Product

	1990	2010	Change
Australia	4.7	5.6	+ 0.9
Canada	6.0	5.4	– 0.6
Chile	2.4	4.2	+ 1.8
France	4.6	5.9	+ 1.3
Japan	5.5*	3.8	– 1.7
Mexico	2.3	5.2	+ 2.9
Poland	4.0	5.2	+ 1.2
South Africa	5.3	6.0	+ 0.7
Spain	3.7	5.0	+ 1.3
United Kingdom	4.4	6.2	+ 1.8
United States	4.8	5.4	+ 0.6
Zimbabwe	12.5	2.0	– 10.5

* Figure is for 1989.
Source: World Bank database, http://data.worldbank.org.

Organized Business Sector

Of our three identified sectors, the organized business sector is the most powerful, given its cross-industry composition, and it consequently receives the largest attention in this chapter. Even so, the philanthropic and edubusiness sectors have, for the past decade, been the most visible drivers of corporate school reform within the United States. One indicator comes from an examination of funding sources for 127 pro-corporate reform organizations, done in 2013 by the progressive advocacy group Class Size Matters. Donations were led by the philanthropies of Gates, backing sixty-nine groups; Walton, forty-two groups; and Broad, thirty groups. Edubusiness and related technology companies had a smaller presence: Dell and Hewlett backed twelve groups each; Pearson and Google, four each. Companies with less of an education profile also appeared—General Electric gave to ten groups; Boeing and JPMorgan Chase, eight each; AT&T, four. The Business Roundtable (BRT) and other business federations did not appear in the Class Size Matters spreadsheet, although several of the listed companies are BRT members. The listing did not purport to be complete.[52]

On the other hand, substantial evidence points to the organized business sector as the long-term ringleader of corporate reform. One clue is the timing of corporate reform's rollout, beginning in the early eighties in the thick of a bosses' revolt that was led by a newly aggressive organized business sector. The correspondence between that revolt's neoliberal/market ideology and the ideology of corporate school reform is more than coincidental. Further evidence explored in this section lies in the central role played by the BRT in consolidating U.S. corporate reform in the nineties, and the continuing role played by the OECD and World Bank in propagating the same model on a global scale. Business federations have also given lead to corporate reform at a city level, with public school closures and the spread of charter schools often linked to gentrification and/or downtown development plans; the Commercial Club of Chicago is a sharp example of such.[53] The treatment in this section focuses on the BRT and OECD—as examples, respectively, of national and global leadership in corporate reform—followed by general reflection on the aims of the organized business sector with respect to school reform.

While corporate reform had its U.S. launch with release of *A Nation at Risk* in 1983, the movement did not adopt a systematic organizing posture until the organized business sector, via the BRT, took the bull by the horns six years later. At their annual summer meeting in 1989, the BRT's big-company CEOs initiated a ten-year national campaign geared to a primary goal of getting every state committed to standards—with tests aligned to the standards.[54] The CEOs each adopted one or more states to promote the cause. Kathy Emery, in a 2002 dissertation, describes the group's work in Maryland:

> The Maryland BRT surveyed candidates during election years and testified in state legislatures. They also reviewed the state test in order to correlate student ability on it to the ability to perform well in the workplace. When MBRT sponsored focus groups of parents, teachers, and principals and discovered widespread concern about the tests, MBRT had the state delay the introduction of the new exams and then used funds from the Anne Casey Foundation to create a 45-member speakers bureau to begin to change the public opposition to the test.[55]

In Washington State, Emery continues, the BRT pushed education reform through Partners for Leadership in Education, funded by Boeing; Microsoft; Washington Mutual Bank; and the timber company, Weyerhaeuser. The group met with newly elected state legislators every two years and served on "cut-score" committees that determine the scores needed to pass state exams. Upon discovering public concern over the reform agenda, Partners launched a media campaign. Emery recounts: "They created a video and handbook to explain the new standards movement to parents and sponsored workshops for editorial writers, members of the chamber of commerce and community 'movers and shakers' on 'how to get the word out to the community.'"[56]

In 1999, State Farm Insurance CEO Edward Rust wrote a progress report on the BRT's education campaign. In Washington, he noted, Boeing CEO Frank Shrontz "worked with Governor Booth Gardner to draft comprehensive reform legislation that passed in 1993." In Kentucky, the CEOs of United Parcel Service; Ashland, an oil refiner; and Humana, a health insurance company, "personally intervened to save school-improvement legislation."[57] The BRT worked closely with the National Governors Association, a collaboration that included several national education summits and the founding of the Achieve think tank that would later drive Common Core.[58] By 2002, when the No Child Left Behind Act (NCLB) encoded a stern testing regime into federal law—together with sanctions leading to shuttering public schools and handovers to charters and private contractors—the BRT had effectively prepared the political ground nationally. Moreover, the BRT, together with the Chamber of Commerce, spearheaded a coalition of fifty business groups and individual companies that helped shape and pass NCLB. "The coalition worked hard to ensure that the law's testing requirements focused on reading and mathematics and required annual snapshots of students' performance," according to *Education Week*.[59]

Today, the BRT still maintains an Education & Workforce Committee, headed by Exxon Mobil CEO Rex Tillerson, and with a recent focus on promoting the Common Core. But many of the state business education alliances it had helped build in the nineties have since receded (one exception is the still vital Massachusetts Business Alliance for Education).[60] Over the past decade, the onus of national leadership for corporate schooling has shifted from the BRT to the edu-philanthropists and edubusiness.

It is not hard to imagine why the BRT might lower its profile on the education reform front following the passage of NCLB. Its task of aligning the country behind standards and tests was largely achieved; the shift toward private management of public schools was now underway; and the organization had many other priorities. Moreover, there is a political drawback when business is visibly in the driver's seat of a business takeover of education. The philanthropists and their foundations can posture more effectively as selfless benefactors of the public interest.

OECD

On a global scale, no organization has been more influential in promoting corporate school reform than the Paris-based Organization for Economic Cooperation and Development. A close rival would be the World Bank, which has long pushed corporate schooling models in the developing world.[61] However, while the OECD gears to its thirty-four member countries, who are primarily in the developed world of the North, the agency is also spreading its wares southward and, as discussed below, consulted closely with Mexico regarding that country's recent education reforms.

The OECD is the world's largest think tank, with 2,500 employees and a $400 million budget. The United States is its top contributor, providing 21 percent of its 2014 central budget, with number two donor Japan giving 13 percent. Established in 1961 with a mission to "promote policies that will improve the economic and social well-being of people around the world," the OECD has adopted a high profile on education issues over the past two decades. OECD's educational trajectory is led by its Programme for International Student Assessment (PISA), a triennial math/science/reading test for fifteen-year-olds and in which over seventy countries now participate. Starting with its first round of tests in 2000, PISA promptly became the world's gold standard for measuring and ranking national school systems. But the OECD does more than test students and rank countries; it also produces education policy papers and recommends how individual countries can improve their PISA results. The OECD's educational prescriptions comport with the U.S. corporate reform model—promoting standards, testing, and privatization[62]—with a notable emphasis on workplace readiness. OECD literature, and the PISA test itself, focus on *competencies,* wherein students perform certain practical tasks that are said to match the demands of the "21st century job market." As the OECD explains:

> Today's labour force has to be equipped with the set of skills and competencies which are suited to the knowledge economies. . . . Governments should make an effort to properly identify and conceptualise the set of skills and competencies required so as to incorporate them into the educational standards that every student should be able to reach by the end of compulsory schooling.[63]

Critics charge that the competencies approach—also known as competency-based education and training, or CBET—narrows curriculum to that which is measurable, while diminishing learning as a process of discovery. Terry Hyland argues:

> Instead of an experiential holistic approach, CBET atomises and fragments learning into assessable chunks, rather than valuing process and experience, CBET is concerned only with performance outcomes, and most significantly, instead of fostering critical reflection and alternative perspectives, CBET offers a mono-cultural view based on the satisfaction of restricted performance criteria directed towards fixed and pre-determined ends.[64]

Researchers have also challenged the validity of PISA as a measuring device. Austrian professors Stefan Hopmann and Gertrude Brinek outline the findings of their 2007 European anthology, *PISA According to PISA:* "Almost all of the chapters raise serious doubts concerning the theoretical and methodological standards applied within PISA, and particularly to its most prominent by-products, its national league tables or analyses of school systems." The "league tables" refer to the country rankings published by OECD. The authors continue: "PISA is by design culturally biased and methodologically constrained to a degree which prohibits accurate representations of what actually is achieved in and by schools."[65]

Despite these and other criticisms, the policy impact of PISA and the OECD educational model across the participating countries has been substantial. In fact, OECD openly regards PISA as a vehicle for promoting the agency's brand of education. In a 2012 study, OECD sought to answer such questions as:

- How influential is the PISA evaluation of national system performance in policymaking processes?
- To what extent are the competencies outlined in the PISA frameworks and instruments promoted in the education system?
- Have PISA-based national performance targets or indicators been established?[66]

Countries who follow the model and boost their PISA scores will reap rewards by way of economic growth, assure OECD economists, who offer impressive projections that mirror the approach of Shultz and Hanushek, cited earlier in this chapter. For example, "A modest goal of having all OECD countries boost their average PISA scores by 25 points over the next 20 years . . . implies an aggregate gain of OECD GDP [gross domestic product] of USD 115 trillion over the lifetime of the generation born in 2010."[67]

OECD employs a school reform strategy pioneered by the Reagan administration and its *Nation at Risk* report. First, international test scores are compared to reveal that nation X is falling behind. Second, it is argued that the mediocre test scores bode ill for nation X's economy. Third, a program of corporate schooling is offered as the urgent solution for the "educational crisis" and for the nation's economic future. In each OECD member country, a cohort of political actors and media outlets reliably converts the latest PISA results into grist for the corporate school agenda. The U.S. education secretary will say: "The United States came in 23rd or 24th in most subjects. We can quibble, or we can face the brutal truth that we're being out-educated."[68] Australia's education secretary will echo: "These are the worst PISA results since PISA began in 2000. . . . They are a serious wake-up call for the Australian education system."[69] And from Britain's education secretary, we hear that top PISA performers such as Shanghai, Singapore, and South Korea are "leaving our children behind in the global race."[70]

Among the many countries witnessing PISA's policy impact has been Denmark, where weak PISA results in 2000 and 2003 gave rise to a "back-to-basics wave" with a strong testing focus.[71] In reference to science education, Jens Dolin at the University of Copenhagen points out that teachers nationally had built a "solid tradition for project-oriented work in science" and a "practical, experimental approach" including role play, alternative written assignments, and use of a portfolio. But now he sees the authentic and project-based pedagogies losing ground as the system presses for "cheap tests and a high PISA score." In meetings with science teachers throughout Denmark, he says, "you hear how the test examples, recently published on the internet, makes them put more emphasis on the content areas covered by the test, and change their focus toward facts and the measurable."[72]

Denmark's experience with corporate-style reform, triggered or accelerated by PISA, has been mirrored elsewhere, as suggested in an Education International survey of national teachers unions in 2006–7. Germany, which was gripped by "PISA shock" after the country's disappointing ranking in 2000, cited a new regime of national standards and "testing testing testing." Ireland remarked that PISA "has been and still is a catalyst for change in favour of more testing and evaluation." In Australia, a government report on *The Future of Schooling* made "considerable use of the PISA data" to show a "long tail of underachievement." The document became the basis for setting national goals that lean toward "testing accountability regimes."[73]

Some governments look to OECD as a consulting service to help devise education reforms, inevitably in the corporate style. In Mexico, a two-year consultation concluded with a 2010 OECD policy document, *Improving Schools: Strategies for Action in Mexico,* which contained fifteen recommendations.[74] The recommendations would be reflected in education reform laws signed by President Enrique Peña Nieto in December 2012 and September 2013. One key reform required new teachers to pass national exams, while existing teachers would have to pass exams every four years to maintain their licenses. Another reform extends "autonomy" to local schools. (School autonomy, as envisioned by such bodies as the World Bank, often translates into shifting school costs to parents and undermining teachers unions.)[75] The Nieto reforms triggered massive and ongoing protests by teachers, who contend that the government is preparing the way for mass firings, union busting, and privatization.[76] The resistance movement does not oppose teacher evaluations per se, but calls for evaluations that are framed within a democratic process toward genuine school improvement.[77]

Though a lead global booster for corporate school reform, the OECD is not a business voice in the straightforward manner of a Business Roundtable. The organization's posture is one of neutrality and evenhandedness, with governance handled through a council of ambassadors appointed by the member countries. Its official advisory bodies include one for the bosses (the Business and Industry Advisory Council) and one for the workers (the Trade Union Advisory Committee). Nonetheless, political economist Richard Woodward sees much evidence of OECD's corporate bias, including in its annual forum, a business-sponsored affair where "speakers representing pro-capitalist, corporate interests" outnumber those from "more socially or charitably orientated organizations," and where "choirs of neo-liberal prophets congregate to eulogize about the benefits of capitalist globalization."[78] OECD's policy positions provide even sharper evidence of the organization's corporate orientation. Its economic model, pushed as fervently as its educational one, is squarely neoliberal, emphasizing greater freedoms for business—especially transnational companies—and fewer protections for local economies and workers. Thus, in a 2006 "jobs strategy" document, the OECD advocates:

- Moving toward "open international trade and investment" and removing "legal impediments to entry of new firms" (that is, developing countries should not be allowed to protect their vulnerable economies from transnational investors).
- Reducing "competition-restraining state control of business operations" (that is, promote privatization and deregulation).
- "Reducing constraints on [job] dismissals for economic reasons" (that is, cut worker protections related to layoffs, such as seniority provisions and severance pay).
- Allowing individual firms to opt out of sector-wide labor agreements that "have adverse effects on employment" (that is, weaken unions).
- Ensuring that minimum wages are "set at levels that do not harm job creation."
- Curbing unemployment, welfare, and retirement benefits.[79]

All posturing aside, the OECD is the corporate sector's top global think tank and policy advocacy center. And PISA is its marketing tool for corporate education policy. At varying speeds and intensity, and with notable inequities between the richer North and poorer South, most of the world has been gravitating toward the OECD/World Bank/Business Roundtable model of schooling.

Sector Aims

For the organized business sector, school reform is a social engineering project. The aim is to mold a citizenry suitable to corporate hegemony's advancement. The sector's interest, we might say, lies with the *content* of schooling, as distinguished from the edubusiness focus on the *profits* to be gleaned from schooling. Here, "content" refers not only to the material in a textbook but also to lessons conveyed through the *process* of schooling—how classrooms are organized, the ways of thinking that are encouraged and discouraged, and who has access to which kinds of schools.

A curriculum that serves corporate hegemony is one that builds habits of subordination and compliance in working-class schools while fostering critical thinking and managerial skills in elite schools.[80] Let's focus our scrutiny on the working-class schools that serve the mass bulk of students. Critics have pointed to the roles of high-stakes testing and scripted curriculum in subordinating and controlling students and teachers alike.[81] More pernicious in promoting the same are government reading standards, in which corporate reformers have also played an active hand. In its *Business Leader's Guide to Setting Academic Standards* (1996), the BRT shows how its members helped revise one of the reading standards in Washington State:

Before revision: "The student reads to construct meaning from a variety of texts for a variety of purposes."
After revision: "The student understands the meaning of what is read."

By omitting the phrase "construct meaning," the revised standard uses "clearer language" and avoids "education jargon," according to the BRT guide.[82] Yet the children of BRT members have wide access to pedagogies that invite them to construct meaning (known as "constructivist" education, with the learner using reading, writing, or math as tools for making sense of the world). As the elite University of Chicago Laboratory Schools explains to kindergarten parents: "Our program builds on young children's curiosity and enthusiasm and is based on the understanding that young children learn best when they can construct meaning in a context-rich environment."[83] Under corporate schooling, working-class students do not enjoy the same privilege, are not asked to make their own interpretations and discoveries. Rather, they are told that there is only one interpretation, which exists inside the text, and their task is to find it and mark the appropriate answer on their worksheet. The lesson for working-class students is that they are not empowered, do not have a say-so about the meaning of things, and that the written word represents an authority to which they are subordinate.

Today, the Common Core, with corporate and BRT backing, continues to teach reading as a process of subordination, notably through its concept of "close reading," focusing students on "what lies within the four corners of the text."[84] As Common Core co-designer David Liben explains, the standards "virtually eliminate text-to-self connections," meaning the students' experiences and feelings aren't important and aren't relevant to what the text means. "In college and careers, no one cares how you feel," he says.[85] By the same token, Common Core's version of close reading discourages students from connecting the text to the world at large, including that of the text's author. As educator Daniel Ferguson points out, such a model fails to equip students as critical readers and thinkers.[86] The tight linking of Common Core with standardized tests also reinforces the conception of reading as the retrieval of one right answer.

The subordinating aim of corporate schooling is further reflected in the extreme disciplinary culture that marks much of the charter school movement. The no-excuses disciplinary model with its behaviorist rewards and punishments—popularized by KIPP, the largest of the corporate-backed charter chains—is also promoted through the leading reform venues for teacher and principal training such as Teach for America (TFA) and Relay Graduate School of Education.[87] TFA trainees get versed in the work of Lee Canter (*Assertive Discipline: Positive Behavior Management for Today's Classroom*). As one TFA alumnus recalls: "It's three steps in action: Give explicit directions, narrate the desired behaviors being done in the classroom, and issue consequences for students not complying. We were encouraged to come up with positive reinforcements [e.g., stickers, candy, school privileges] for students who did comply."[88] The authoritarian and behavioristic discipline is not limited to charter schools, however; reformers are also introducing the model into the regular public schools. One study describes a K-8 public school in Baltimore, fictitiously named Belleview, that practices the no-excuses pedagogy:

> The primary teachers at Belleview exercised control over every aspect of the students' school day. All student talk was explicitly restricted and occurred only as responses to the teachers' questions or directives. Very often the response pattern involved whole-class unison answers. We observed virtually no instances of student-initiated talk that reflected authentic communication, collaboration, critical evaluation or problem solving. This level of control went beyond what might be considered typical day-to-day management of a classroom. . . .
>
> [The teachers] constantly reminded students that they needed to earn points each day by being good listeners. During a class discussion in which students were asked to make predictions about a story, Jamie [a teacher] stated that, "I see a lot of people are not earning their threes this morning, so then you can just

stand along the wall at recess time this afternoon." A "three" indicated that students were demonstrating proper classroom behavior. That same day, Jamie warned students that anyone who was squirming or talking would lose ten minutes of their lunch period. Such rules and consequences were a regular part of the primary classroom environment at Belleview.[89]

The compliance lessons are aided by a neoliberal individualist ideology, once articulated by Margaret Thatcher: "They are casting their problems at society. And, you know, there's no such thing as society. There are individual men and women and there are families."[90] So, for example, when progressives argue that low test scores are reflective of social conditions, and that schools and communities need more support, corporate reformers dismiss these as excuses, countering that students must simply be trained in character and "grit."[91] As for the teachers struggling to close the achievement gap in under-resourced schools, the reformers similarly recommend a can-do attitude. TFA advises corps members to focus on the Big Goal (such as 80 percent of students passing the test), to "assume personal responsibility," and to "work relentlessly."[92]

The corollary to such individual solutions is fault-finding and victim-blaming. Students, teachers, and schools that don't meet achievement targets—however relentlessly they may try—are deemed failures under corporate reform, and sanctions will be applied. On a wider plane: working-class communities and predominantly working-class communities of color that encounter a dearth of jobs and affordable housing are considered failures who lack the will or grit to succeed.[93] Meanwhile, corporate interests that helped engineer a scarcity of living-wage jobs and the downsizing of social programs gain advantage from the individualist narrative, avoiding responsibility or scrutiny and diverting attention from our economy's systemic ills.

Vital within corporate reform's social engineering mix is the reinforcement of social stratification—notably by class, race, and language.[94] NCLB, for example, claimed to champion equity by requiring schools to demonstrate the yearly achievement growth of four student subgroups: low income, ethnic/ racial minorities, special needs, and English learners. The federal law, which did not address the school funding inequities that affect student achievement, produced harsher conditions for all the targeted student groups. Test-driven pedagogy would make it harder for teachers to individualize and humanize instruction, or to bring students' lives and cultures into the curriculum. Closings and school "turnarounds" with mass staff dismissals would make schools in communities of color less stable and secure, and more reliant on inexperienced and temporary staff. Charter schools would exacerbate patterns of segregation and the push-out of special-needs students and English learners. NCLB would also diminish federal support for bilingual education, with English learners unfairly expected to pass the same tests taken by native English speakers, and references to bilingual education stricken from the Department of Education altogether.[95]

Social stratification comes with ideologies of superiority—white over black or brown, English language over Spanish, European over non-European heritages—that extend relative privilege to the favored groups. Grassroots solidarity becomes harder to build. Corporate control is bolstered when diverse cultures are marginalized. In the words of educator Harold Berlak, "a vibrant cacophony of voices on what constitutes truth, knowledge and learning" is replaced with "one set of answers, and only one."[96]

Whereas organizations such as the BRT and OECD bring national and global goals to school reform, another segment of the organized business sector is constituted locally and with somewhat different priorities. In Chicago, corporate reform has been driven by business's power hitters at the Commercial Club. The club's key education report, *Left Behind* (2003), offers a boilerplate corporate perspective, with "failing" schools blamed on an inflexible union that protects under-performing teachers, and with the proposed remedy of non-union charter schools that will spur improvement through choice and competition.[97] But the club's primary aim with corporate reform, as Chicago professor Pauline Lipman asserts, lies in real estate profits as part of an elite urban restructuring. The Chicago model dismantles public schools and public housing in majority low-income black and Latino neighborhoods, and then targets new housing and charter schools to more white and affluent populations—all surrounding a downtown envisioned as a world-class corporate and tourist center.[98] Variations of the model can be found in New Orleans, Philadelphia, and elsewhere.[99]

The example of the Commercial Club doesn't forestall the social engineering, ideological, and curricular priorities that appear to be primary for national and global business interests; but it does add another texture. Sociologist William Domhoff distinguishes between local "land-based" elites whose income is based in rents and mortgages, and "national-level corporate capitalists" whose income derives from the production and sale of goods and services. The land-based elites tend to organize themselves as "growth coalitions," who maximize their profits through intensified land use. Applying Domhoff's scheme to the school reform movement, we can identify two subsets within the organized business sector—a national segment driving school reform primarily for social engineering purposes, and a local segment focused on the real estate profits to be gleaned from school privatization (an objective of the edubusiness sector). Domhoff adds that his categories aren't airtight and that, in the largest cities, one can find major corporations and extremely rich families capturing profits both from land use and production.[100]

Edubusiness Sector

For edubusiness, the aim is straightforward: turn schooling into profits. But that doesn't tell us precisely what the game plan is. Edubusiness takes many forms—selling tests, curricular packages, and technology; contracting to manage schools or to provide a range of other services (data analysis, consulting, transportation, food, custodial); operating for-profit and nonprofit charter chains; leasing/selling/lending in the charter real estate market. Is one form more important than another? Is there one that best signals where edubusiness and corporate reform as a whole are heading? This section offers a few ruminations, with particular attention to the U.S. charter industry.

Much critical attention goes to the testing industry and its profiteering, with global education giant Pearson the dominant player.[101] However, while the tests are a centerpiece of corporate reform strategy, they make up a relatively small slice of the edubusiness target from a revenue standpoint. A 2012 report estimated that standardized tests were costing U.S. public schools $1.7 billion annually, or just a quarter of 1 percent of K–12 spending.[102] Even if Common Core winds up doubling that figure, and test-prep materials are included in the package, we might be looking at 1 percent of expenditure. A much bigger prize, one that stands to benefit more diverse sectors of edubusiness, would be school privatization joined with intensive labor cost-cutting. Staff salary and benefits constituted 70 percent of the 2010–11 U.S. public school budget, or $423 billion.[103] Converting labor savings—derived from a non-union, deprofessionalized workforce—into profits is a bedrock aim of the charter school movement.

Although charter schools are indeed cutting labor costs,[104] converting that into school profits—or "positive year-end balances," in nonprofit terminology—is not simple or straightforward. A new charter school will contend with a few years of start-up and growth costs. And even for the established charter, much of its labor savings may be routed to vendors or entities beyond the school. One way to regard charter schools is not as profit-producing entities in themselves, but as sieves through which various investors outside the school access public school dollars. We'll look at three interrelated routes for this money outflow: charter chains, real estate, and online instruction.

Charter Chains

Owing both to the complexities of running a school and the challenges of recruiting students and maintaining full enrollment, many charter entrepreneurs prefer to affiliate with chains, which offer their name brands, packaged curriculum, management services, and financial assistance or guidance. While the early charter movement consisted mostly of freestanding independent schools, the field's center of gravity has since been shifting toward the chains. Nationally, charter chains enrolled 24 percent of charter school students in 2003–4, with that figure rising to 44 percent by 2011–12. Among the chains themselves can be found a further industry trend: a shift away from the for-profit chains and toward the nonprofits. In the period just cited, the for-profit share of charter chain enrollment fell from 75 to 51 percent, while the nonprofit share climbed from 24 to 49 percent.[105] Although the for-profits do predominate in certain states such as Florida and Michigan, the nonprofits seem to enjoy the long-term edge, owing in part to the edu-philanthropists, who direct almost all their charter giving to the nonprofit chains.

The nonprofit chains, which the industry calls charter management organizations (CMOs), have a business model in which affiliated schools pay management fees that sustain the central office. For example, the KIPP Infinity Charter School in New York City pays KIPP 11 percent of the per-pupil revenue that the school receives from public sources, with 10 percent going to the regional office for "back-office functions" and 1 percent going to the national office as a license fee.[106] Few, if any, of the CMOs have built networks large enough to sustain the central office without substantial philanthropic subsidy. But the CMO business model envisions "going to scale" and eventually achieving self-sufficiency based on the management fees. The building block is the school site, explains Kevin Hall, president/CEO of the Charter School Growth Fund, an organization that distributes philanthropic dollars to a portfolio of some fifty CMOs. "The site's got to throw off cash," he says.[107]

The for-profit chains are different, since they receive little philanthropy. Many supplement their management fees by functioning as landlord, and sometimes lending agency, for their network schools. This can include aggressive rent gouging. A *Miami Herald* investigation found that the Florida-based Academica, the country's largest for-profit charter chain, charged several of its schools rents exceeding 20 percent of revenue.[108] (That contrasts with a median charter facility cost of only about 6 percent of revenue nationally.)[109] The rents were in addition to management fees. Worse is the Virginia-based Imagine Schools, which, the *Columbus Dispatch* reports, charges several of its Ohio schools rents exceeding half of school revenue.[110] Both Academica and Imagine play a hand in recruiting people to serve on the boards of their network schools, leading to conflicts of interest and boards that neglect to question the exorbitant rents.[111]

Here we can see two slices of public school dollars diverted from schools and into edubusiness hands. One slice, via management fees, goes to charter chain offices vested with a mission to take their networks to scale. The other, covering charter facility costs, is grabbed by real estate operators and lenders, some of whom are also charter chain operators.

Real Estate

The real estate business generated by charter schools is not limited to the activity of the for-profit chains, but involves a growing sector of landlords, builders, and lenders working with diverse segments of the charter movement—chains and independents, for-profits and nonprofits. The real estate vendors and lenders serve the 78 percent of charter schools that occupy private properties as renters or owners, whereas the remaining 22 percent are situated in school district facilities.[112] One investor active in the field is former tennis pro Andre Agassi, who has partnered in a facilities fund to "capitalize on and promote the movement for U.S. charter schools." The fund builds facilities and then leases them to charter operators, with a later option to buy the building.[113]

Some investors focus on the lending side of the transaction. Increasingly, charter operators raise capital to build new schools by issuing bonds, with $2 billion worth issued in 2014 alone.[114] Given their relatively high risk, charter bonds yield higher returns, making them attractive to savvy investors. Professor/blogger Julian Vasquez Heilig learned that Texas charter schools were paying an average interest of 8 percent for bonds, compared to just 3 percent paid by local school district bond issuers. But what makes the bonds even more attractive is that charter investors can qualify for a federal New Markets Tax Credit that adds up to 39 percent over seven years.[115] Critics such as Heilig and New York reporter Juan Gonzalez believe that the charter bond and lending market helps explain why Wall Street hedge fund managers have donated enthusiastically to charter schools while launching influential corporate reform lobby groups such as Democrats for Education Reform (DFER).[116] Charter bond investors can reduce the risk of default by growing the charter market: "As more charter schools open, a smaller percentage of them are being forced to close," notes the *Wall Street Journal*.[117] Indeed, in March 2015,

hedge fund manager and DFER co-founder Whitney Tilson key-
noted a New York City symposium on "Bonds and Blackboards:
Investing in Charter Schools," aimed at stirring up more buying
of charter bonds.[118]

Online Instruction

A third significant area of public school dollar diversion is
online instruction. In fact, no component of corporate reform
receives more edubusiness excitement and boosting than does
online instruction and education technology generally. The 2014
annual conference of the International Society for Technology
in Education, held in Atlanta, drew eighteen thousand attendees
and five hundred vendors.[119] While online instruction vendors are
penetrating the public school districts, the trail is being blazed
in the charter sector. An education consulting firm observes, "It
has been the charter school sector and specialized state virtual
schools that have introduced a sea change in digital instruction
models that is now finding its way back into the traditional school
district environment."[120]

The highest profit margins are in the full-time virtual schools,
in which students connect online from their homes. K12 Inc.,
the top virtual school vendor in the United States, charged its
biggest client—Agora Cyber Charter School, serving students
across Pennsylvania—product and service fees constituting 55
percent of the school's total expenses in 2012–13.[121] Agora, in
turn, presses for labor cost savings by assigning teachers huge
student loads. Agora teachers report handling between 70 and
100 students at the elementary level, and 300 students at the secondary level. The 300-student load in secondary is aided through
an "accelerated schedule" that compresses a year of study into
a half-year; thus the teacher handles two loads of 150 students
each over the course of the school year.[122] On the other hand,

K12 has recently suffered reversals of fortune, losing Agora and major affiliates in other states due to poor student performance and other problems.[123]

Given the inherent limitations of full-time virtual schools— high dropout rates and the difficulty of sustaining students' motivation when they study alone at home—much of the industry touts "blended learning," which integrates online instruction at physical brick-and-mortar schools. With blended learning, enthuse Terry Moe and John Chubb of the Hoover Institution, education can be "customized" and "freed from geographic constraints." Students can have "more interaction with their teachers and with one another," and "sophisticated data systems can put the spotlight on performance . . . and sharpen accountability."[124] Others are less upbeat. Gordon Lafer from the University of Oregon reports on a Milwaukee, Wisconsin, school run by Rocketship Education, a nonprofit chain of K–5 schools and national pioneer in the blended learning field. Starting in kindergarten, Rocketship students spend two hours of each day in the school's learning lab, where the focus is online learning. The lab is staffed by tutors who, Lafer observes, have "no certification and whose only required credential is a high school diploma." The lab arrangement allows the school to use five fewer teachers than it would with a fully certified staff, yielding an estimated $500,000 per year savings. The school further saves by relying on an inexperienced, high-turnover teaching staff, most of them from Teach for America. Finally, Lafer points out, the school's pedagogy "revolves relentlessly around state standardized tests," both in the classroom and the learning lab, while "teachers' salaries and promotions are determined in large part by the improvement in their students' test scores."[125]

The features that Lafer criticizes—test-driven, cost cut-focused, deprofessionalized—no doubt help attract Rocketship's strong bench of corporate donors including Netflix CEO Reed Hastings and the foundations of Dell, Broad, and Walton. One of Rocketship's backers, the Charter School Growth Fund (CSGF), partnered with Hastings in 2010 to acquire DreamBox Learning, an online K–5 math program that is used at Rocketship schools. CSGF followed the acquisition with a $30 million "next generation" initiative that promotes DreamBox and blended learning among the CSGF portfolio of fifty CMOs. The organization seeks also to move blended learning into the public school districts, and to win state legislation toward this end. A report co-sponsored by CSGF lists the policies that states "must get right to maximize blended learning's transformational potential," such as

- Eliminating state caps on the enrollment of students in online or blended-learning programs or courses;
- Eradicating rules that restrict class size and student-teacher ratios; and
- Lifting state rules around certification and licensure to let schools slot paraprofessionals or capable but non-state-certified teachers into appropriate assistive or instructional roles.[126]

Philanthropic Sector

Since most corporate reform drivers engage in some level of reformer philanthropy, let's define the philanthropic sector as those drivers who are particularly active in giving. The sector encompasses diverse objectives, and we cannot draw a simple equation between the aims, say, of Gates, Walton, Fisher, Dell, and the philanthropic hedge fund managers. Ultimately, their aims must be teased out by examining the evidence for each philanthropist. This section takes a glance at two of the most prominent philanthropists.

Eli Broad

With a net worth of $7 billion, Broad has given over $600 million to school reform since 1999. His influential Broad Center has trained and placed dozens of people, most with a background in business rather than education, as urban school district superintendents, all versed in the corporate schooling model. Another Broad project seeks to expand charter school enrollment in Los Angeles, to encompass half of the students in the city's school district by 2023.[127] Though some suspect that Bill Gates, with substantial Microsoft holdings, gives to school reform so that he can cash in later through school technology sales, such an edubusiness argument would be hard to sustain for Broad, who has no comparable concentrated investment. "Between my portfolio and that of the foundations," Broad writes, "we have more than 200 investments, none of which amounts to more than 5 percent of our holdings."[128]

An alternate interpretation, that Broad's school reform goal lies in corporate hegemony, also looks doubtful. Even if corporate hegemony does bode well for Broad's long-term portfolio returns, accruing wealth doesn't appear to be his priority. In 2010, he and his wife, Edythe, signed the Giving Pledge, a project conceived by Gates and Warren Buffett, in which the super-wealthy commit the majority of their wealth to philanthropy. In addition to education, the Broad Foundation gives heavily to bioscience research and the arts. Such actions appear to be more consistent with someone who wants to do good for the world (as Broad conceives the good), than one with a corporate hegemony focus.

A helpful piece in understanding Broad's philanthropic motives is his embrace of "venture philanthropy," a model that reigns among the edu-philanthropists, borrowing from the field of venture capitalism. Whereas traditional philanthropy takes a relatively hands-off posture toward grantee organizations, venture philanthropists bring an investment-return perspective, picking projects that support their own strategic goals and then closely monitoring grantee performance.[129] "It's crucial that you apply an appropriate set of metrics to your giving," Broad advises prospective donors. "If you're in a position to be generous enough to make grants, it can only help to know from the start what results you and your grantee want to achieve. . . . There's nothing hard-hearted or domineering about holding those to whom you give accountable."[130]

With Broad investing toward clear-sighted strategic goals, but with the evidence casting doubt on edubusiness or corporate-hegemonic motives, a reasonable interpretation would be that his goals are ideological and visionary. Market forces have well served Broad, the product of a lower middle-class family who would earn riches. Now he believes that market forces can build better schools and a better world. What gives charter schools the "competitive edge," he theorizes, is their accountability: "Students perform or the schools are closed." Moreover, as charter enrollments swell, "market forces will pressure neighboring district public schools to improve."[131]

Broad's outlook and school reform model certainly do facilitate corporate control and hegemony, and his giving is no doubt appreciated by the BRT and the organized business sector. But Broad's pursuit of neoliberalism as a prescription for a better world—based on economic freedom and individualistic bootstrap initiative—is not quite the same as the BRT's pursuit of neoliberalism as a strategy for enhancing corporate power. For many school reform philanthropists who haven't a clear edubusiness stake—as do the foundations of Dell and Hewlett, or hedge fund managers enthusing over the charter bond market—investigation will likely uncover priorities that are heavily ideological and neoliberal-visionary.

Bill Gates

Top philanthropist Gates walks a fine line between the edu-business and ideologue camps. Many critics observe his huge donations to Common Core, with its heavily digitized curriculum. They connect this to his Microsoft holdings, valued at $14 billion in fall 2014, and see evidence of a clear financial stake. In fact, during a March 2014 interview with the *Washington Post*, Gates was asked directly whether "business interests" figured into his funding of Common Core. He fired back: "This is giving money away. This is philanthropy. This is trying to make sure students have the kind of opportunity I had. . . . It's so, almost . . . outrageous to say otherwise. . . ."[132] Gates's response wasn't quite in the spirit of full disclosure, since Microsoft is directly engaged in Common Core–generated business. Just weeks prior to the *Post* interview, a collaboration was announced combining Pearson's digitized Common Core curriculum with Microsoft's Windows 8 operating system.[133] At the same time, Microsoft closed a deal to equip Miami-Dade County Public Schools with 100,000 Windows 8 devices (laptops and tablets).[134]

On the other hand, Gates has been selling off his Microsoft holdings at a rate of eighty million shares annually since the mid-nineties, moving the proceeds to his foundation. "If Gates continues that pace," *Computerworld* reported in November 2014, "he will exhaust his Microsoft holdings in just under four years."[135] Gates's gradual divestment of Microsoft in favor of his foundation, to which he has contributed over $28 billion,[136] seems to signal that changing the world has become more important to him than profits. Indeed, his writings and speeches do suggest a man on a mission—albeit an authoritarian mission that many believe is destroying young people's spirits. "I find it stunning that the educational schools are not training teachers to use the KIPP way of teaching classes," Gates remarks on his blog.[137]

Conclusion

This chapter challenges three interpretations of corporate reform that are current among public education advocates—one that focuses on edubusiness; a second that identifies the problem as primarily ideological; and a third that points to white supremacy as the leading force behind reform. This chapter incorporates what is valid in these progressive analyses: part of the reform leadership does orient to edubusiness; market ideology may indeed be central for some reform drivers; and racism and other forms of stratification are clearly integral to the reform package. But the chapter centerpiece points to the organized captains of industry, who are using school reform as a social engineering project to advance corporate hegemony as part of a broader hyper-capitalist trajectory birthed in the 1970s. The hegemonists work in close alliance with edubusiness along with a cohort of philanthropic market missionaries. What are the ramifications of this alternative analysis for an educational justice movement?

First, the chapter provides the movement a more compelling case against corporate reform than others that have been offered. Most notably, it accounts for those important reform drivers who are not out to get rich off schools but have other objectives.

Second, the alternative analysis may encourage us to think more strategically about the classroom and school as a terrain for challenging corporate social engineering. The demands for an education that is democratic, critical, multicultural, and multilingual—long forwarded in professional conferences, social justice teacher groups, and the pages of *Rethinking Schools*—belong at the center of a broad public education movement.

Third, if the takeover of education is a class-wide corporate project, and integrally linked to more general aims of neoliberal capitalism, then such would underscore how large is the task of an educational justice movement. It is unlikely that our progressive goals for public education can be realized within the confines of a single-issue movement. One of the points highlighted by Joel Jordan in chapter 5 is that education organizing can and should connect schools with communities and with broader agendas for social justice.

2

Teachers Unions that Partner with Billionaires

Howard Ryan

When I first became a union leader, I was quick to identify the enemy, fire up members, and wage war for what I believed to be right. Eventually, I learned that if you set out looking for a fight, you'll find one—but you probably won't find a solution.

—RANDI WEINGARTEN, President,
American Federation of Teachers[1]

We've become accustomed to having a peacetime chief. . . . But what I'm trying to get people to understand now is that we are at war. And we need a wartime chief.

—AGUSTIN MORALES, teacher and education activist[2]

THE DIVERGENT VIEWS OF RANDI WEINGARTEN and Agustin Morales—with the former proposing education reform through "labor-management collaboration" and the latter through a militant fightback against corporate interests—represent one important debate within the teachers unions. This chapter will address this and more. The teachers unions can provide a vital centerpiece for an educational justice movement. No other grassroots education stakeholder can begin to match the resources or breadth of the unions, with a combined four million members between the larger National Education Association (NEA) and the smaller American Federation of Teachers (AFT). Yet, with important exceptions led by the bold example of the Chicago Teachers Union (CTU), the teachers unions are not quite part of an educational justice movement. AFT/NEA leaders at national, state, and local levels have, to varied degrees, aligned themselves with corporate forces. Where they do criticize elements of the corporate school agenda—high-stakes testing, school closings, charters, Teach for America—their protestations are muted. The wide-ranging analysis of corporate school reform carried out by such academics as Wayne Au, Stephen Ball, Pauline Lipman, and Kenneth Saltman does not generally have teachers union equivalents in the United States.[3] Here again, CTU represents an important exception, producing a rich series of critical reports since the union's transformation in 2010.[4] But for teachers unions to realize their enormous potential for movement leadership, they must first fully acknowledge and frankly assess the corporate takeover of public education. And second, they must commit to empowering teachers and joining hands with community allies in a broad challenge to the corporate juggernaut.

This chapter addresses manifestations of corporate alignment in the teachers unions—including union leaders collaborating with school reform billionaires and accepting grants from them—and how these interfere with effective union leadership for public education. The unions' posture and strategy with respect to charter schools and privatization is taken up by Joel Jordan in chapter 5. Here, we'll give particular attention to standards, testing, and teacher evaluation systems, looking at AFT/NEA national policies as well as contract provisions bargained locally. The chapter goes on to distinguish between two competing models of teacher unionism—a *service* model and a *social-movement* model—with the social-movement approach integral to the building of a powerful educational justice movement.

Standards, Tests, and the Union Partnership Strategy

The teachers unions' partnership approach was signaled in 1997 by then NEA president Bob Chase. Too often, NEA's gains had been won "through confrontation at the bargaining table or, in extreme cases, after bitter strikes," he remarked in a speech to the National Press Club. "These industrial-style, adversarial tactics simply are not suited to the next stage of school reform…. It's time to create a new union, an association with an entirely new approach to our members, to our critics, and to our colleagues on the other side of the bargaining table."[5] Today, the partnership model's most articulate proponent is AFT president Randi Weingarten, who writes:

> Frankly, collaborating is harder than confrontation. Many people are more comfortable with the us-versus-them posture. Consultation takes time. Considering the point of view on the other side of the negotiating table can require moving out of one's comfort zone. And while some see compromise as capitulation, what it does is enable the seeding of trust and good will, not the ceding of authority and responsibility. It's not easy, but it is effective.[6]

Certainly, no wise unionist would oppose collaborating with management when the two parties have broadly shared goals. The problem with the AFT/NEA approach is that it includes partnering with the lead drivers of corporate schooling. Here are some examples:

- Weingarten and other teachers union leaders have attended strategic retreats hosted by billionaire corporate reformer Eli Broad, and have taught at Broad's superintendents academy.[7]
- Top corporate reform funder Bill Gates spoke at the AFT's

July 2010 convention and, that same month, gave the union a $4 million grant to support its innovation fund and its "teacher development and evaluation programs."[8]

- In 2011, NEA's then president Dennis Van Roekel co-authored a *USA Today* column with Teach for America founder Wendy Kopp. Van Roekel and Kopp's proposals included tying the evaluation of university teacher preparation programs to the test scores of students taught by the program's graduates—a policy also supported by the Obama administration.[9]

In 2014, responding to member complaints, Weingarten announced that the AFT's innovation fund would no longer accept Gates grants.[10] Yet the individual relationships are symptomatic of a deeper kind of partnership that manifests in AFT/NEA education policies as well as in the contracts bargained for the members.

Let's consider the critical arena of standards and tests. As noted in chapter 1, corporate interests have framed education reform as a matter of imposing standards and tests from above, *not* as a democratic process involving fully funded schools, teacher/parent/community alliances, and locally driven forms of school transformation. The teachers unions aligned with this corporate perspective early on. In 1991, both AFT president Albert Shanker and NEA president Keith Geiger joined a thirty-two-member council tasked to advise Congress on the "desirability and feasibility" of national standards and testing. The council's report advised in the affirmative, while adding that the standards must be voluntary, not federally mandated.[11] The council did acknowledge the need for quality school conditions, recommending that the states establish "school delivery standards" to ensure that "students do not bear the sole burden of attaining the standards."[12] However, the council viewed standards—and assessments linked to the standards—as the "cornerstone" of systemic reform.[13]

In words that hauntingly prefigured the federal No Child Left Behind Act of 2001 (NCLB), which would fiercely bind public education to tests and test scores, the report envisioned "tests worth teaching to," an assessment system that could "measure and hold students, schools, school districts, states, and the Nation accountable for education performance."[14]

Shanker brought particular verve to the standards-and-testing bandwagon. Under his watch, in 1995, AFT launched an annual report, *Making Standards Matter*, to "help ensure that the standards movement in this country succeeds."[15] The 1996 edition opined that "students who are not meeting state standards should not be passed from grade to grade and they shouldn't be handed a high school diploma."[16] The report measured each of the fifty states in terms of their progress in setting standards that met AFT criteria, and in terms of their linking the standards to high-stakes tests. The report worried that "less than half of the states require or plan to require students to pass high school graduation exams linked to their standards," and that only nine states had graduation exams linked to standards in "all four core subjects"— math, English, science, and social studies.[17] The report did urge that schools provide struggling students with "substantial extra help."[18]

When NCLB upped the ante by using low test scores to punish schools and communities through a destructive ladder of sanctions, the teachers unions objected to the over-testing and under-resourcing. But corporate reform's driving assumption— that top-down standards and high-stakes testing are the starting place for making better schools—was still not frontally challenged as such. In February 2004, with the membership restive over NCLB's test-and-punish focus, AFT's then president Sandra Feldman sent a letter to union vice presidents urging caution: "Our major concern ... is that we do not throw out the baby with the bath water on education policy."[19] In a follow-up newsletter to local leaders, she added: "The goals of the No Child Left Behind Act . . . are goals the AFT has long supported—high standards for all children, with tests to measure whether the standards are being met; qualified teachers in every classroom; and help for students and schools that are lagging behind."[20]

Common Core

Today, the Common Core State Standards (CCSS) epitomize all that is wrong with the standards/testing paradigm. First, the standards were developed through a corporate-dominated process that involved few educators. CCSS lead architect David Coleman, with virtually no background in teaching, worked on CCSS through a Gates-funded think tank, Student Achievement Partners. The other CCSS think tank, Achieve, has a deep bench of corporate sponsors.[21] When CCSS designated two work groups (one for mathematics, one for English language arts) to spearhead writing the standards, all but three of twenty-nine work group members were employed either by testing companies or corporate-funded think tanks.[22] Second, the draft CCSS standards received wide criticism from educators, whose concerns were not reflected in the final version. A 2010 statement signed by over five hundred early childhood health and education professionals warned that CCSS's narrow focus on discrete reading and math skills would restrict children's development by pushing out hands-on and play-based learning.[23] Other educators warned about CCSS's requirement that all kindergarteners learn to read, when many are not developmentally ready;[24] its requirement that students master materials with higher text complexity;[25] and its interpretation of "close reading," which discourages students from connecting a text to their own thoughts and experiences or to the world.[26] Third, as Diane Ravitch points out, CCSS backers declined to field-test the standards before implementing them nationally.[27] Finally, CCSS places even more emphasis on testing than did NCLB, and as a CTU position paper argues, the negative impact will bear most heavily on students of color: "The experience of NCLB suggests that the students most likely to be behind—those who are poor, African-American, Latino, and/or go to segregated schools—are also the ones most likely to have their schools turned into test-prep factories so that children meet the demands of success metrics."[28]

Despite the wealth of researcher and teacher testimony challenging CCSS, both NEA and AFT are stalwart supporters of the new standards. Moreover, the national unions approach this critical topic with the exaggerated claims of a public relations campaign, rather than acknowledging criticisms and weighing the evidence. Here are illustrative excerpts from "10 Things You Should Know about the Common Core," published in the fall 2013 edition of NEA Today:[29]

- "Educators desperately want to reclaim the joy in teaching— which means creative lesson plans, meaningful exploration of topics, and inspiring the joy of real learning in our students," says NEA President Dennis Van Roekel. "Common Core could help achieve that if the implementation is done correctly."
- "The standards make things equal for all children in the U.S.," says Colorado teacher Cheryl Mosier. "We're not going to have pockets of high-performing students in one area compared to another area. Everybody will have a very high bar to meet, but it's a bar that can be met—with supports [in place] for all teachers."
- "Drill and Kill" Curriculum Could Be History.

Members pushed back against the CCSS puff piece with a storm of commentary on the NEA website. Said one: "I am terribly disappointed that my union ignores the valid criticisms and concerns of the very teachers it supposedly represents." And another: "Very unhappy with your sheer disregard for those of us in the trenches and the children that we are fighting to protect from the ruination of public education."[30]

The teachers unions can and should embrace *authentic* standards. As explained in a recent policy statement of CReATE—a network of Chicago-area education professors—authentic standards are student-centered, holistic, and culturally responsive; are research- and community-driven, rather than market-driven.[31] An exemplary set of standards for the English language arts was jointly developed by the International Reading Association and National Council of Teachers of English in 1996, and reaffirmed in 2012. Their standards reflect the democratic, learner-centered pedagogy that Debra Goodman describes in chapter 6 in regard to the whole language movement. Students "conduct research"; "communicate their discoveries in ways that suit their purpose and audience"; "apply a wide range of strategies to comprehend, interpret, evaluate, and appreciate texts"; and, in other ways, students figure things out and share what they learn, supported by a resource-rich environment.[32] There are also authentic alternatives to assessing students, teachers, and schools.[33]

It is crucial that the teachers unions provide leadership in these areas, rather than hewing to corporate agendas and frameworks. While the AFT and NEA criticize over-testing and pressures to teach to the test,[34] they also support policies that contribute to these problems. CCSS has sharply increased the number of tests in school systems that were already test-flooded by NCLB.[35] New York City teacher/blogger Katie Lapham estimates that her first-grade class loses two weeks of instruction to testing and test prep as a result of CCSS—and that is above and beyond the time lost to testing prior to CCSS. Even though federally mandated testing doesn't start until third grade, the principal at Lapham's school insists that teachers implement all of the various optional tests in grades K–2 so that students are better prepared for the rigorous

CCSS testing they will face in third grade.[36] The linking of test scores to teacher evaluations, a practice supported by many AFT/NEA leaders, likewise pressures teachers toward a test-prep focus.

Partnership Strategy and Teacher Evaluation

Corporate reform proponents emphasize teacher evaluation as much as they do standards and tests. Evaluation systems have been redesigned to give management tighter control over teachers' labor, to determine teachers' raises through performance-based pay programs (also known as merit pay), and to facilitate teacher firings. The new systems have certain prominent features. First, "student growth," measured primarily by test scores, is now a mandatory part of teacher evaluation in most states. For example, the weight of student growth in evaluations is 20 percent in Texas; 35 percent in Arizona and Tennessee; and "at least 50 percent" in Colorado, Florida, Georgia, and Michigan.[37] Second, the new systems are configured to reduce the number of teachers who are given overall satisfactory ratings. Third, the systems terminate allegedly ineffective teachers faster than in the past.

Given the many state laws that now mandate linkage between teacher evaluation and test scores, an effective challenge to such policies necessarily requires state-level organizing. Yet such state-level departures would not be viable without huge change and invigoration at the local level. Two teacher evaluation systems— one adopted in New Haven, Connecticut, in 2009; the other, in Washington, DC, in 2010—set the pace nationally for a test-linked and punitive approach to evaluation. Both were bargained by the local teachers unions and before applicable state laws were enacted. As a starting point for developing alternatives, it is worthwhile to review the impact of these systems. The posture of union-management partnership that accompanied their adoption deserves examination as well.

New Haven, CT

In her keynote at the AFT's 2012 convention, Weingarten told of a transformation in New Haven, Connecticut. The leaders and members of the New Haven Federation of Teachers (NHFT) "are partnering with their district to overhaul teacher development and evaluation and to turn around low-performing schools," she said. "Together, they reached a new agreement that uses multiple measures to assess teacher performance and focuses on helping all teachers improve throughout their careers. It's a far cry from the shaming and sanctioning of teachers based on a single test score or a drive-by observation, which do nothing to improve teaching and learning."[38]

The centerpiece of the contract signed by NHFT in 2009 was an evaluation system called TEVAL, which became a template for Connecticut legislation as well as a national model. TEVAL linked teacher assessment to students' test scores, but with the scores incorporated through student growth goals determined by each teacher. For instance, one teacher goal might be that her students' math scores will grow by 10 percent over the course of a year. Student growth comprises roughly half of the evaluation. TEVAL also reduced job security: a tenured teacher will find her job at risk with a single unsatisfactory evaluation. Teachers deemed to be low performing do receive advance notification by the end of October, according to the TEVAL guidebook, allowing time to improve before the final "summative" evaluation is issued at the end of the school year the following June. Along with notification, at-risk teachers are provided an "intensive plan of improvement" with "frequent support sessions." But if teachers do not improve sufficiently by the end of the school year, "they will be subject to sanctions . . . including termination."[39]

Local union leaders claim that the TEVAL model is working well. David Low, NHFT vice president and math/physics/ocean engineering teacher at a vocational high school, cites a more collaborative environment in the schools. "The level of professionalism and how teachers get treated hopefully has increased because we're asking administrators to take a view of how things are going and how they can help, rather than 'Here's what you need to be doing, and here's what I saw that's wrong.'"[40] NHFT president David Cicarella, who was honored by the White House as a "Champion of Change" in 2012, says that the new contract has been "great for teachers, principals, and central office." The union had a "tremendous amount of input" in its development: "It's probably more our document than the district's. So even though there is a lot of pressure, a lot of accountability, it's more fair now."[41] Similarly, Weingarten tells of a New Haven school meeting, held two years after the new contract's implementation, in which she, then education secretary Arne Duncan, and local officials met with teachers, who talked about "the voice they have, the empowerment they feel, and their passion to help children."[42]

But in my interviews with New Haven teachers in August 2012, I detected a pall of fear, particularly in the city's academically low-rated schools. Critics of the new contract, who spoke to me on condition of anonymity, described a more stressful, test-focused, and bullying environment, where new tiering systems assist the targeting of schools and teachers. A tier one school is safe, while a tier three is in for deep scrutiny; a level five teacher is "exemplary," while a level one—"needs improvement"—faces potential termination. The teacher rankings, ostensibly aimed at supporting professional development, have fostered fear and division, says one middle school teacher. "You have these conversations like, 'Well, what's your ranking? Really, she gave you a two? You should totally be a four.' Or: 'You're a three, I'm a three. But I'm way better than you.'" One teacher complained to her: "My test scores are fine, and I'm meeting my goals. But when I go to my debriefs [with an instructional manager], it's 'Why wasn't that kid participating? Why aren't you doing this? Why aren't you doing that?' " [43]

A veteran elementary school teacher sees more bullying of staff under the new contract. She recalls being subjected to a surprise classroom observation after speaking out at a school staff meeting: "Here they come in my room. Sometimes they bring a whole entourage, like five people." The observation was followed by a critical report, the teacher recounts: "She did this and this wrong. She didn't have her objective. She didn't follow through with this guided reading lesson." [44] A year after my visit to New Haven, a local retired teacher, in a letter to Diane Ravitch, cited conditions that mirrored my own findings. New Haven teachers "are now plagued by endless testing and data paperwork overload," she wrote. "To make matters even more difficult, this is occurring in a school climate of fear and mistrust." [45] TEVAL forced out thirty-four teachers in its first year of implementation. [46]

Washington, DC

The D.C. evaluation system, called IMPACT, was part of a 2010 contract that the AFT-affiliated Washington Teachers Union (WTU) signed with then D.C. schools chief Michelle Rhee. IMPACT included certain elements seen in New Haven, such as slashed job security and 50 percent of teacher ratings tied to student growth (primarily test scores). It also added performance-based pay to the mix, with a rating of "effective" or better required for salary step increases, and teachers rated "highly effective" eligible for bonuses. As in New Haven, the D.C. contract bore the imprint of partnership—with district administration and with corporate interests. The foundations of Eli Broad, the Waltons, Julian Robertson, and Laura and John Arnold—all leading corporate reform backers—supported the new contract with $64.5 million in donations. This would pay for retroactive general raises totaling 21 percent, along with funding the bonus program.[47] Upon reaching a tentative agreement, the parties launched an unusual union-management joint public relations campaign aimed at convincing teachers to ratify the deal. This began with a press conference headed up by Rhee, Weingarten, and WTU's then president George Parker. In a joint written statement, the trio declared, "We worked through our differences to come up with a plan for education that best serves the needs of D.C.'s schoolchildren." [48] This was followed by a media and leafleting blitz under the slogan, "Good for Students, Fair to Teachers."

But the new evaluation system produced even harsher results than seen in New Haven. In July 2010, a month after ratifying the new agreement, WTU members received a rude awakening as 241 teachers were fired, many because of "ineffective" IMPACT ratings.[49] Over 700 teachers with "minimally effective" ratings received written warnings, putting them at risk of dismissal the following year. The firings bolstered Rhee's national reputation as a tough-minded advocate for kids. Many D.C. teachers, however, would come to see IMPACT as a tool for cultivating fear, punishing outspoken teachers, and weakening the union. In a 2011 survey, only 2 percent of 450 responding WTU members considered IMPACT "an effective way to evaluate the performance of teachers as it relates to student achievement."[50]

IMPACT featured a scoring system that lent an image of scientific objectivity while ensuring that a growing cohort of teachers were ripe for termination. Teachers needed to earn a minimum of 250 points, within a scale that ranged from 100 to 400, in order to be rated "effective." In prior years, 95 percent of D.C. teachers were rated satisfactory or above. But in IMPACT's first year, only 82 percent of teachers were found to be effective or highly effective.[51] In 2012–13, schools chief Kaya Henderson,

TABLE 2.1: IMPACT Rating System as Revised in 2012–13 School Year[54]

Rating	Points
Ineffective	100 to 199
Minimally Effective	200 to 249
Developing	250 to 299
Effective	300 to 349
Highly Effective	350 to 400

who had replaced Rhee, announced that the district's definition of teacher effectiveness needed to be "more rigorous" in order to "dramatically accelerate student achievement."[52] Therefore, the minimum score for an effective IMPACT rating was boosted from 250 to 300 (see Table 2.1). The number of teachers rated effective or better promptly dropped further that year, to 73 percent.[53] The remaining 27 percent faced relatively rapid dismissals, even if they were tenured and veteran teachers. "Ineffective" teachers are subject to immediate termination. "Minimally effective" teachers are at risk the next year if they do not rise to the "effective" level. Teachers who are "developing" but less than effective have two years to shape up or face termination.[55]

One of IMPACT's sharp critics is Elizabeth Davis, a thirty-six-year veteran information technology teacher who was elected WTU president in 2013. Davis recalls how she happened to receive a low IMPACT score one year. Her evaluator had arrived late to her classroom and instructed Davis to begin her lesson over again, explaining, "I want to hear you read the lesson objective." Davis refused, pointing out: "My students are in the process. They've already started their activity." The students were busy creating brochures using Microsoft Publisher, and their objective was written on the board. The evaluator nonetheless marked Davis down for refusing to begin her lesson over again. Davis believes that IMPACT also interferes with culturally sensitive teaching: "Every child comes to us, no matter their reading level, with some knowledge. Some teachers are really good at finding out how to connect what they want to teach to what the child already knows, making it relevant to every child. But now doing so can hurt you, since what might be relevant to the child and their growth might not be on a standardized test."[56]

The IMPACT system and stepped-up teacher firings, joined with years of closings and privatization of D.C. schools, would bring particular harm to D.C.'s majority black community. Starting in the 2008–9 school year, Rhee had begun using staff layoffs as opportunities to replace higher-paid, veteran black teachers with lower-paid, inexperienced white teachers, many of them Teach for America (TFA) corps members. (Both Rhee and her successor Kaya Henderson—who resigned her position in 2016—are TFA alumnae.) Among those ousted by IMPACT in 2010 was sixteen-year teacher Malvery Smith. Smith remembers the summer meeting where she and two hundred other fired teachers were being advised by their union. The meeting was 98 percent black, she says, "and strictly veteran teachers." One day that same summer, Smith was at a school to give a WTU professional development class when she happened to notice another class taking place in the same building. "They were having a meeting in the small auditorium upstairs," she recalls, "and I looked in to see what was going on. I saw one black teacher and twenty-four white teachers." Smith learned that the class was part of a TFA training program; the attendees would likely be among those taking the jobs of D.C.'s fired black veterans, including Smith herself.[57] While hundreds of mostly women black teachers, economic pillars in their community, have been stripped of their jobs, thousands of black students have been deprived of experienced teachers who, as Davis puts it, know how to connect classroom material to students' knowledge and lives.

Competing Models of Teacher Unionism

No doubt, one reason that many teachers union leaders adopt a partnership strategy—or what is effectively a posture of surrender to corporate reform—is that there appears to be no way to resist. WTU activists had tried to press George Parker to replace the union's ineffectual quiet bargaining with a more militant organizing posture, but to no avail. As past union vice president and president Nathan Saunders recalls: "George would say to me, 'You need to get on board, because this is going to happen with us or without us.'"[58]

The perception that resistance is impossible is, in turn, tied to a particular model of unionism. Traditionally, U.S. teachers unions, and unions in other fields as well, have focused on "member services." This means bargaining over salaries, working conditions, and employee rights, along with helping individual members with their grievances on the job. Another arena of activity—advocating for public education and social justice, building broad-based community alliances—has, with exceptions, not been a historical priority of the teachers unions.[59] Under the dominant service model, the union is akin to an insurance policy: members pay dues; union leaders and staff provide protection and bargain contracts. Insurance, travel, and product discounts are included. Only limited member engagement is expected. The service model characterized CTU prior to the ascension of new leadership in 2010, as a Chicago middle school teacher explains:

> I just paid my dues. . . . There was no room for the membership to need to do anything, because "we'll take care of it.". . . There wasn't any education about trying to get the community involved. The union was not fighting against the damage that was being done by Chicago's policy of closing schools.[60]

If union members are seen and see themselves only as service recipients and not as organizers and leaders, then union officials bring no clout to the bargaining table and have no means to challenge corporate interests. The partnership option logically follows.

An alternate model called *social-movement unionism* also provides traditional member services. But it does so in the context of member engagement, leadership development, and the building of grassroots union-community coalitions.[61] Such was evident when a transformed CTU arrived at the bargaining table in November 2011 with a giant forty-member team, representing the diversity of the union's membership.[62] An elementary school teacher comments on the new model while looking back on the 2012 CTU strike: "Before the strike I saw them [the union] as an entity up there to go to. Now I see them as within my building. I mean it's in myself, it's my other colleagues. . . Now I feel more connected to the union."[63]

While the choice between a service or social-movement model is relevant to all unions, the implications are particularly far-reaching in K–12 public education. Teachers unions are the voice for teachers and other staff—counselors, clinicians, librarians, paraprofessionals—covered by the contract. But they do not represent students, parents, or community—constituencies who equally deserve a democratic voice in schools. What responsibility do teachers unions hold for helping these other groups gain such voice? How can the stakeholders make common cause? These and similar questions weigh heavily on teacher unionism and education organizing strategy. In two historic conflicts that well deserve study—one in the Ocean Hill-Brownsville neighborhood of New York City in 1968; the other in Newark, New Jersey, in 1970–71—black communities demanded a stronger voice in neighborhood schools. They wanted better school conditions, curriculum reflecting black history and perspectives, and teachers who were more attuned to students and communities of color. While the community demands might have presented the local AFT chapters with opportunities to explore new alliances, or to broaden beyond the union's narrow service model, they were instead regarded as a threat. Battles ensued pitting black against white, union against community, leaving behind tensions and racial wounds that have yet to heal.[64]

Today, teachers need allies as never before, as do students harmed by test-driven curricula, and communities destabilized by school closures, housing crises, and jobs crises. Here again, CTU's social-movement approach offers promise. The union's collaborative work with the community is conducted partly through a CTU community board, explains the union's staff coordinator and influential visionary Jackson Potter.[65] The other part is through the relationships that CTU member-leaders develop at school sites with parents, local school councils, and neighborhood organizations. CTU and its community partners organize joint forums and conferences, while they mobilize together against school closures and other attacks. CTU invites community organizers to help train union members in how to work with the community. At the same time, says Potter, the union can help the community groups build their own memberships. "How do we create settings where you get access to our members, who have access to the parents who you want to talk to?" Ultimately, he observes, "We want to help the community groups build up their organizations, and then we want their help to build up ours."[66]

We might say, then, that the two competing union models conceive teachers differently in relation to the community they serve. The service model regards teachers as professionals operating at a certain remove from the community. Its orientation is reflected in the oft-heard union wisdom, "Keep the members happy." The social-movement model, by contrast, emphasizes teachers' jointness with the community: a common plight, a soli-darity. The welfare of members is integrally linked to the pursuit of justice for all.

Union democracy is another critical distinction between the service and social-movement models. Even in unions with solid constitutional practices such as fair and open officer elections and regular assemblies with transparent decision making, top officers and staff normally operate with broad discretion in the daily run-ning of the union. A genuine grassroots democracy requires not only constitutional procedures but also member engagement and leadership development on many levels.

One union that is currently in process of shifting from a ser-vice-based to a social-movement approach is the Massachusetts Teachers Association (MTA), an NEA affiliate with 110,000 members in K–12 and higher education. For years, MTA lead-ers had a pattern of making backroom deals that compromised member interests. In one such case, in spring 2012, the pro-corporate group, Stand for Children, was threatening to place a "Great Teachers Great Schools" referendum on the state ballot. The measure would make teacher performance evaluations, rather than seniority (that is, years of service), the primary basis for determining who stays and who leaves in cases of layoff or transfer. Teachers union contracts traditionally rely on senior-ity as the key criterion in layoff and transfer decisions, a method that contributes to a stable teacher workforce while avoiding the management favoritism and other vagaries that come into play in performance evaluations. Other provisions of the referendum would limit teacher access to tenure, make it harder for the union to defend dismissed teachers, and eliminate the union's right to bargain on a host of issues.[67]

When MTA leaders learned of Stand for Children's plan, they "did not inform the membership, much less mobilize it," recounts sociology professor and MTA board member Dan Clawson:

Instead the president and vice president engaged in secret back-room negotiations with Stand for Children. When the board of directors first learned about this—thanks to persistent questioning by a handful of board members—the president insisted that the entire discussion take place in executive session; board members were forbidden to tell the rank-and-file what was going on.[68]

MTA leaders eventually negotiated a deal that avoided the ballot measure, but with the union agreeing to legislation that sharply reduced the impact of seniority in layoffs and transfers. Clawson comments: "The union's mantra, heard often under the old leadership, was 'it could have been worse.'" [69]

One impact of the union's deal with Stand for Children was an intense member discussion about the need for a different kind of union. This included rapid growth of an MTA dissident caucus, Educators for a Democratic Union (EDU). In 2014, EDU recruited teacher educator Barbara Madeloni to run for MTA president. Prior to this, Madeloni had earned a national reputation for her bold opposition to corporatizing measures in teacher education at the University of Massachusetts-Amherst.[70] The Madeloni-EDU campaign drew many lessons from Chicago's Caucus of Rank-and-File Educators, which had swept the CTU union election in 2010. "The idea of it," says high school history teacher Jamie Rinaldi, "was we're going to run a campaign that almost presents that we're a parallel union. What could the union look like? We started with coffees in people's living rooms. And then we built those up to house parties. And we had meetings where we talked about struggles that different locals were going through, and what sort of policies should inform the campaign."[71]

Madeloni won an upset election victory at the union's annual meeting of delegates in May. That fall, the union faced its first crisis under the new leadership. The Massachusetts Department of Elementary and Secondary Education (DESE) unveiled a set of proposals that would tie teachers' licenses to their performance evaluations. The licenses must be renewed every five years. Under one proposed option, a teacher who received a single evaluation of "needs improvement" during the prior five years would be denied renewal of her license, destroying her teaching career.[72] MTA's response to DESE reflected a sharp break from the union's past. "Madeloni did not initiate backroom negotiations and seek an orderly retreat," notes Clawson, but "she immediately and decisively opposed the new licensure proposal, and gave an eager membership ways to act":

> More than five thousand members sent emails, and two rallies were scheduled, with buses rented and members signed up to attend the last two of DESE's "Town Hall" meetings for their proposal. Instead of choosing which bad option to support, the campaign was titled "None of the Above."[73]

Rather than face busloads of angry teachers, DESE canceled its last two town hall meetings and promptly rescinded its proposals. Clawson remarks that an enlivened membership was crucial to nixing the plan, but "so too was a newly installed, fighting leadership." He adds with caution that the victory was a temporary one and that similar proposals could be revived "as soon as DESE and corporate reformers think we are napping."[74]

A second Madeloni initiative would lay groundwork to challenge test-driven education, while also helping establish the union's new participatory model. MTA's legacy in this regard should be noted. In order to qualify for Race to the Top money, Massachusetts had, like many other states, passed legislation in 2010 tying teacher evaluations to student test scores. The old MTA leadership had gone along with this,[75] and MTA members now faced intensified pressures to teach to the test. So, starting in fall 2014, Madeloni and union vice president Janet Anderson traveled around the state holding community forums with teachers, parents, and students. The forums asked questions such as: How does standardized testing impact student learning, engagement, and love of learning? How does the teacher evaluation system impact teacher workload, professional development, and job security? Information gleaned from over two dozen forums would provide a basis for the union's strategic planning.

Madeloni, who is the "wartime chief" referenced by Agustin Morales in the epigraph for this chapter, is one of those union leaders who dares to name the prevailing threat while also asserting an alternative vision for better schools and a better world. "We come into office during tumultuous times—indeed, dangerous times," she wrote in the union's magazine, *MTA Today*, shortly after her election:

Corporate players, looking to privatize public education, profit from the public dollar and bust our unions, have imposed business ideology on public schools through high-stakes testing, charter schools and technocratic accountability systems.... Ours is not simply a fight against corporate "reforms," as some would frame it. Ours is a struggle *for* a vision of public education as a place for joy, creativity, imagination, empathy and critical questioning so that students enter the world ready to participate in democratic communities.[76]

Part II

Organizing through Resistance

3

A School Community Says No to Privatization

BEIDLER ELEMENTARY SCHOOL, CHICAGO

Howard Ryan

> I just thought that this is my second home. I come in early and I stay late. I have a love for what I do, and I love the children I teach. So we started making signs, and I started getting teachers and parents together to fight for our school.
>
> —JESSIE HUDSON, special education teacher

THE SPRING OF 2011 SHOULD HAVE been a time for celebration at Jacob Beidler Elementary School.[1] The West Chicago pre-K through 8 public school had been in academic upswing for several years, thanks to a stable environment and seasoned staff. Serving over four hundred students—95 percent black, all low income—Beidler had rapidly climbing scores on the Illinois Student Achievement Test (ISAT), high student attendance, high parent satisfaction. It had won the state education board's Academic Improvement Award four times since the award's creation in 2003, and was well on its way to a fifth award for 2011.

This year was like no other, however, because after more than a decade of struggle, Beidler was getting a $2.2 million campus park. Beidler students had always had to make do with recess in the street in front of the school. While the new park would mean safer play for all the students, it would especially mean a lot to the proud members of the Beidler Special Olympics team. The team had long conducted its spring practice in the muddy, gravelly vacant lot behind the school. "Before the children would go out, I would have to check the area, make sure there were no condoms or broken bottles," explains special education teacher and school union delegate Jessie Hudson, who has served as Beidler's Special Olympics head coach for twenty years. Hudson adds, "It was never what you call real safety, because there was always glass and everything out there." The campus park would end these problems, replacing the vacant lot with a running track, jungle gyms and swings, a basketball court, astroturf, trees.

It was indeed a great year for Beidler. But in late March, just days after construction on the park began, it abruptly halted.

Beidler Targeted for Privatization

On March 21, Beidler reading teacher Latina King left school for the day and was preparing to enjoy her evening, when she received a call from Hudson that left her staggered. She recalls, "I was in such disbelief that I walked down the street to a 7-Eleven to actually read it in the newspaper." What she read is that the Chicago Public Schools (CPS) board had announced plans to "consolidate" by moving Beidler's students to nearby Willa Cather Elementary School. The Beidler building would, in turn, be given to an all-boys charter high school, Urban Prep Academy, which was currently housed on the second floor of Cather. The Beidler staff could apply for jobs at Cather or elsewhere, but their future employment was not assured. "Consolidation" was a euphemistic term: CPS planned to close Beidler and hand the building to a charter operator. Several other school closures/consolidations were also proposed, affecting fourteen schools and 4,800 students in total. Citing a $720 million deficit, CPS claimed that Beidler and other schools were underutilized and that the district needed to operate more efficiently.

CPS had been issuing annual lists of "school actions"— closures, consolidations, turnarounds—since 2004, when former mayor Richard Daley and his public schools chief Arne Duncan (who later served as U.S. education secretary) launched Renaissance 2010 (Ren2010), a six-year plan to open one hundred "high-performance" schools while closing sixty "failing" neighborhood public schools. Two-thirds of the new schools would be privately operated, publicly funded charter or contract schools; the others would remain CPS schools, but with selective enrollment. Ren2010 was a corporate project: its blueprint was a 2003 report, *Left Behind,* produced by a committee of the city's elite Commercial Club. The report bemoaned the low test scores in CPS schools and prescribed "increasingly large doses of parental choice." CPS needed "more charter schools—publicly funded but independent, innovative schools that operate with greater flexibility and give parents whose children attend failing schools an option they do not now have."[2] The report also blamed the teachers union for lagging school performance: "The entire collective-bargaining apparatus has been designed less to improve teaching or student learning than to protect the interests of teachers."[3] The Commercial Club supported Ren2010 with a "fundraising and strategic partner," the Renaissance Schools Fund. The fund, in turn, was connected to a new charter school promotion group, New Schools for Chicago, that would "expand the pipeline of quality operators" and make recommendations to CPS as to which charter schools should be selected.[4] Critics called the new group a CPS "secret cabinet."[5]

While the Commercial Club touted Ren2010 as a plan for upgrading school performance, studies in Chicago and nationally suggest that the largest impact of charterization has been to exacerbate educational inequity.[6] A 2012 Chicago Teachers

Union (CTU) report notes the growing resource disparities in public schools since the city's school system fell under strict mayoral control in 1995. The disparities sharpened further under Ren2010, creating a two-tier school system. "Selective enrollment schools, turnarounds and charters received state-of-the-art facilities, equipment, and supplies, while neighborhood schools serving low-income students of color deteriorated."[7] If city leaders were concerned about school performance, why weren't they directing more resources to the schools in greatest need? When not citing low performance as its rationale for school actions, CPS claims underutilization—its rationale of choice in spring 2011. How the addition of more charter schools—or, in Beidler's case, the conversion of a neighborhood school to charter—addresses underutilization goes unexplained by CPS. CTU observes that many of the new charter schools are placed in areas where existing schools have been closed.[8] Meanwhile, Chicago's charter schools perform no better on average than the neighborhood schools they replace, even while they tend to enroll the higher-achieving students and often push out the more academically challenged students.[9]

The Commercial Club's real aim with Ren2010, argues Chicago education professor Pauline Lipman, lay in using charter and selective schools to support downtown development, real estate ventures, and white gentrification in communities of color.[10] The Beidler closure and charter conversion plan appeared to fit such a pattern. In 2007, *Business Week* identified Beidler's neighborhood, East Garfield Park, as being one of "America's Next Hot Neighborhoods."[11] Many area warehouses and commercial buildings had been converted into lofts in the past decade, attracting more affluent and white residents. Moreover, Beidler itself was an attractive facility, located just a block from a city train station. Its main brick building had been built only ten years before, replacing an asbestos-contaminated building. It had a lovely all-purpose room that doubled as a lunchroom and gym. "Urban Prep's basketball coach was down here scouting us out," recalls Jolene Galpin, who teaches first and second grade at Beidler. "He asked, 'Hey, can I come in and check out your gym?' And our principal said: 'No, you can't. What are you doing here? Are you kidding me?'" The coming campus park would further enrich the property. Beidler's Local School Council (LSC) president, Bettye Sherrod, who has put her grandchildren and foster children through the school, points out that the LSC and staff had worked hard to upgrade the school: "We have lab rooms, computer rooms, art and music rooms. We went out and got those things ourselves. And now they want to turn it over to a charter?" With a predominantly black staff and student population, the Beidler community saw the district's move on the school as a form of racial dispossession, as Hudson explains. "All these white people are moving into this neighborhood, and they want our school because they see that we have this. Right off the train they see this beautiful building and this park."

There were other elements of harm and injustice in the proposed school giveaway. One was academics. Beidler's test score growth—from a 23 percent "meets or exceeds" on ISAT's composite measure in 2002 to 64 percent in 2010—was in no small part the result of a mostly veteran staff working together over many years, winning resources for the school, and providing a community anchor that allows trust building with students and parents.* This would all be put at risk by students' forced transfer to another school and the displacement of staff. Indeed, a 2007 study of school closures in Chicago's Midsouth area found that schools receiving transferred students lacked resources and staffing for the influx, reporting "a climate of uncertainty,

---

*This is not intended to endorse a reliance on standardized test scores to measure a school's progress. Test scores are referenced here and elsewhere in the book, despite limitations, as the measure that is most widely available.

demoralization, tension, and stress affecting students, teachers, and families."[12]

The Special Olympics team played an important role in Beidler's academic and environmental advances, tending to the needs of the most challenged students. Hudson talks about what Special Olympics means for the students involved: "Special needs children look to each other and tend to stay within the perimeters of their circle. But when they get involved in Special Olympics, they launch out and start talking to other students. 'Oh, I know her!' They remember each other from year to year. And what I love about it is that color is no issue with them. No color barriers or anything, and everybody's hugging each other."

Beidler's special needs students were now worried about their new campus park. Hudson's classroom has a window looking out on the vacant lot that was being converted. "The men had been out there working every day, drilling away, and the building would be rattling," she recounts. "Then all of a sudden, the construction just stopped, and everybody started getting scared. It was so gloomy and sad. I had to pull my shades down because the kids would just take their chairs and sit by the window and cry." The closure of Beidler would not only mean the loss of a long-awaited park, but could also mean losing Special Olympics altogether. Not every school has a Jessie Hudson—a certified Special Olympics coach with a passion for the program. Hudson was also supported by seven other Beidler teachers who volunteered as assistant coaches for the program. This infrastructure of support would be swept away by CPS's proposal.

Another grievous risk—and a central concern at Beidler if the students were transferred to Cather Elementary—was gang violence. Chicago education activists have repeatedly warned CPS about the dangers of increased violence when schools are closed and students are forced to cross neighborhood and gang lines to attend different schools. CPS has stepped up its school actions despite such warnings, and spikes in violence have resulted.[13] On September 24, 2009, Derrion Albert, a sixteen-year-old honor student at South Chicago's Fenger High School, was beaten to death when he was caught between fighting youth factions. The beating was caught on cell phone video, picked up by major media, and widely broadcast. Chicago police acknowledged that Albert's slaying was related to the mixing of students from different neighborhoods, according to an NBC report, which also connected the slaying to the school closures under Ren2010. "You have a trail of blood and tears ever since they launched (Renaissance 2010)," said Tio Hardiman, director of the anti-violence organization, CeaseFire Illinois. "There's a history of violence associated with moving kids from one area to another."[14] School closures are enmeshed with Chicago's racial politics: the vast majority of the closings target the predominantly black and Latino South and West sides, promoting neighborhood destabilization and violence. The Derrion Albert tragedy remains a symbol of racial injustice in these communities.

The Beidler community was very aware of such dangers, as the proposed closure would force children to cross gang lines to attend Cather. People were especially mindful of what happened to Carl Garner when he was a Beidler seventh grader in 2010. Carl went with a few friends to a hot dog stand that was across the street from Cather. Carl's mother, Tina Garner, describes the incident:

> Carl and his friends were approached by a group of five boys. These were older high school boys. Carl is big for his age. If you saw him in the seventh grade, you would think he was in high school. He's six foot three now and wears a size fourteen shoe. The high school boys hit one of Carl's friends and knocked him out. They tried to hit Carl too, and he hit back before they could really jump him.

The hot dog stand was only two blocks from the Garner home, but "it's different gangs in different sections of the West Side," Garner explains, "and I guess when you cross that street and go around the corner, you're crossing a gang line." Carl himself wasn't hurt. But the incident became common knowledge at Beidler, especially because Tina Garner, a local homeowner who put all three of her children through Beidler, is very active at the school.

One further injustice came into play for Beidler and the other targeted schools: CPS had allowed only a tiny window for community input. The proposed school actions were announced on March 21; final decisions were made in mid-April. During the school board's March 23 meeting, CTU president Karen Lewis challenged CPS for its short notice of school actions: "Last spring, [CPS CEO] Ron Huberman vowed that parents and educators would be involved in the planning of any proposed school actions. That didn't happen. Again. And he promised more advanced warning. In the past, January was the dreaded announcement month. This is March. Two months *less*, when more was promised."[15] The Beidler community had a great deal at stake, and very little time.

Getting Organized

At an 8:30 a.m. staff meeting on March 22, Principal Ewing announced that the school had been targeted for closing, adding, "It's time to fight for Beidler." Ewing, who planned to retire at the end of the school year, faced certain constraints as an administrator without union protection, but "she did support us in whatever way she could," says King. Union delegate Hudson would assume the helm of the campaign to save Beidler. Hudson had never been an activist as such, and wasn't sure what would be required. But she knew how she felt: "I just thought that this is my second home. I come in early and I stay late. I have a love for what I do and I love the children that I teach. So we started making signs and I started getting teachers and parents together to fight for our school." King became Hudson's right hand, "taking on a leadership role sort of behind the scenes," as King explains. "I wasn't out there speaking. But whatever Ms. Hudson said she needed, I was there." Hudson, King, and Ewing were joined by Galpin and assistant principal Tony Teague to form an ad hoc campaign leadership team.

One of Hudson's first calls went to CTU which, under the new CORE (Caucus of Rank-and-File Educators) leadership that had won the union election in 2010, had established an organizing department whose duties included helping schools fight CPS closures and turnarounds. The department assigned Christel Williams, a former school paraprofessional and now full-time CTU organizer, to assist Beidler. Williams began meeting with the most active Beidler teachers to help them think strategically and, as she puts it, "get them to believe that we could win this." Williams wanted the team to identify people's strengths and delegate responsibilities. "These teachers had gifts that had not been unwrapped, maybe certain talents that hadn't been challenged before." She also advised the team to document Beidler's accomplishments and document the problems with CPS's plan. For example, one teacher researched local gang territories and put together a map that was later presented to the school board, showing the dangerous blocks that Beidler students would have to navigate if transferred to Cather.

The Beidler teachers were quick studies. Hudson headed up parent outreach. King handled emails and made all the flyers. Marian Prude, a fourth-grade teacher, ran a media committee to reach out to TV and newspapers. She also made sure teachers had supplies to make posters and banners. Galpin ran a data committee to document issues and prepare presentations. Says Hudson: "We put flyers in Walmart, neighborhood stores, churches, put them in mailboxes. We got petitions going at our front desk downstairs. Whenever we had something, any type of program for the children, we always had petitions out. And sometimes parents would take petitions. We were just out there, made ourselves known. 'Oh, we heard about Beidler.' 'Yeah, we know about Beidler.'"

Staff meetings became organizing centers, as King describes: "We just said, 'Hey teachers, we need your students to make these posters whenever you get a chance. And you can use the supplies from Ms. Prude.' We also told the staff that if you had time on your prep period, get on the phone. Call parents, call as many people as you can." King adds that organizing Beidler was more than a full-time job: "We were here day and night. And when I say night, I'm talking like eight, nine o'clock at night. We would order food; those who would stay late called home. We would have maybe three or four more teachers who would stay and say, 'What do you need me to do?' And then we would say, 'Hey, can you finish calling these people in this list? I need to go finish these flyers.'" The project churned. Williams and the other CTU staff organizers turned their attention to other schools on the hit list that needed greater support.

And the Children Shall Lead Them

The teachers waited a few days before telling students about the threat to their school. "We didn't want the children to become upset and change the whole atmosphere," King explains. But news had already begun filtering to students through their parents. Toward the end of the first week, teachers started having conversations with their classes. King remembers talking with her own students: "The kids would say, 'Well, my mother said I'm not going to Cather. That's too far away. It's too many gangs. We gotta cross over.' They expressed their concerns—how far a walk it would be, the gangs, mixing in with the other children from Cather, the teachers would be different. They didn't want to experience that. And I told them, 'That's why we all need to fight.'"

Days after the Beidler closure was announced, a small group of parents took their own initiative and picketed in front of the school with signs reading "Save Our School." Meanwhile, the campaign leadership team was planning a big march around the block for after school on April 1. And they wanted the students to have an active role. "This is not just teachers fighting. This is everybody fighting," says King. "The students wanted to be involved, so this was a great way to put them in charge of their school." Teachers distributed poster boards and crayons, and the school became a civil rights workshop. King notes: "The kids got a kick out of it because they get to draw. This is perfect for them. So they came up with their own slogans. Teachers would take a look and approve it. I had sixth grade at the time, so I had some artists in there. They would first draw their vision on paper and then transfer from paper to the poster board. Security gave us wooden sticks to hold up the posters." Because students in the upper grades (6, 7, and 8) move from room to room for different subjects, it made the poster production inefficient. So the leadership team organized one day on which the upper grades remained in their homerooms for the entire day. The teachers coordinated so that the homeroom teachers would teach all subjects, and the students were prepared with the assignments they had to do. This allowed more time for poster making while preserving traditional instruction as well.

Teachers also gave students letters inviting their parents to join the march, including permission slips for parents to sign to allow their children to participate. About 95 percent of the students returned signed slips. On Friday, April 1, students and staff alike came ready for the action wearing their bright green

Beidler T-shirts and polo shirts. Some parents joined in as well. King describes the march around the block and its orderly implementation:

> School is over at 2:45. So about 2:20, we started rounding up all of the children who had permission. We called down each class one by one, starting with the little ones. We lined them up inside the main entrance, class by class behind each other. So we waited until the 2:45 bell rang. Then we dismissed the children who were not participating. Then once we got everyone out of the building, we began our march. Somebody had a bullhorn. Somebody started yelling "Save Our School!" and everybody just joined in.

Media representatives, including a crew from a Spanish-language TV station, greeted marchers as the green wave exited the building, five hundred strong. When the march turned down busy Lake Street, continues King,

> People were pulling over, asking what's going on. When we explained, then some people joined. Some people blew their horns. Some people just got out and stood and watched. We got the attention of everyone who was there. After the march, children came back to the front of the school where we had a DJ and a short rally. The DJ played some songs requested by the principal that were children-appropriate. The principal and assistant principal talked to the children and parents about saving our school. Then we collected the posters the children had made so we could use them again.

The leadership team stayed very late that night planning their next moves.

Community Allies

The campaign reached out to allies and found precious support. Early on in the project, King and Hudson contacted Beidler's past principal, Geraldine Moore. Moore recommended they get in touch with Reverend Paul Jakes, who runs a small church in East Garfield Park. A prominent Chicago activist and one-time mayoral candidate, Jakes had helped Moore in the struggle to get Beidler's campus park built. He took King's flyers, distributing them to his congregation and to his network of ministers. He connected the Beidler team with Pastor Benjamin Turk, whose church is across the street from Beidler, and the campaign would hold community meetings there. Jakes also had a friend, the late Paul Davis, who ran a public relations firm. Unbeknownst to the Beidler team, Jakes and his fellow ministers pitched in to hire Davis to handle media outreach for the Beidler campaign—beyond the outreach that Prude and her media committee were doing. This helped the Beidler campaign receive consistent news coverage. But perhaps Jakes's largest contribution was his powerful presence at public meetings and actions. "He was like our speaker," says King, "the big guy who leads the marches and who you see talking on TV. He gets people inspired and focused."

Hudson found a very helpful community organization through the family of a student. The student's grandmother's sister was a member of Action Now whose mission is "to organize working families and strengthen their voices on issues of racial, social and economic justice." Hudson recalls: "One of their organizers came out and spoke with me. He said, 'Before we go any further, would you like to join?' So I joined Action Now. I still pay ten dollars every month. The organizer talked about how terrible it is for charter schools to just come in and try to take over. So I said, 'My main thing is how can you help us?' He said, 'Whatever you need us to do—march with you, pass out flyers, things like that.'

So, whenever we had flyers at the school, they would take some." Action Now is also an important ally of CTU in the citywide fight against school privatization. Their blue-shirted members bolster public actions, and their speakers are often at the rally podium or press conference.

The Beidler team also reached out to elected officials. King describes how parents made a useful connection with a local alderman. LSC president Bettye Sherrod and another LSC member, Gwendolyn Cox, "kept calling and calling Alderman [Walter] Burnett, and they couldn't get in touch. They finally got in their car and drove to his office. Burnett and Alderman [Jason] Ervin were the two that came out to support us. They were instrumental in getting our campus park started."

King adds: "That's when the senior citizen home over here got involved as well." Residents of a nearby senior center were concerned about Beidler's prospective conversion to a high school, with new problems posed by an older student population. They became allies in the campaign and helped lobby elected officials. Alderman Burnett raised these concerns during his public remarks opposing CPS's plan, as the *Chicago Sun-Times* reports: "Burnett said he shut down a basketball court less than a block from the school because it was disrupting a seniors' center across the street. But under the latest plan, 'I'm going to have a whole bunch of high school kids disturbing the senior center again,' Burnett said."[16]

Democratizing a CPS Meeting

CPS representatives came to Beidler on the evening of March 31 to share information about the district's consolidation plan. A CPS flyer had announced the session as a community meeting but, as King explains, the district wanted to discourage parents from coming: "They sent us word that the meeting was only for staff." The Beidler team ignored that instruction and mobilized all-out for the meeting. When CPS school relations officer Jose Alvarez walked into the Beidler all-purpose room for what he thought would be a simple informational meeting, he faced what was essentially a rally to stop a school giveaway. "There were over a hundred parents there," says Tina Garner. "We had the alderman there. We had a couple of committeemen. We had news people." Galpin adds: "I had contacted Rosalind Rossi from the *Sun-Times* that day and asked her to come out. They came and interviewed our assistant principal, took a tour around the building and took pictures."

The Beidler team not only mobilized for the meeting, but came prepared with their own program. "It was actually funny," Galpin reflects, "because, when the team from the central office came here, they had not intended for Beidler staff or anyone having our own presentation." But Ewing had typed up an agenda and began to review it for the meeting. "And first," she announced, "we'd like to begin with a parent and LSC member, Bettye Sherrod. Then we're going to have one of our teachers, Ms. Galpin, do a PowerPoint presentation on some data that we've pulled together." At that point, the CPS officials halted the meeting and took Ewing aside for a private discussion. They told Ewing, "We didn't intend on it going this way," to which the principal replied: "Well, we have prepared this information and we want you to hear what we have to say. It's not just about you and what you have to say." CPS allowed the locals to make their presentations.

The Beidler team's data left the CPS officials without a rationale to support their plan, as Ewing recounts: "When they realized that Cather's scores were just a point or two off from ours, they couldn't use low performance as an excuse anymore. Then they tried to say our building was underutilized. Well, we went through and did an analysis of all the buildings in the area. Not only were their scores lower than ours, but their buildings had even a lower enrollment than we had." She points out: "They should have just been honest in the first place and said your building is so nice that we want to put a charter school in there."

CPS then heard from Tina Garner. "I'm a homeowner and a taxpayer. I pay over three thousand dollars a year just for property tax alone, not to mention homeowners insurance and everything else. This is the only school that my kids have ever been to, and I've been in this neighborhood since 1985. And I find that this is a safe school. There have been no incidents of abductions, gang-banging. No drugs are sold in this facility. Since I've been coming here, I go to the parent meetings and I volunteer, and the outcome has been great for my kids."

Reverend Jakes then spoke and, according to the *Sun-Times*, repeatedly drove the audience to its feet as he blasted the CPS proposal as "insulting," "appalling," and "dangerous." Pointing out that the CPS plan would force Beidler kids to cross three gang territories to get to Cather, he added: "We want to be clear. We do not want another Derrion Albert killing. We will not stand for it in East Garfield Park."[17]

The following week, on Thursday, April 7, the Beidler community held a second march, this time joined by Beidler alumni, clergy, Action Now, and other supporters in a half-mile parade to a city community center—the Garfield Workforce Center. This was a grander affair, led by a sound truck contributed by Reverend Michael Stinson and with police escort. Jakes, who helped plan the action with the Beidler team, notes its strategic significance: "We wanted to march to a city institution to bring some media attention and really embrace the whole picture of what is devastating to not only the children, but to the whole community. Because we're really looking at the other NATO: The Neglected, the Abused, the Totally Overlooked. That's what would happen if they did what they wanted to do with this school, causing a whole shift with employment, parents losing ability to get to their children quickly."

The next evening, the Beidler community gathered across the street from the school in the basement of Pastor Turk's Central Memorial Missionary Baptist Church. They were joined by representatives from other targeted schools. Hudson remembers being lifted by the deep sense of community among the fifty attendees: "Everybody was sort of hanging on to each other, I think because we were in our first meeting with all the different schools. The thing that was so moving was the singing of the songs, the joining of the hands. Sometimes when we go to meetings we don't know what to expect. It just took me back to Dr. King's day—we shall overcome."

Victory!

On the morning of Monday, April 11, 2011, Beidler parents, teachers, and students filled three buses bound for downtown, where the board of education was holding a hearing on the Beidler-Cather consolidation. Filling the buses was itself an achievement, in that it was during spring break and would require a whole day's commitment. "I knew it was going to be hard getting the parents to actually come to the school, get on the bus, and go downtown," says Beidler science teacher Syreeta Epps. So she engaged her students in recruiting their parents. Epps has a practice of holding classroom raffles every two weeks. "It's honoring the group as a whole and mostly concentrating on behavior, not so much the academics." The winners get little gift cards and treats, and she brings enough so everybody wins something. Epps adapted her raffle for the April 11 turnout: students who signed up their parents to attend the board meeting got to participate in the raffle. From among the twenty-five students in Epps's homeroom, this brought ten to twelve parents along with their children, which she felt was "huge."

Beidler's green wave flooded CPS headquarters. Says King: "When we all walked in, we packed out two rooms. We had the room where the board meeting was held and then another floor was full of people." Many people wanted to speak on behalf of Beidler, so parents, teachers, and students all made sure to get on the speakers' list for the meeting.

But as soon as the meeting started, something unexpected happened. King recalls: "They announced—at the very beginning of the meeting—that they were not going to consolidate Beidler and Cather. But we could remain to testify to have it on record. So everybody who had signed up to speak stayed to speak. It was just as emotional, as if CPS hadn't announced anything. I think we had just been going through so many marches for those weeks."

Ewing told the hearing: "Forty-three years after Martin Luther King died, prejudice still exists. African Americans and Hispanics are targeted for consolidation. Elected officials demoralize neighborhoods and schools." Galpin testified that Beidler is not under-enrolled. Citing a national norm of 135 square feet of school space per student, Galpin pointed out that Beidler's utilization was at 75 percent and Cather's at 80 percent.[18] By contrast, if Urban Prep moved into Beidler, their utilization would be a mere 35 percent "even if their enrollment increased to 225 next year." She challenged the board: "How can schools in more affluent neighborhoods remain open with enrollment of less than two hundred students? Students should not be squeezed in classrooms so CPS can open another charter school."

Eighth-grader Carl Garner told the hearing: "I'm a big little kid and I want to live to see tomorrow. I want to go to college and be a lawyer or doctor. But I can't do that if I'm afraid for my life and getting attacked just to go to school." His sister Kira, a seventh grader, said, "I think Beidler is a safe haven for this community." Kira participates in the Special Olympics, her mother explained to me the following spring, "and that's where she is today with Ms. Hudson."

"We came back to the school afterward," King remembers. "Everybody was there, and people were texting other people, 'Hey, we won!'" Reverend Jakes congratulated everyone: "We have a victory. You should be proud of yourselves. You came out, you supported your children's education. It was worth it all." The Beidler team had prepared a raffle to thank the parents for giving their day. Bettye Sherrod won an Xbox video game unit, which she passed along to her grandson. The Xbox is a reminder of their success, she says. "It was kind of saying, 'You guys, y'all did all right.'"

Beidler finally got its new campus park the following October. Present at the ribbon-cutting were the two principals, Geraldine Moore and the newly retired Shirley Ewing, who had fought for over ten years combined to have the park built. Also present were Alderman Burnett; Beidler's new principal, Charles Anderson; and Beidler's staff and students. "When they cut that ribbon and I saw the kids running in the park, I just cried," Hudson remembers. "I was just so, so happy for them that they have somewhere to play. The children were so happy."

Reflections

Public schools are sites of democracy, however imperfectly, and Beidler had a history of democracy in action. Teachers led by Hudson had taken the initiative to build a Special Olympics program. Sherrod and other parents had worked with the school to bring "lab rooms, computer rooms, art and music rooms," and they had fought and lobbied to win a campus park. In 2011, the entire school—staff, students, and parents—engaged with community support to defend what they had built. And their voices prevailed.

Still, things do not remain at peace at Beidler, nor in the scores of other Chicago schools that remain threatened by the privatizers. In fact, it is hard for any public school nationally to feel a sense of security—particularly in low-income communities—in the face of corporate predators, defunding, and high-stakes testing. "We're still not out of the woods," says King. "They're going to be looking at us with a magnifying glass once our latest scores come back." Though Beidler was saved in spring 2011, four other schools were shut down. After the election of Mayor Rahm Emanuel that year, the targeting of schools in the city's South and West sides would intensify, even while community opposition deepened. Thus, in 2012, CPS carried out seventeen school actions—closures, phase-outs, and "turnarounds" that replace school staff. In 2013, the bleeding was far greater with seventy-two actions: fifty schools were shuttered; five underwent turnarounds; and seventeen more were "co-located," wherein charter schools are given space within regular public schools.[19] These would smooth the way toward sixty new charter schools projected in a five-year CPS plan.[20]

Nor did Beidler's success against privatization neatly translate into a stronger teachers union at the school. Galpin observes: "In that moment, there were some people who were ready to fight and save our school. But now, a year later, you don't see that same sort of spark from teachers." While Hudson is proud of the organizing work that saved Beidler, it's not something she looks forward to doing again: "It was hard getting people to do things, hard getting teachers to stay after school."

On the other hand, several Beidler teachers discovered their leadership capacities. Hudson has long felt it her calling to become a principal, and has taken the required school leadership coursework. But after the Beidler campaign, she sees herself "in a different light." Now, she says, "I see that leadership does not always come in the form of being principal or assistant principal. Leadership comes in other aspects, to be able to move people and make a difference. I didn't do it by myself. But to know that I played a part in us still being here at the school, and not as a principal but as a mere teacher, that just moves me as far as leadership is concerned." King notes her own engagement as co-leader: "My mind was going twenty- four/seven. Even getting home and trying to sleep, it was like, oh, another idea popped in my head. We need to do this."

Teachers also saw how the struggle changed the students. King observes: "They saw the seriousness of this, because they were actually involved in it. They got a chance to feel what we were feeling. Some children were upset, some actually cried. It changed the children a lot, because I don't think they realized how much Beidler meant to them." Epps too was inspired by "having the kids mobilize like that, and having them fight for something they want and actually get it. That's the part that I loved about it the most."

Garner reflects on the campaign's achievement from a parent's perspective: "I hope my grandbaby will go here. I'm glad that there's still a school here for her to go to." Garner's house is on the same block as the school and within sight of the school entrance. "We can stand on our porch and watch our kids walk to school and walk home."

Hudson remarks on Beidler's Special Olympics team finally practicing in their new campus park. "We never had a safer year than this one. I can't even compare it to what it was in the past. If you fall, you're okay because you're not falling on concrete and gravel. They run and it's just like kites soaring in the wind."

4

Uniting to Serve Students in the Face of a Hostile Principal

KELVYN PARK HIGH SCHOOL, CHICAGO

Howard Ryan

One of Mrs. Diaz's favorite statements in our staff meetings at the beginning of the year was, "If you don't like it, I'm happy to sign your papers. You can just leave, because this is the way things are going to be." Everybody would just sit silently looking down and be very tense.

—JAMIE YUHAS, art teacher

ERIC WAGNER WAS PUZZLED WHEN Victor Ochoa, discipline dean and new union delegate, invited him to join the Professional Problems Committee (PPC).[1] Though Wagner was in his tenth year teaching history at Kelvyn Park High School (KPHS), he had never heard of the PPC. "What do we do?" he asked Ochoa, who replied, "Well, we're going to meet with the new principal."

Principal Mariana Diaz (not her real name) brought fresh challenges to KPHS upon her arrival in fall 2009. Situated in Northwest Chicago's Logan Square Neighborhood, KPHS at the time served over 1,500 predominantly Latino students. But like most public schools in the city's low-income West and South sides, KPHS struggles with short resources and sees its enrollment slipping each year with the introduction of more charter schools. As such, it is vitally important to have an administrator who is in step with the school's needs and is willing to work to bring more resources. Diaz instead brought an aggressive budget-cutting agenda—a practice that union activists believed was aimed at impressing Chicago Public Schools (CPS) administration. The principal began the semester by firing the school copy room's two staffers—one of whom was a volunteer—and putting the room under lock and key. Plus, any teacher wanting copies would have to go through Diaz and justify their request. Teachers would be limited to five hundred copies per year; that figure later became two thousand, but was still enormously stingy. Wagner estimates that a typical high school teacher makes 25,000 copies per year, and the figure is higher for teachers with advanced placement courses. Diaz also refused to fill open teaching positions, preferring the cheaper route of relying on day-to-day substitutes. While saving money, the turn toward substitutes would deny students access to well-planned instructional units and to teachers who build meaningful relationships with groups of students to help them learn. Due to a resulting unfilled science position, five classes of KPHS freshmen spent their entire first year of science with substitute teachers. That same year, the school lost a history teacher and a music teacher. They weren't replaced either.

Diaz would test the KPHS community in many more ways. Ochoa and Wagner were undeterred as they came to the school year's first PPC meeting, written union agenda in hand, and waited in a conference room for the arrival of Diaz. They waited a long time. The room was baking hot because the thrifty principal had turned off the school's air conditioning. Diaz finally arrived forty minutes after the appointed time and informed the two teachers that they had fifteen minutes to present their business. Ochoa handed Diaz a copy of the agenda and began enumerating the points of concern. He was about to read point number three when Diaz interrupted: "You say this is what the teachers are concerned about. Let me tell you about your teachers. The level of instruction at this school is horrific. Those are your teachers, Mr. Ochoa."

Ochoa and Wagner looked at each other, and Wagner piped up: "First of all, Mrs. Diaz, I've never seen you come by my classroom. We come in here trying to talk to you, and we've been waiting for forty minutes. Then you show up and insult the staff?" Prior to becoming an educator, Wagner had served for five years as an army paratrooper, and he still maintains a certain military bearing and combat readiness. At that point, the school bell rang and Wagner left to teach class. Ochoa finished out the PPC meeting with Diaz ranting about how bad the staff and school were, and how she was going to straighten things out and lay down the hammer.

True to her word, Diaz bore down on selected faculty members in the coming weeks. Several teachers complained about the bullying to Jerry Skinner, a seventeen-year KPHS veteran and chair of the English department. One said, "She came into my classroom and used sharp words on me in front of the kids." The school's general environment went into a tailspin after Ochoa left for a counseling position at another school. Rather than hire another discipline dean, Diaz assigned discipline oversight to her assistant principal, who handled the duties with laxity. At the same time, Diaz instructed the discipline office to question teachers who issue discipline referrals—"Have you called the parent?" or, "What are you doing that's causing the problem with the student?" Teachers would write referrals for misbehaving students; the students would go to the discipline office, which promptly sent them right back to class where they misbehaved again. More fights were breaking out, more chaos; the school was becoming less safe.

Diaz also issued a policy that made things less safe for student athletes, advising an October coaches' meeting: "I don't want to see coaches driving students home. And you will not have a job here if you do." Skinner, who coaches wrestling, explains: "By the time we get done with practice, it's sometimes seven o'clock; by the time we get back from meets, it's eight or nine o'clock. We are in a poor neighborhood. You don't want students walking home at night." CPS allows coaches to drive athletes home, according to Skinner. "You need to show proof of insurance and have a driver's license." But for that whole year, he says, "I just let my kids walk home."

Skinner sees Diaz as part of a new breed of principals who gear to a business model of schooling. "They seem to be getting training which says that inner-city schools are failing institutions with failing teachers. They don't seem to trust the staff's expertise, don't want to learn from us." The teachers, for their part, were unprepared for an administrator who took the offensive. "People were just confused about what to do," says Wagner. "Morale was very low. People were scared for their jobs." KPHS teachers were accustomed to a relatively stable climate under protection of their longtime delegate, the late Allegra Podrovsky, a respected music teacher and unionist. "She was like four feet tall but strong and forceful," Wagner remembers. "She knew everything about the union and the contract." On the other hand, Podrovsky was trained in the Chicago Teachers Union's traditional service model of unionism, which did not emphasize member engagement. "There wasn't a lot of reaching out to staff or keeping them updated," says Wagner. "It was kind of like, 'I'm the delegate. Don't worry—whatever is union stuff, I take care of it.'" KPHS union meetings were small, infrequent, and not very inspiring. "It was mostly a lot of complaining and not a lot of what can we do about it," comments math teacher April Truhlar.

To create an effective response to Diaz, the teachers would have to fashion a new kind of union at their school.

New Union Leadership

KPHS had no lead union delegate after Ochoa's departure. Teachers approached Wagner and Skinner about filling the position, both being respected as outspoken teachers. But they were reluctant. Wagner was teaching an extra class—in world studies, requiring an extra prep—while he also advised an after-school Social Justice Academy that engages students in community service. Skinner, a former wrestler, devoted many hours to coaching the wrestling team. He also didn't feel confident about jumping into the lead spot. He approached the associate delegate, music teacher Henry Reichert, about becoming lead: "I'm willing to be your associate, and maybe learn from you. But I want that learning process." Reichert declined, however, preferring his secondary post.

In early January, at the invitation of fellow English teacher Liz Brown, Skinner attended an education summit sponsored by the Caucus of Rank-and-File Educators (a faction within the Chicago Teachers Union) and allied community groups that were fighting for quality schools and challenging privatization. At one of the workshops, an elementary school delegate described her school's struggle against a hostile principal. "I remember her account vividly," says Skinner, "because it actually seemed worse than at Kelvyn Park. She was meeting with the principal over some disputes when the principal directly threatened her: 'I will see you fired if you keep on doing this.'" Workshop attendees shared experiences from their schools and swapped strategies. It was "all very eye-opening" for Skinner. After the event, he thought further about becoming lead delegate, and consulted with his wife, who had also attended the summit. "Look," he told her, "I have fifteen years' seniority at the school. I've been a good union member. But there are problems now, and I've let other people correct them in the past. I need to do it."

Meanwhile, Wagner was taking his own initiative. As a history teacher, he was particularly aggrieved over Diaz's restrictive copy policy because he liked sharing historical documents with his students. Diaz had defended her policy by accusing the staff of rampant fraud and abuse. In response, Wagner conducted research and discovered that KPHS was in the bottom 5 percent of district schools in copier usage. He also found a positive correlation between schools' higher copier usage and their standardized test scores. In the days leading up to a late January all-staff meeting, Wagner distributed to staff a summary of his research findings. He drafted a short statement that he planned to give at the all-staff meeting and got some editorial tips from Skinner. Wagner came to the Friday meeting fully prepared, bearing a box with several binders, including articles on how a resource-rich environment helps low-income students of color achieve academically. Wagner had a lot riding on how the staff reacted. "My thinking was that if the staff doesn't back me up," he says, "I'm getting my resumé together and getting the hell out of there, because otherwise this wasn't worth fighting for."

Diaz knew what was coming and came with a counter-plan: she simply would not allow Wagner's presentation. When her challenger stood up in the meeting to ask for time, she ordered, "Mr. Wagner, will you please sit down."

"I have five minutes on the agenda for this," he protested.

"You are not on the agenda," she retorted.

Wagner took his seat. But later, when the agenda opened up for question and answer, Skinner lent an assist. "As an education professional," he declared, "I'd like to hear what Mr. Wagner has to say." A few others spoke up from the floor—"Why won't you let him speak?" Diaz, at a loss, took several minutes to consult with a

CPS mentor who was at the meeting. She then announced, "Mr. Wagner, you can make your presentation." Wagner presented his research and then tested his audience. "If you think we need to scrap this copy policy, if you support change to give you back the materials that you need to teach, then I'd like you to stand up." As if responding to a virtuoso performance, almost everyone in the room—teachers, security guards, lunch ladies, janitors—rose to their feet and gave a long, hearty applause. Art teacher Jamie Yuhas recalls that the moment almost brought her to tears. "Well, Mr. Wagner, I wish the staff would stand up and clap for me," was the principal's response. Change would not come quickly.

The presentation and show of solidarity at the all-staff meeting may not have swayed Diaz, but it did lift staff spirits. This was evidenced by the record turnout at an after-school union meeting the following Friday at The Levee, a local bar. Forty of the school's ninety teachers came to welcome Skinner as the new lead delegate. Skinner opened the meeting with a prepared statement in which he praised the staff, who had seen much harsh criticism from their new administrator. "There is no substitute for the dedication and experience that you, the faculty and staff of KPHS, bring into the classrooms of our school every day." He backed up his praise by showing how KPHS test results had, for the prior three years, measured favorably when compared to a neighboring school. He distributed copies of his statement, including an attached sheet with the comparative test data in reading, math, and science.

Skinner also distributed a staff survey that he would collect over the next two weeks. KPHS staff had rarely been surveyed by their union, and they embraced the opportunity. Math teacher Truhlar comments: "It was exciting for me to be able to just have my voice heard on paper. 'What's important to you? What are we willing to fight for?'" Skinner compiled the results and emailed a report to the members. Here are some remarks from the survey:[2]

When I first began at KP, the staff and administration were extremely cohesive and supportive. Now teachers feel blamed and unrespected.

I wish the rules were enforced so I could spend more time teaching and less time disciplining.

Many amazing programs that we worked years to develop have fallen apart due to staff shortage issues.

Too much time trying to figure out how to make copies, opening doors for tardy students while being aghast at the behavior in the halls.

As I try to develop myself as a teacher, I look to my administration to provide guidance and consistency. This has not been the case.

I have never seen so many fights in my life. I don't feel safe.

Skinner was surprised by the depth of staff response: "I knew things were bad, but I thought, okay, a minority are having a hard time. But then hearing from so many people—teachers in their tenth or twentieth year at Kelvyn Park saying, 'I never experienced it like this.'"

Skinner and Wagner teamed up to give leadership at KPHS. They not only wanted to right the various wrongs imposed by the new principal, but they also sought to build a more positive union culture. Wagner—who initially engaged as a PPC member, then served for two years as associate delegate, and then replaced Skinner as lead delegate—describes some of the changes. There was more communication: "We started giving email updates to staff every week or two—what's going on in the union, things in the news about labor. 'We've filed grievances on this and this. We have a meeting with administration and we're going to bring up this and this issue.'" Union meetings became regular and more accessible. "We made sure it was a day when everybody got off at the same time, and we published an agenda beforehand." They alternated meeting times and locations to maximize participation. "We'd have a meeting in the school lunchroom and then the next one at a bar after school with drinks and pizza. Some people were more comfortable with meetings in the building, some more comfortable going to the bar, so we would switch it up." They made the meetings themselves more productive. "We would tell people not to monopolize conversation, because there are certain people that would sit there for like twenty minutes and harangue. Let's move on and keep the thing going." They consulted with members to help craft solutions to problems. "I'm a history teacher; Jerry is an English teacher. If something is going bad in the math department, we don't have a clue. You're a math teacher. Why don't you tell us what it is, and what you think we should do to fix it? You're the expert on that." They made people feel included and listened to. "I just walk around the building and ask people how they are doing, and if they do stop you in the hallway, just taking the time. Even though I've got fifteen other things to do just like everybody else, it's taking the few minutes with the person and sitting down and talking with them."

Members responded to an open and proactive leadership. "After the PPC meetings, they'd tell us what issues were discussed: boom, boom, boom, and boom," says special education teacher Elaine Allen. "And 'we're gonna wait and see what she does with *this*'—the copy machine, the discipline." Truhlar adds: "They also encouraged us to protect ourselves and collect evidence. Like, if you sent this kid to the dean, and they were sent right back to you, you need to write that down. Not just to protect ourselves, but to support our cases and our grievances that we have as a school." Skinner and Wagner's initiative compelled others to engage, Truhlar observes. "It can't just look like these two people are the only ones who have the problem. They had to prove that this is systemwide. And for me, it was like, 'How am I not gonna go to a meeting or do what I can to support this, when they're fighting for me? It's just a matter of respect.'"

Going Through Channels

The staff survey gave the KPHS union leadership a mandate to fix numerous problems, of which the top three were the copier policy, unfilled teacher positions, and discipline. Skinner and Wagner believed in using the available channels and exhausting them before going outside the channels. But that still left a lot of discretion: which channels should be pursued and how so. Their first course was to raise the issues at the PPC. The five-member PPC team, led by Skinner and associate delegate Reichert, presented their case to Diaz, including documentation to support each item. Diaz was unimpressed. Regarding the copier policy, she said that students should be taking notes; they didn't need extra copies.

The PPC team considered their next move. Parent-teacher conferences were coming up, where parents come to pick up their children's grades. Why not use that opportunity to notify parents about the school problems? suggested Skinner. Someone else knocked that idea down: it might violate some rules. Maybe they should go to the principal's boss instead? The team liked that idea. Diaz's boss was Rick Mills, a CPS area officer and retired army colonel. Wagner, with a military background, volunteered to hold the meeting with Mills. "But I want to show that I have support from the staff," he said. "I don't want to just say it and complain." To back up Wagner, the team wrote a "Petition Requesting Advice and Assistance," outlining the top three problems created by Diaz. The petition was promptly signed by sixty-five teachers, an impressive showing. Skinner called Mills's office to schedule the meeting for Wagner, but the meeting would be two weeks away—plenty of time for Diaz to learn about it and take countermeasures. What else could they do in the interim?

Skinner decided that the March 17 meeting of the KPHS Local School Council (LSC) would be an appropriate venue. This was a twelve-member body with six parent representatives, two community representatives, two teachers, one student, and the principal. Skinner didn't expect much from the venue, having heard that "a lot of principals have LSCs in their pockets." Chicago's LSCs actually have proud origins: community activists worked hard to include the creation of LSCs as part of a 1988 Illinois school reform law. The bodies gave parents and community a real voice in neighborhood schools, including oversight of discretionary funds and school improvement plans, and the right to evaluate, hire, and fire principals. But in 1995, another state law sharpened mayoral control of Chicago schools, and CPS moved to squelch LSC power—with the district's new test-driven accountability system expediting the process. Schools that didn't meet test benchmarks were placed on probation; CPS then claimed that the LSCs lose their authority at the probationary schools.

State law makes no provision for removing LSC authority at probationary or low-performing schools. CPS was *interpreting* the law, and that interpretation has been challenged, says Adourthus McDowell, an education organizer with South Chicago's Kenwood Oakland Community Organization (KOCO).[3] But because CPS assumes responsibility for training LSC members, its perspective holds sway in most LSCs. On the other hand, where LSC members have access to alternative training—such as through KOCO or the West Chicago community organization, Blocks Together—the bodies remain a powerful voice for parents. At many schools, LSC power depends simply on whether its members find the resolve to question the principal. "I was told that we're supposed to have a lot of power," observes Hector Basave, who was LSC president and the father of two KPHS students during Diaz's tenure as principal. "But it seems like at Kelvyn Park, there was no power at all. It was more like people were intimidated. It's hard to fight the principal when not too many members would speak up." Language was one barrier, says Basave, as several of the LSC members spoke only Spanish.

Each monthly LSC meeting has a public participation section on the agenda, and visitors can sign up to speak. Skinner thought that a timely topic would be Diaz's latest staffing move. In late February, a veteran history teacher had left KPHS for a job at the U.S. State Department. Rather than hire another experienced history teacher, Diaz had managed to cover for the lost teacher by juggling the schedules of ten teachers. While saving money, Diaz's approach disrupted many classes in mid-semester. Plus, two English teachers (including Skinner) and a physical education teacher now had to teach history—a subject they had never taught, or hadn't taught in many years. Skinner approached the other affected English teacher and the P.E. teacher, asking if they thought the new arrangement was fair to the kids. When they said it was not, Skinner asked if they would make statements to the LSC, and the two teachers agreed to do so.

On the day of the LSC meeting, the two other teachers were unable to attend, so Skinner took their prepared statements and attended the LSC on his own. What Skinner saw as he waited for his opportunity to speak did not look promising. The body was taking nominations for the election of new LSC officers. People were saying, "Yes, I'm a nominee. I've always liked being at the school, and things are working really well with Ms. Diaz." After two hours, when Skinner was finally allowed to speak, he felt plenty discouraged: He thought, "Well, get it over and leave, you schnook." Skinner read his statement to the assembled group: "I was told that I would be taken out of my eighth-period English class and made to teach a temporary American history class. Though I'm dedicated to doing that, I do not think I'm as good a teacher as a full-time history teacher that should be hired." He then read his colleagues' statements, which were similar in content.

"And all hell broke loose at that meeting," says Skinner. Community and parent representatives who had appeared rather docile were now asking questions. "Wait. The kids are being taught social studies by someone who's never taught it?" Diaz promptly responded: "Let's make this clear. I have complete confidence in my staff." But the letters from teachers, admitting that they couldn't do as good a job as an experienced history teacher, had their own power. KPHS teachers discovered they had allies.

The teachers would become regulars at LSC meetings. At their April meeting, LSC members learned of the broader problems—growing reliance on unqualified or substitute teachers, out-of-control discipline—with statements from the chairpersons of science, social studies, business, and music. The body also heard from a student leader, senior class vice president Elizabeth Medina, who gave a statement protesting the lack of teachers and lack of safety at the school. LSC members gradually became more suspicious of the principal. They would ask the teachers: "Why are we finding this out now? Why haven't you guys been coming and talking to us?" Skinner told them: "Yeah, we're sorry. We should have done that."

Meanwhile, CPS officials were trying to contain the emerging troubles at KPHS. Colonel Mills canceled the meeting that Skinner had scheduled; Skinner faxed the signed petitions to Mills's office notwithstanding. Mills did send a senior CPS official, David Gilligan, to meet with the KPHS staff on April 28. On the night before that meeting, Gilligan called Wagner to ask,

"The principal will be there, right?" Wagner knew that this would be unproductive. "No, the teachers' plan is to meet with you," he countered. "If you come here and the principal is at the meeting, then the meeting's off." Gilligan relented.

More than sixty teachers packed the faculty lunchroom to meet with Gilligan the following day. The turnout amazed Skinner because the meeting was after school and uncompensated. Gilligan's initial stance was to use CPS insider language to argue that various staff positions weren't budgeted, and that therefore nothing could be done about the staffing situation. What happened in response pleased Skinner and Wagner very much: teachers who had never been known to speak out were doing so now. Somebody from the reading department challenged Gilligan: "No, no, you don't understand. We turned in the documents and we know the funds are budgeted." Another teacher pitched in: "I'm the head of the special ed department, and I put in the paperwork with the state. We're supposed to get these two positions." Gilligan was outmatched, and he had given more teachers an opportunity to find their voices and bring their expertise to the table. Two dozen teachers remained in the lunchroom for a second meeting that included Diaz, who took a defiant stance. Gilligan's aim with the meetings was perhaps to let the staff blow off some steam. Neither he nor Mills were interested in forcing the hand of Diaz, who, after all, was imposing a budget austerity favored by CPS.

On May 12, another group took leadership in the KPHS educational justice struggle, and they weren't going to rely on official channels. Elizabeth Medina and 150 other seniors marched out of the building chanting, "What do we want? Teachers! When do we want them? Now!" Some handcuffed themselves to the gates in front of the building. CPS officials rushed out to KPHS to meet with the students, listen to their problems, and encourage them to return to their classes. Many of the student leaders were politically active in other venues, such as the Logan Square Neighborhood Association. They had joined the Chicago Teachers Union (CTU) in protesting school closures downtown at CPS headquarters. Four students had interviewed on a youth-oriented radio show, calling attention to the school's safety and staffing issues. KPHS administration responded to the student walkout by suspending three students, and then interrogating Skinner, whom they groundlessly accused of inciting the student action. Gilligan returned to KPHS in the wake of the walkout, telling Skinner, "We better have some more meetings." Gilligan met with a small group—Skinner, Wagner, and administrators—three times before the semester's end.

Just prior to the group's second meeting, Wagner happened to notice a bunch of discipline referral slips strewn on the ground outside his classroom, which is located directly below the second-floor discipline office. The forty slips, which hadn't been processed, were dated as early as September 2009. Diaz had long been asserting that KPHS discipline problems were on the decrease, and she had data to support her case. Now the union had smoking-gun evidence to support teachers' complaints that the school was taking no action when they referred students to the discipline office; many referrals weren't even entered into the computer, as CPS policy required. Gilligan's jaw dropped when he was presented with the unprocessed referrals at the meeting. A subsequent investigation found that a disgruntled student had likely thrown the slips out of the discipline office window the prior day. The meetings with Gilligan produced several agreements. A discipline dean would be hired and would meet with staff the next school year. KPHS would develop a better program for in-school suspensions (where suspended students remain in the school, such as in study hall). Teachers who issue disciplinary referrals would receive a written acknowldgement and report of action taken. On other issues: Diaz agreed that all vacant staff positions would be filled, and that coaches would be allowed to drive student athletes home at night.

The broad problems from the 2009–10 school year continued into 2010–11, however, and few of the agreements from the Gilligan sessions were honored. At a September 23 PPC meeting, the union pointed out that the position vacated by English teacher Liz Brown, who had accepted a staff position with CTU, hadn't been filled. Diaz explained that she had to wait for official notification of Brown's resignation before she could fill the position. Skinner later learned, on the contrary, that Brown had submitted her written resignation and that CPS had approved the vacancy for filling. On the discipline front: no dean had been hired, and the promised written acknowledgments for student disciplinary referrals were not being issued.

But another factor had been added to the mix the past summer, and it would make a critical difference in the KPHS struggle.

Loss of Girls' Volleyball

Mireya Dones, a KPHS sophomore and proud member of the conference-winning Lady Panthers girls' volleyball team, received a shocking text message at the end of the 2009–10 school year. Mike Nguyen, fourteen-year gym teacher and a hard-driving, devoted volleyball coach, was notifying the team that they would not play the next school year. "I started calling all my friends and like, oh my God, what's going on?" recalls Dones. "The principal said there wasn't enough funds for girls' volleyball—which was a lie because we found out that there was." Dones has played volleyball since elementary school; she had natural talent, and the sport became her passion. "I love playing—it makes me a different person when I'm on the court," she says. "And the team becomes like a family." Coach Nguyen had paid for Dones and a teammate to attend a three-day sports performance camp. "In order to get in the camp, you have to be really good," comments

Dones's mother, Maritza Rios. Rios had played volleyball during her youth but stopped playing after she married at sixteen. "When Mireya told me she wanted to be on the volleyball team," she says, "it made me really happy because that could have been me." The sport also keeps her daughter focused on her studies, as an alternative to drugs or the party scene. Dones explains: "It made me a better student, because if you don't have good grades, then you can't play on the team."

Nguyen also lost his job that summer—joining 1,200 teachers who were laid off by CPS, which alleged a $600 million deficit. Several hundred teachers were later rehired after a judge upheld CTU's lawsuit claiming that the layoffs had violated union seniority rules. But Nguyen was not among those retained. At a July 8 meeting of Kelvyn Park's LSC, a dozen student athletes and parents requested that Diaz take proactive measures to save girls' volleyball. Diaz refused all suggestions and moved to cut other athletic programs as well. When sixty student athletes and coaches—from football, volleyball, and cross-country track—packed the LSC meeting of September 29 to protest the loss of girls' volleyball, Diaz told the assembly that she had done everything she could to save the team. "It's the coach's fault," she added. "He was fired and left things disorganized."

The following Monday, a delegation of thirty students, parents, and teachers met with the local alderman. His office could only accommodate ten people at a time, so the delegation met with him in three shifts. Students told the alderman about the loss of girls' volleyball as well as a host of other problems at the school. One said, "I have a class with thirty-five kids"—reflecting the citywide classroom overcrowding produced by the CPS layoffs. Another reported: "Student IDs haven't been handed out—anyone can walk into the school. We are not safe."

On October 22, Diaz met with the coaches to say that all school athletics would have to be canceled for the year, that there was no money left for buses or to pay game officials. Mills had allocated $1,000 for athletics transportation and this had already been spent, she explained. But they had $19,000 for transportation the prior year, protested school athletic director Kai Heinecken, who submits a budget request for the department each May. Where was the rest of the money? "She was basically declaring a war," Skinner remarks.

The following week, on October 27, a small delegation from KPHS arrived at 6:00 a.m. for the monthly board of education meeting at CPS headquarters. Skinner was joined by LSC president Hector Basave; Mireya Dones came with her mother and a teammate, Andrianna Alvarez. They had come extra early to ensure getting on the speakers' list. Prior to the start of the meeting, a CPS staffer approached Basave and, addressing him in Spanish, suggested that he discuss his concerns with her privately, rather than taking these in front of the board. The LSC leader stood his ground: "I came here at six in the morning. I have a statement to read to the board. I have some documents to present, and I am presenting them. Then after that, we meet."

When it came his turn to speak, Basave handed the board copies of a three-page chronology outlining the school's past year of troubles under Diaz. He said:

> I am speaking for the students, parents, and teachers of the school, and I have brought a two-hundred-page binder to document what I have to tell you. We are worried and frustrated by our working relationship with our board-appointed interim principal. . . .
>
> It is not what she has done, but also what she has failed to do. She has failed to hire teachers that our school should have to educate our students. She has failed to make the school a disciplined and safe place. . . . Teachers have signed petitions, and students have protested over this failure. Our great conference

champion girls' volleyball team lost its entire season this year, and there's not adequate support for the other teams at the school. We have gone to other people for help and now we are coming to you. Please take a good look at what is going on at our school.

Andrianna Alvarez addressed the board about the loss of girls' volleyball, with teammate Dones standing at her side: "We were going to do our best to win a conference and city championship for our school. Many of us were hoping to make the all-city team and perhaps win a scholarship to college and continue our career. But we are here today to tell you that all the things that we hoped and dreamed and worked for will now never happen because our volleyball season has been canceled." When Alvarez began to speak of Coach Nguyen, "who will always be more a father than a coach to us," she broke down in tears. The board president waived the normal two-minute limit for public speakers and said, "Take all the time you need." CPS had made a decision to take the Kelvyn Park community seriously.

CPS CEO Ron Huberman told the KPHS delegation that he'd like them to meet with Calvin Davis, director of CPS sports administration. When Davis later met with the KPHS coaches, he said, "You guys don't have any more money? That doesn't sound right." After that came a meeting with Mills. This was followed by a "discovery" that KPHS had $290,000 in unallocated funds. The athletic budget for buses and game officials was reinstated. It was too late to start the girls' volleyball team in the current year; but Coach Nguyen was rehired that fall and the team would resume the next school year. The vacant English teacher position was filled. And there would be no more restrictions on making copies.

All this was substantial progress, though things were far from satisfactory at KPHS. The environment was more stressful because of classroom overcrowding. The school discipline problems would particularly take time to turn around. In November, a teacher had a wastebasket thrown at her, striking her in the face. That same month, a campus police officer tasered a student amid a huge fight on the school's third floor. Skinner and Wagner filed a grievance backed by a hundred pages of supporting documents, citing the school's general violation of teachers' contractual right to a safe and healthy work environment. In early December, Diaz received clear direction from her CPS mentor, "I want the grievances to stop—whatever it takes." Diaz finally moved to fill the vacant discipline dean position and, in a peace offering, invited Skinner to sit in on the interviews.

Postcript: Next Generation of Union Leaders

Diaz was eventually replaced by another principal. Though equipped with better people skills and not the bully that Diaz was, the new principal seemed to follow a similar business model and was slow to trust her staff. One prominent issue was that KPHS staff and parents had been working on a community plan for the school in partnership with the Logan Square Neighborhood Association. The principal was not cooperating with the endeavor. On the other hand, KPHS union leaders had learned from their struggles with Diaz, and they were more proactive after that experience. "We will probably speak up too early instead of too late," says Skinner. "I wonder if things could have been different if we had taken on Mrs. Diaz more forcefully from the very beginning. Maybe we would have had a really ugly fight in the first month, and everything would have been ... not perfect, but better."

Skinner and Wagner's union vision is deeply democratic, and one of their objectives is to spread leadership—in particular, to develop the leadership of younger and women teachers. "We know the future of this union is these young teachers, who are often the least engaged," notes Skinner. The two leaders took notice when some of the non-tenured teachers (i.e., new teachers without job security) would show up to the LSC meetings. "They would sit there directly confronting the principal," says Skinner. "Eric and I were very motivated and inspired by that."

One up-and-coming leader was April Truhlar, who was in her fifth year of teaching math and had recently gained tenure. "Whenever we have staff meetings," Skinner notes, "she is the person who asks the tough questions. She is not sitting around waiting for Eric or me to do it." In summer 2011, Truhlar agreed to chair a union contract committee at the school. "The way it came to be," she explains, "is that the CTU reached out and asked each school to form a committee of people to look at our current contract, talk to the stakeholders in our school and community, and decide what we like, what we think should change, and then report that back to the CTU." The initiative was part of a wider contract campaign preparation, with the CTU contract expiring the following June. Truhlar, who had led a committee meeting with twelve teachers the day before our interview, continues: "This is a way teachers can sit down and kind of hash out how they feel about what's going on. It's with Jerry and Eric's support, but independent of them. So I'm hoping that, for people who are not going to the union meetings, we can give them some voice through this also—through interviews, surveys, just informal discussion."

A second new leader was seven-year art teacher Jamie Yuhas, who volunteered with the KPHS Social Justice Academy. Wagner points out that Yuhas, like Truhlar, was more effective than himself or Skinner, as "two older white guys," at reaching the younger, more union-skeptical teachers. "She brings a different segment because she hangs out with a lot of younger staff socially, and she would tell me that some of them had negative impressions of the union. Some people would see me as like a hard-edged character and be a little bit intimidated. But they are more apt to talk to her." Yuhas became the associate delegate in 2012, and Wagner replaced Skinner in the lead position.

Yuhas reflects on the organizing terrain among the younger teachers. "Some people had an outlook that Wagner and Skinner were a little too intense, or maybe they were blowing things out of proportion. Or some of the women teachers would say, 'You're being way too harsh toward this woman principal.'" She adds that these critics were actually only a small group. "For the most part, people were like, 'Awesome. We have these great people fighting for us, and every which way.'" But the naysayers "would be leaders at our school in other ways, like on curriculum committees. So that's why it was important to me to get them on board."

Yuhas had personal assets that helped her reach the younger teachers, being closer to their age and with a calm disposition. But she also recognized her own limitations. As the daughter of a union steward at the Caterpillar plant in Pontiac, Illinois, a hundred miles south of Chicago, Yuhas has union in her blood. And that is not always an advantage. In June 2012, with CTU looking for a solid yes in an upcoming strike authorization vote, Yuhas was having difficulty making her case with a friend and co-worker who was raised in an anti-union family. Even while the two were out for fun, they would butt heads in the same arguments over and over. Her friend viewed Yuhas's pro-union stance as a product of the latter's upbringing—"Oh, that's why you care." Yuhas describes how her friend was finally reached:

> I think the turning point was her speaking to this other teacher who she didn't see as a pro-union person, but as a hard worker who would do anything for the students, super-dedicated. She respected his opinion, and when he challenged her and said, "That's not a good perspective that you have," she changed her

mind. I think she probably still has a distaste in her mouth about unions and still isn't a hundred percent. But there was one day when she wore a red dress to school, and it was a CTU Solidarity Friday where all the members are supposed to wear red. I told her, "Wow, you're wearing a red dress. That must be just an accident." And she says, "No, I actually did it on purpose."

The members at KPHS voted 100 percent yes on strike authorization, or very close to it, according to Wagner. That organizing achievement was truly a team effort.

The union at KPHS suffered two organizing setbacks in summer 2012. First, Truhlar left the school for a teaching position at a suburban high school. Then Yuhas lost her position due to staff cutbacks that CPS attributed to declining enrollment. With the union's help, she stayed on with a one-year appointment as a small learning communities coordinator, but her future at KPHS was uncertain. Sometimes organizing is like the work of Sisyphus—you push the boulder up the hill, only to have it roll down again and again. Hopefully, Truhlar and Yuhas's work bridging between older and younger generations will continue to be part of the school's union culture.

Wagner reflects on the transformation at KPHS: "We stood up and called out the administrators in front of everybody, and guess what happened? We didn't die." Special education teacher Pat Peterson adds: "They stood up. Then we had confidence to stand up with them."

5

How to Fight Back: Teachers Unions against the Corporate Juggernaut

Joel Jordan

THOSE ALIGNED AGAINST THE CORPORATE assault on public education confront a problem of daunting complexity. The attack rolls out in manifold ways: high-stakes testing; teacher evaluations based on student test scores; attacks on teacher job security; privatization through charter schools and vouchers; increased racial segregation; loss of local voice in schools owing to mayoral, state, and federal takeover. Moreover, it is integrally linked with the wider global assault on working people through austerity and a weakened public sector, all in pursuit of corporate profitability and capitalist stability. Then there is the organizational barrier within the teachers unions, whose leadership, especially at state and national levels, has been unwilling to confront these issues by organizing their members and allies to fight back. Finally, what fightback has materialized—against high-stakes testing and against the growth of charter schools—has tended thus far to focus on particular aspects of the corporate onslaught without clearly pointing toward a broader, comprehensive strategy.

The purpose of this chapter is to take these crucial issues and challenges into account in framing a strategic approach to the fight against corporate school reform that could be useful to students, parents, and educators in the front lines of the struggle.

Putting the Assault on Public Education in Context

Let's start with what we are actually up against. As Howard Ryan demonstrated in chapter 1, corporate school reform has been led by an alliance of edubusinesses out for profit, business federations aiming at corporate hegemony, and philanthropists motivated by a market-based world vision. All these interests are increasingly hegemonic within the Republican and Democratic parties, which mainly differ over the extent to which they want to weaken or eradicate public education and teachers unions altogether. Though it is true that corporations have always attempted to influence public schooling toward a corporate model, such efforts have grown enormously in recent years. Why is this?

One aspect is the corporate response to the continuing crisis of capitalism, triggered by the fall in manufacturing profits and investment beginning in the 1970s, and the subsequent rise of financial investment with finance/banking the new dominant force shaping government policy. This "financialization" of the world economy has been coupled with a politics of austerity carried out by the leading capitalist nations, culminating in the banking crisis of 2007–8 and the Great Recession. These developments have had a dramatic effect on the workforce, with declines in higher-wage manufacturing jobs and union jobs; more unemployment and low-wage, precarious employment; and attacks on workers' pensions and health care.

The economic shift has been accompanied by a rise of neoliberal ideology committed to rolling back the egalitarian gains of the movements of the sixties and seventies, as well as the social welfare gains begun during the Great Depression. In public education, those gains included trends toward student-centered, project-based instruction geared to developing critical thinking skills; anti-racist, anti-sexist curriculum; bilingual education and dual-language programs; affirmative action in hiring; opposition to tracking within schools; and increased federal funding for low-income students, special needs students, and English language learners. In a period of relative prosperity and growth, up to the 1970s, the elites could concede such reforms when demanded by the progressive social movements of the day.

But now, as skilled and professional jobs dry up amid the decline of these movements, the elites are less committed to investing in public education or fostering egalitarian goals based on an optimistic view of economic progress. Instead, they had to find new methods of enforcing class- and race-based stratification to prepare students and society to accept the tough times ahead, but at the same time not appear socially discriminatory. The chosen strategic alternative, exemplified by the bipartisan No Child Left Behind Act of 2001 (NCLB) and the U.S. Department of Education's Race to the Top, was the imposition of a test-based *meritocracy*, whereby state and federal assistance to low-income and English language-learning students would increasingly be replaced by market-based individual rewards and punishments centered on standardized test scores. A meritocracy assumes that life success is determined solely by one's personal merits, disregarding the role of inequitable social structures.

The meritocratic strategy combines several related tactics: (1) to artfully wrap the imposition of rewards (for example, merit pay, federal grants) and punishments (school closings or mass teacher firings, loss of local control), couched in the language of civil rights, an approach that can appeal to communities of color concerned about low expectations for their children in the public schools; (2) to reassert authoritarian modes of instruction and the narrowing of the curriculum (constant test prep, excessive focus on reading and math at the expense of other subjects, militaristic "no-excuses" discipline), all in the name of high expectations and academic rigor; (3) to enforce this regime through publicly funded or subsidized, privately run, unregulated, and mostly non-union charter and voucher schools designed to cream the best students, especially in communities of color; and (4) to foster competition and division as a way of discouraging communities from collectively demanding increased education funding to lower class size and counselor loads; establish a rich, varied curriculum; and expand support services.

In sum, the overriding aim is to promote the age-old Horatio Alger ideology that holds isolated individuals responsible for their educational and economic success or failure, and not the corporate and political elites for perpetuating an increasingly unequal, hierarchical society.

The Teachers Unions

In the face of this lavishly funded and politically powerful corporate campaign, one might have expected the teachers unions—the National Education Association (NEA) and the American Federation of Teachers (AFT)—to have launched a fightback against education funding cuts, deskilling of teacher work, the loss of members due to the rapid growth of non-union charter schools, and the growing use of invalid standardized student test scores to evaluate teacher performance.

But such was not to be. Notwithstanding the narrow differences between the NEA and AFT, they share essentially the same bureaucratic "business union" approach of U.S. labor unions as a whole. Thus, the teachers unions tend to avoid the risks to their treasuries and to their own leadership by organizing their membership; allying with parents, students, and community; and militantly confronting school districts and state and federal governments. Instead, they typically rely on quiet and increasingly ineffective channels of advocacy, such as routinized local collective bargaining, lobbying, legal action, and accommodation to the limits set by Democratic Party politics and policies.

This state of affairs is institutionalized through a sharp division of labor between local unions and their state organizations, with local unions responsible for local collective bargaining agreements and local school board elections, and state organizations responsible for legislative lobbying and coordination of statewide political action. In practice, this division of labor works to the disadvantage of the local unions because state governments, not local districts, make the laws that most affect public education, including school funding, seniority, credentialing, teacher evaluations, scope of collective bargaining, and privatization. So, while the local unions are focused on local issues, the state organizations typically take the line of least resistance in state capitols on the more important issues mentioned above.

In 2012, for instance, the California Teachers Association (CTA/NEA) opposed the efforts of the much smaller California Federation of Teachers (CFT/AFT), under its newly elected progressive leadership and community allies, to put an initiative on the state ballot establishing a millionaires' tax to at least partially restore funding for education and other public services that had been slashed as a result of the recent banking crisis. Instead, the CTA backed a more regressive, competing initiative supported by Governor Jerry Brown that would have raised less money for California schools. CTA leaders argued that supporting the governor's plan would give the union more influence with the governor. The fact that Brown, in the face of the popularity of the CFT-backed initiative, chose to scrap his own plan and strike a compromise deal with CFT to put a mostly progressive tax initiative on the ballot (Proposition 30) indicates just how (in)effective CTA's strategy was.

Another and more infamous example of the "inside game" was the AFT's invitation to billionaire Bill Gates to be the keynote speaker at the 2010 AFT national convention, despite his foundation providing millions for non-union charter schools and promoting teacher evaluations based on student test scores. The purpose for inviting him was not to challenge him (see President Weingarten's adulatory introduction on YouTube), but clearly to ingratiate AFT with Gates, arguably the most influential non-politician in the United States on education issues.

As well, the national teachers unions, especially the AFT, have frequently intervened in local contract negotiations where they have argued for making concessions to the corporate reform agenda—especially around teacher evaluations based on student test scores—rather than organize a fight against it.

To the extent that the teachers unions have attempted to organize against corporate attacks, it has been mainly confined to two spheres of activity: community engagement and the organizing of charter school educators. Unfortunately, both of these organizing trajectories have been conducted within a limited strategic frame.

The AFT, through the Alliance to Reclaim Our Schools (AROS), has, to its credit, engaged community-based organizations (CBOs) in cities throughout the country around a comprehensive social justice program, including support for sustainable community schools; opposition to privatization and high-stakes testing; adequate, equitable school funding; and a living wage for all working families. Moreover, the AFT has taken the lead, with some NEA participation, in bringing together mainly urban teacher union locals and CBOs, to engage in "walk-ins," whereby educators, parents, and students gather before school to celebrate their school's achievements, raise demands for needed school improvements, and decry school privatization. In February and May of 2016, hundreds of schools participated in these national days of action. While progressive locals are attempting to use these actions as opportunities to further engage their members, parents, and students, it is not likely that these mobilizations will lead to change in the actual priorities and politics of the state and national teachers unions. One need look no further than AFT and NEA's rush to support Hillary Clinton's presidential run, despite her continuing support for charter schools and national standardized testing via the Common Core.

Both the NEA and the AFT are committed to organizing charter school educators into the union. But, despite the best efforts of many excellent charter school organizers, the lack of a larger NEA/AFT strategic orientation to the charter phenomenon means that charter schools have continued their rapid growth, bringing harm to public schools and to communities. This harm includes documented patterns of racial discrimination and segregation in charter schools; shortchanging English learners and students with special needs; and the setting up of two-tier school systems, in which the public tier (regular neighborhood schools) suffers perpetual under-resourcing. The harm also includes the defunding/depopulating/closure of district schools, with students' lives and neighborhoods destabilized and stable teaching careers under attack.[1] This strategic myopia is most evident in the failure of the affiliates to directly confront the fundamental threat to public schools that charter schools pose. Like the proverbial deer in the headlights, the NEA and AFT have been virtually paralyzed both by the claim that charter schools are public schools because they are publicly funded and by the support for charters within the Democratic Party. So, except for AROS, the unions have done little to alert their members regarding the impending danger, much less mobilize them to take action.

Now that charter schools are an established fact in most states, the NEA/AFT efforts to unionize charter school educators suffer from the same myopia. In their desire to convince charter school educators to unionize, the national unions are reluctant to criticize the competitive, essentially *private* charter school model for fear of alienating charter school educators, even if charter expansion comes at the expense of district schools. Rather than address this conundrum, the affiliates tend to adopt a "pure-and-simple" conception of union organizing justified by the right of workers to organize, whether charter or district teachers. Such a strategy ignores the larger regressive social purpose of the charter school industry, which is to destroy the public school system and replace it with private corporations at public expense.

Progressive Alternatives

In response to the failure of state and national teachers unions to aggressively organize against the corporate agenda, educators throughout the United States are increasingly organizing at the local level to fight not just for bread-and-butter issues like salaries and benefits, but also for "social justice" issues like class size, wraparound student services, restorative justice, parent engagement, reducing counselor loads, and opposing high-stakes testing. The 2012 strike of the Chicago teachers, coming on the heels of a union election victory by candidates from the Caucus of Rank-and-File Educators (CORE) two years earlier, set the stage for successful contract campaigns centered on "the schools our students deserve" in Chicago; St. Paul, Minnesota; Portland, Oregon; and Los Angeles, as well as the election of social justice-oriented caucuses and candidates to union office in many other NEA/AFT locals around the country.

These developments have made possible the formation of a national rank-and-file progressive teacher network—United Caucuses of Rank-and-File Educators (UCORE)—which has held yearly national conferences since 2013, representing over twenty local unions and caucuses under the auspices of Labor Notes, a national media and resource center for labor activists. In its infancy, UCORE has chosen primarily to offer assistance to caucuses in formation, rather than project itself as a national opposition caucus within the NEA/AFT. As UCORE grows, however, it will have to rise to that challenge, as well as think through what kind of state and national organizing strategies make sense as an alternative to those of the current state and national leaderships. UCORE-affiliated caucuses are well positioned to begin taking on national strategic questions, drawing upon their extensive local experiences, mostly in large urban areas.

Strategic Challenges

The teacher unions, and public education advocates more generally, face several strategic challenges. Foremost among them is the need to move beyond single-issue and local campaigns. As we have argued, the attacks on education are not isolated but are one piece of a systematic national corporate attack on working people, especially low-income people of color. So, to expect components of the attack on public education to be adequately resolved one by one, or in one locality, is unrealistic.

Related to the challenge of breadth is one of depth. We have already noted, in the case of the teachers unions, the failure of electoral or lobbying efforts—absent an organizing and mobilizing strategy connected to it to give it power. Yet for education activists on the front lines, the issue of how to build powerful campaigns around education issues that combine union militancy with deep engagement with parents, students, community, and other workers remains a work in progress. Let us see how this plays out in several arenas.

1. High-Stakes Testing

High-stakes standardized testing, introduced federally by the No Child Left Behind law, underpins all the corporate reforms that have been undertaken since, including corporate-run charter schools, teacher evaluations based on student test scores, Common Core standards, school closings, drill-and-kill test prep, narrowing of the curriculum, and the disempowerment of school councils and district school boards. So it is encouraging to see the growth of a national movement to boycott standardized tests, which many students and parents regard as an unnecessary imposition on precious school time and as an unfair and inaccurate barometer of teacher effectiveness.

One problem is that this movement is primarily centered in white, better-off communities. There is considerably more support (though it is eroding) for standardized testing in black and Latino communities, because of their historical experience with discrimination in the public school system. Standardized test scores can appear to more accurately reflect student learning than teacher-given grades, especially if those grades are seen to reflect teachers' low student expectations. This reduces the effectiveness of testing boycotts as a strategy.

Another problem with building a movement to boycott testing is that teachers are under considerable pressure to test students—not just because they can be disciplined for not doing so, but also because such high stakes are often attached to the tests (affecting, for example, their own evaluations and the school's reputation and funding). This all makes boycotting as a *strategy* problematic in that it depends on massive numbers of individual acts of disobedience in order to undermine a test's operability, usually in the absence of broad active teacher support.

Also, often missing in the testing boycotts is a clear alternative to the testing regime. Yet a clear alternative is precisely what is needed to win parents, especially in low-income communities of color, away from the lure of the testing regime with its erroneous claims of fairness, objectivity, and high-performing/high-scoring charter schools. A current plan backed by the Broad and Walton foundations seeks to recruit half of the students in the Los Angeles Unified School District (LAUSD) to charters; the plan is based almost exclusively on proving that students at Los Angeles-based charters score significantly higher than comparable district schools on the California Standardized Tests (CSTs).

It is not enough for teachers unions and school districts to counter that charter schools cherrypick students to achieve these test scores, as true as that is. In the absence of a movement to dramatically improve public education for everyone, many parents will try even harder to make sure their children are the ones who are picked. What could have profoundly more positive results would be for teachers unions to promote programs that engage teachers in collectively developing lesson plans and performance-based student assessments, and which can engage and ultimately convince parents that the quality of education their child is receiving is superior to that provided by a school that "teaches to the test." As of now, however, even the most progressive teachers unions have yet to put adequate time and resources into professionalizing teaching, much less utilizing it as a weapon against test-crazed school "reform."

2. Teacher Evaluations Based on Standardized Test Scores

Here the problem is that even the most progressive teachers union locals that are trying to eliminate the use of test scores in teacher evaluations are usually hamstrung by state and federal policies. For example, the 2012 strike of the Chicago Teachers Union (CTU) was partially over this issue: the union opposed the use of any test scores in evaluating teachers. The problem was that state law required a minimum of 25 percent of teacher ratings to be based on test scores. This meant that CTU, forced to negotiate from a position of weakness, could only minimize the use of test scores, not eliminate it altogether. On a federal level, Race to the Top's requirement that states implement test-based teacher evaluations or lose federal funding also hampered the ability of local unions to negotiate supportive rather than punitive evaluation systems. The 2015 re-authorization of the Elementary Secondary Education Act, which leaves jurisdiction over teacher evaluation to state governments, does little to alleviate pressure on most teachers union locals.

Here again is where the conservative, bureaucratic character of the state and national teachers union affiliates comes into play. Rather than organize a fight against these regressive evaluation schemes on the state and federal levels, the affiliates tend instead to capitulate, looking for the least objectionable compromise without organizing and mobilizing for a fight.

So, ultimately, any progress must come from a strategy that begins to break down the bureaucratic division of labor between union locals and state affiliates. To do so, the progressive teachers union locals and caucuses must begin to build alliances with one another in each state to begin a fightback. Locals cannot do this on their own. This is what UCORE has the potential to do.

3. Charter School Organizing and Accountability

Organizing to stop or even slow down charter school expansion presents difficult problems for even the most progressive teachers union. Apart from AROS, the NEA and AFT's strategic priority is to unionize charter school teachers as a way to maintain union density in the wake of charter school growth. The underlying theory of action has been that such unionization would serve as a disincentive for charter expansion, since most of the charter operators are anti-union.

By itself, though, this strategy is inadequate. First, it is very unlikely that charter school organizing can keep up with the rapid pace of non-union charter school expansion. Charter school organizing is slow and labor-intensive. The labor force is young and constantly changing, while the charter industry is well organized, well funded, virulently anti-union but politically popular. The unionizing effort is also unlikely to gain much support among district teachers as long as they see charter schools and their employees as direct competitors for their jobs and livelihood.

Second, a charter unionizing strategy does not, in itself, address the many problems associated with charterization, such as destabilization and depopulation of district schools caused by charter expansion, patterns of segregation and discrimination in charter schools, and weak accountability and public oversight over charter schools.

A second challenge to building a movement against charter school expansion is its limited organizing potential. Most public school educators and parents do not see the growth of charter schools as a direct threat to their school, unless they are subject to a co-location, whereby a public school is forced to share space with a charter school. Even then, teachers and parents at co-located schools tend to see the problem as one of forced co-location, not necessarily in the broader terms of an encroaching privatization movement. Political education within the union can only go so far to correct that. In particular, teachers at district schools are far more easily organized and mobilized around issues that they see as directly affecting them—class size, salary, benefits, evaluations, and so on. Consequently, the negative impact of the growth of charter schools on district budgets cannot be fought in isolation. It must be married to a broader strategy that addresses the immediate concerns of district educators and parents, as well as charter school educators and their allies.

With this broader approach, United Teachers Los Angeles (UTLA) is preparing to launch a campaign for 2016–18 that integrates a strategic orientation toward fighting for public school improvement while simultaneously fighting privatization. In the summer of 2015, a document leaked to the *Los Angeles Times* revealed philanthropist Eli Broad's plan to sharply expand Los Angeles charter school enrollment to 50 percent of the city's public school students over the next eight years.

In response, UTLA, along with the other LAUSD unions, many community-based organizations, and elected public officials, urged the LAUSD school board to pass a resolution opposing this plan and calling instead for sustainable community schools that serve the needs of students and the community. As a result of this pressure, the school board unanimously passed such a motion on January 12, 2016.

While the school board motion represented an important public relations check in the seemingly relentless drive of the charter school juggernaut to increase charters at the expense of local district schools, it would be too early to call it a turning point. Because of legal restrictions, only a few school districts in California have yet been bold enough to refuse authorizing charter schools. Most districts, including LAUSD, have continued to authorize charters even when doing so threatens district financial solvency because of declining enrollments in the district schools.

UTLA is therefore developing a strategy to wage a multi-faceted campaign—through collective bargaining, community campaigns, school board motions, and political action—that simultaneously calls for expanded support for high-needs schools, especially through lower class size and increased support personnel, as well as charter school accountability.

The UTLA strategy, while it entails challenges, has distinct advantages. First, it offers material support to the very schools that are most threatened by charter school penetration. The Broad plan, for instance, explicitly targets schools in certain high-needs Los Angeles communities for charter expansion. The demand for resources that can significantly help these district schools can serve as a rallying point for parents, students, and teachers who now will have a positive and authentic reform alternative to the claims of charter school "reformers."

A second advantage of the UTLA strategy is that calling for special assistance to high-needs schools is a clear social justice demand with racial justice implications, because the students in these hyper-segregated schools are overwhelmingly students of color. As such, community-based organizations that have historically criticized UTLA and the district alike as insensitive to the needs of students of color and therefore supported some measure of charter expansion, can potentially be drawn in to support this effort.

A third advantage is that, in this time of scarce public resources, a focus on the highest-needs schools, as opposed to all district schools, has the practical advantage of costing less. Especially considering the great cost, for instance, of reducing class size, targeting such improvements to a more limited cohort of schools can potentially be achieved at the local level, with support from the state.

Of course, this strategy presents challenges to union leaders subject to potentially competing demands, such as from members in non-high-needs-schools whose lead priorities may be salary raises or lower class size. For example, in some more affluent Los Angeles schools not subject to federal Title I class-size limitations, class sizes are actually higher than in most high-needs schools. However, the fact that the district is going bankrupt because charters are expanding mainly in high-needs communities serves as an effective argument for shoring up the schools in those communities. It is also a demand that is rooted in a commitment to social justice. Ultimately, for this strategy to succeed, these "affirmative action" demands must be combined with demands that address the need for redistributive policies that benefit everyone by expanding the public pie, paid for by the rich and by large corporations. Otherwise, competition for scarce resources will prevent the solidarity needed to win either kind of demands.

So, while UTLA is by far the largest teachers union in the state, with approximately one-tenth of the entire state teaching corps, its leadership knows that local school districts have limited authority and that a statewide coalition committed to a similar strategy is necessary. In 2015–16, UTLA and several other California teachers union locals that are most affected by charter school growth have been exploring an organizing strategy for holding both charter schools and district schools publicly accountable and equitable under state law, while campaigning for resources especially for high-needs schools. The campaign would not be anti-charter school per se, especially since many union members throughout the state work at charter schools that are also district schools. Nor would the campaign focus exclusively on charter school accountability, which would open the campaign to the charge of bias in favor of school districts that have failed and continue to fail students, particularly in low income communities of color.

As conceived, the campaign will therefore be multifaceted, taking on and coalescing around issues of direct and pressing concern to district educators, parents, students, and other district employees, as well as to their counterparts in the charter school world. The focus would be on policy changes that are winnable at the school board and state levels, complementary to collective bargaining but not subsumed within it. The project would also seek out issues that are common to all urban district locals so that the initially local campaigns can be unified later on. As proposed, such issues could include:

- Limiting high-stakes testing, which drives curriculum and instruction in charter and district schools alike.
- Democratic participation of all stakeholders in school decision making.
- Student and parent bill of rights, including due process in student disciplinary matters.
- Impact of charter school authorizations on surrounding schools and district funding.

- Support for educator professional development and alternative assessments.
- Wraparound services.
- Funded class-size reduction based on student need.
- Due process for all employees, such as in disciplinary or termination cases.

The key point is that any campaign that focuses on charter school accountability must be embedded in a broader focus on public school improvement that is clearly counterpoised to the public school status quo and is capable of mobilizing a broad coalition of forces.

Concretely, the leadership of these locals, most of whose contracts expire in June of 2017, have recently decided to take the unprecedented step of promoting a coordinated bargaining campaign across their locals. The idea is to convince local members of the need for a common bargaining agenda focused on demands for more resources for high-needs schools and for charter school accountability, and then to take part in joint actions in late 2017 or early 2018 in support of that agenda. By working together, each local would enhance its own local bargaining power, but also exert increased political pressure on the legislature and governor to provide needed resources for urban schools and hold charters accountable. Ultimately, these actions could help push candidates in California's 2018 gubernatorial election in a more progressive direction and provide momentum for an anticipated progressive school funding initiative on the 2018 ballot.

Of course, such an ambitious campaign could not be successful without the necessary assistance (legal, research, public policy) from the teachers union affiliates, especially the California Teachers Association (CTA) with over 300,000 members. Since the current modus operandi of CTA, like most other state affiliates, is based on legislative maneuvering, not organizing and mobilizing, the progressive local unions initiating this campaign will also have to wage an internal campaign within CTA to move this project forward.

Outstanding Issues and Questions

The bulk of this chapter has focused on thinking through the fight against corporate school reform, with a focus on teachers unions. The fight *against* corporate schooling, however, presses us—teacher unionists as well as all public education advocates—to define more clearly what we are *for*. One key area needing development in this regard is how to integrate social justice curricula into a more general struggle for school transformation. Another closely related key area is how to integrate the struggle for school transformation into an even broader struggle for social transformation.

Instruction and Curriculum

Over the past few decades, a sizable group of mostly younger teachers—many of color—have developed networks devoted to promoting student-centered, anti-racist, social justice-oriented pedagogy. Unfortunately, this vibrant movement has been mostly isolated from the teachers unions, and for a few reasons. First, teachers unions tend to shy away from recommending any particular type of instruction, as veteran teachers especially are understandably suspicious of any mandate that might conflict with their chosen instructional approaches. Second, most teachers unions, except the largest, lack the capacity to establish a viable professional development program. Third, many social justice-oriented teachers are focused narrowly on their own classroom instruction and aren't necessarily engaging in their unions or in school organizing issues.

Teachers unions can no longer afford an eclectic or agnostic approach to classroom instruction. The corporate approach is clear in its preference for authoritarian, didactic, conformist modes of teaching to poor and working-class people, the purpose of which is to perpetuate an obedient, complacent population. Such authoritarian modes of instruction even appeal to many low-income parents of color who believe that "no-nonsense" modes of instruction develop self-discipline and weed out disruptive students who detract from a positive learning environment. If teachers through their unions are to be champions for students and communities *outside* the classroom, they must be willing to do the same *inside* their classrooms by building on the actual experience and knowledge of their students. Where possible, progressive unions could begin this process by bringing together like-minded social justice educators to create professional development programs for salary point credit on a voluntary basis that, with the union's support, could begin to transform the classroom culture in many schools.

In like manner, as an alternative to the drill-and-kill testing regime, teachers unions must be the foremost advocates for teacher professionalism based on collaborative team practice, including preparing lessons and assessing student performance. For this to happen, more time must be found in the school day for individual and collaborative planning time, allowing for more art, music, drama, physical education, and other enrichment subjects and activities that have been curtailed in recent years.

And, at the level of the school, teachers unions must be the foremost advocates for collaborative principals capable of ensuring a stable, healthy, clean, and orderly school climate that fosters an authentic collegial and supportive professional relationship with faculty combined with high standards. Many districts, left to their own devices, will replicate class and race hierarchies by rotating hostile school administrators though inner-city schools, creating instability and demoralization among teachers, students, and parents alike.

Union efforts to transform high-needs schools cannot simply focus on improving school conditions, but must also address the actual relationship between students and teachers and, by extension, the professional relationship among teachers and between administrators, teachers, and students. To put it bluntly, if some teachers continue to lecture students as their one and only mode of instruction, smaller class size won't improve student learning.

Community Empowerment

One overriding mantra of the corporate austerity agenda is the false claim that education is the economic salvation for society, as opposed to full employment, universal health care, affordable housing, low-cost child care, and other government-initiated anti-austerity reforms that would significantly improve the quality of life for all. By itself, education cannot eradicate the poverty, unemployment, poor health care, racism, and class oppression that more than anything determine student outcomes and opportunities.[2]

To take on the corporate school reform agenda at its roots, teachers and their unions have to flatly reject the education-as-cure-all proposition and become instead the foremost champions for jobs and services in the communities in which they teach. In fact, not to do so continues to set up schools and teachers for failure under a testing regime that inevitably assigns lower scores to students in poverty. No improvement in the teaching profession or in public education as a whole can remotely compensate for continuing austerity and its effect on students, whether through the widening income gap, stagnant wages, mass incarceration, or shrinking investment in jobs and social services.

As long as the myth of public education as social savior continues in its present form, teachers will be made scapegoats for all of society's ills.

Unfortunately, like the rest of U.S. labor, the state and national teachers unions, with few exceptions, are ill prepared to build a movement that fights either for their own members or for the broader needs of working-class communities and communities of color. That task must be undertaken by grassroots forces—unionists, parents, students, community-based organizations, and other allies—prepared to expose these myths and begin the necessary work of linking schools with communities in a way that builds political power toward social change. Schools are ideal central locations for such organizing because they exist in every community and can bring the entire community together. At best, however, most current thinking about community schools has narrowly focused on the provision of "wraparound" health and other services at the school, rather than utilizing the school as a location for organizing the community to demand decent housing, health care, safety, and so on.

Transforming an educational movement into a broader movement for social justice is a strategic task that will be difficult for unions, even the most progressive, to initiate on their own unless they develop a sufficient core of visionary, sophisticated rank-and-file activists capable of organizing within their unions and making common cause with parent, student, and community allies. Given the immense and often conservatizing day-to-day pressures on union officers, the leadership development role of rank-and-file caucuses within the unions becomes that much more important, both locally and nationally.

Fortunately, there is much to build on, as the upsurge in militant and progressive teachers union activism and caucus-building continues unabated, serving as an inspiration within the labor movement and as a potentially powerful ally with other social movements in the fight against corporate domination and racial injustice.

Part III

Organizing through School Transformation

6

Critical Literacy, Democratic Schools, and the Whole Language Movement

Debra Goodman

IN THIS BOOK'S INTRODUCTION, Howard Ryan highlights democratic goals for public education and identifies school transformation as an organizing priority. This chapter provides a vision of democratic school transformation, drawing upon insights from progressive education, particularly whole language. Whole language builds upon a long history of progressive education, including John Dewey's democratic schools and experiential learning, Lev Vygotsky's social constructivism, the critical pedagogy of Paulo Freire, and since the 1960s is further informed by a half-century of research on reading as a language process.[1] While the term *whole language* is no longer widely used,[2] it is important to consider why whole language is worth a second look—not only as a pedagogical framework but as part of an organizing strategy that involves professional teachers with knowledge and agency.

In the 1980s and 90s, whole language was a growing movement of "empowered professionals" coming together in teacher support groups to explore first-hand learning experiences with meaning making at their center, and to resist approaches that reduce literacy learning to mastery of a sequence of skills.[3] Whole language teachers advocated for students as language learners and created curriculum building upon students' background knowledge.[4] They acted upon understandings of families and communities as culturally and linguistically rich—pushing against pedagogies that devalue the home culture and language of students, particularly poor children and children from immigrant families or communities of color. Here, I draw upon the stories of amazing teachers and my own experiences teaching within a community of whole language educators.[5]

When children are encouraged to express themselves within a community of learners, their responses are often unexpected and delightful. In Figure 6.1, Amber, a first grader, uses three symbol systems—written language, art, and music—to create a joyful text. Her work reflects her experiences, such as observing musical notation while sitting beside her grandmother as she played the piano. While writing a heartfelt message, she draws upon linguistic tools including speech balloons and exclamation points.

FIGURE 6.1. Amber's Composition

Amber created this text in a whole language classroom at Detroit's Dewey Center for Urban Education, where teachers, parents, and learners were "changing the story" of an inner-city public school.[6] The Dewey Center, and other whole language classrooms and schools, thrived during the late 1980s and early 90s, an era when community-based "empowered schools" were encouraged and even enjoyed district resources and state grants. In whole language communities, reading and writing were embedded in meaningful and purposeful activities; teachers and learners investigated critical issues and themes without worrying about boundaries between subjects; and kids had significant input about topics, texts, materials, and schedules.

Since the 1990s, progressive education has suffered broad attack, as part of the wider corporate initiative to discredit teachers and dismantle public education. Critical attention around the corporate takeover of schools has focused on privatization and high-stakes testing. But another crucial piece involves what happened to literacy education during and since the No Child Left Behind era, in which a democratic teachers' movement under the banner of whole language was systematically attacked and undermined by mega-publishing interests.[7]

Today, as administrators and teachers struggle with state and national policies and increased high-stakes testing, there has been a torrential increase of mandated programs that narrow the curriculum. Literacy in many classrooms has regressed from Amber's joyful message to an earlier era of tapping and barking out sounds and words with no connection to meaning—let alone real-life events. Sand tables, water tables, blocks, and dramatic play have disappeared from pre-schools and kindergartens, replaced with worksheets and scripted phonics programs.[8] Literature discussion and long-term, multifaceted inquiry themes and projects are gone, replaced by a focus on literal text meaning and short standardized tasks assigned to all. And working-class and immigrant children—students who need the nourishment of literature-rich classrooms and creative learning experiences—are most likely to be subjected to stripped-down curriculum and drill-oriented direct instruction.[9]

Education in the United States has a history of competing promises: democratic goals of free public schools for civic life versus goals that are business-driven.[10] When I've asked parents about their hopes when they send kids off to school, they say they want their children to become lifelong learners, cultivate a love of literature and the arts, make friends and collaborate with others, explore their own talents and culture through a rich and varied curriculum, and learn side-by-side with caring and creative teachers. Today's mantra of producing students who are "college- and career-ready" narrows the focus to job preparation, offering students, even young children, a distant—and often out-of-reach—future if they apply themselves now.

Like most teachers, I entered teaching with democratic ideals, believing that all children are learners, and hoping to cultivate that kernel of curiosity and wonder in every child. Current educational policies and corporate-driven reforms are undemocratic by nature; they restrict the rights of teachers to teach and learners to learn. Whole language, regardless of the label, offers a vision of what can happen when teachers are empowered professionals with agency over classroom decision making and support for professional learning. The following sections describe a whole language theoretical framework and the history of whole language as a pedagogical movement.

Whole Language Theoretical Framework

When I was a reading specialist in Detroit, a colleague, Mr. Cohen,[11] asked me to evaluate Brenda, a fourth grader who was "on grade level" within the school's basal reading program but failed the "end-of-level test" required to move to the next reading book. Mr. Cohen had Brenda go through the workbook exercises a second time, but she failed the test again. I asked Brenda to read through the test with me to see if test-taking strategies would be helpful. However, I learned that she did not have the background knowledge and conceptual understandings to make sense of the passages and answer comprehension questions. So I suggested that Brenda come to my Reading and Writing Center during the classroom reading block. For a month, she read books of her own choosing. Every few days, during a reading conference, she talked about her reading and read a few pages to me. At the end of the month, Brenda passed the end-of-level test.

Brenda's story illustrates several premises underlying whole language pedagogy. Learners develop proficiency through reading and writing whole, meaningful texts for enjoyment, learning, and other purposes. Rather than marking literacy development in a stairstep series of leveled readers or books, children are engaged in reading extensively and intensively.[12] Daily opportunities for reading self-selected texts (even magazines or comic books) build conceptual understandings and proficiency, while cultivating lifelong readers. In contrast, common instructional practices—in Brenda's case, workbooks focusing on decontextualized skills—take time away from actual reading and are not particularly helpful. In fact, they make learning to read more difficult. Ken Goodman points out, "Learning language in the world is easy, and learning language in school should be easy, but it is often hard."[13]

While whole language builds upon the foundations of progressive education, it began as, and remains strongly informed by, an extensive research base of language and literacy. This includes research on the socio-psycholinguistic nature of the reading process; writing as a recursive process; sociolinguistic and ethnographic perspectives on literacy as practices within communities; and critical pedagogy.[14] Drawing upon this research, whole language educators developed a pedagogy and curriculum resting on the following premises:

- Reading and writing are language processes involving meaning construction, or making sense.
- Texts are written by authors and actively interpreted by readers. Readers bring meaning to the text based on experiences with the world and experiences with other texts.
- All learners come to school with linguistic and cultural resources and rich experiences with literacy in homes and communities.
- Literacy learning is supported by engagement, which occurs when learners are responsible for their own learning and see the possibilities for acting on their world.
- Children can learn to read and write—in the same relatively painless way that children learn to speak and listen—through social activities and learning experiences involving whole written texts.
- Children learn language conventions as they are immersed in meaningful and purposeful experiences involving literacy.

Contrasting Theories of Literacy Learning and Teaching

As Brenda's story illustrates, whole language developed within a context of contrasting perspectives and practices about literacy learning and teaching. In 1980, 90 percent of U.S. classrooms used *basal readers*—commercially produced reading anthologies and reading programs—with district and state adoptions providing considerable profits for a shrinking number of companies. Brenda's basal program included grade-leveled anthologies (readers), two consumable workbooks, and a thick teacher's manual detailing every aspect of instruction. Underlying basal reading programs was a view of reading as a discrete set of skills (i.e., decoding, vocabulary, comprehension). Within this perspective, reading and language arts instruction meant skills practice assignments (phonics worksheets, handwriting practice, spelling practice, and so on). Minimal time was devoted to actual reading and writing.

Whole language educators rejected the premise of basals—teaching reading as a set of skills. They refused to group students by ability or assign labels (poor, remedial, etc.) that limited their access to meaningful texts and influenced their identity as readers. They rejected basal readers' excerpted texts and controlled vocabulary—and thus rejected unnatural language that made reading more difficult. Whole language teachers replaced seatwork and worksheets with a wide range of texts selected by the reader based on interest, topic, author, or genre. Instead of round-robin reading and comprehension questions, readers discussed literature in small group, mixed-ability "book clubs," and shared writing in authors' circles similar to professional authors.

In 2001–2009, the era of President Bush's lead educational initiatives—No Child Left Behind (NCLB) and Reading First—government policies countered the move towards literature and reading/writing workshops, instead pushing "phonics-first" approaches with phonics taught outside of the context of actual reading and writing. I detail the *political* intentions below—how definitions of literacy as a set of abstract skills, easily measured with high-stakes tests, laid the groundwork for proving that schools were failing and how business needed to step in and clean things up. *These policies were devised outside of debates about research and practice in language education.* Curt Dudley-Marling and Patricia Paugh point out, "Even the two federally sponsored reports that are most often cited in support of explicit phonics instruction . . . are clear that such instruction *must be imbedded in a rich and varied program of reading"* (emphasis in original).[15]

While NCLB and Reading First have been discredited, these policies continue to be influential, particularly in low-income communities. As Dudley-Marling and Paugh describe it, "the rich get richer" and "the poor get direct instruction."[16] Publishing conglomerate McGraw-Hill's convoluted recommendation for selecting a reading program illustrates how reading instruction reproduces social class structures. *Literature-based* programs, says McGraw-Hill, "work well in districts where students begin formal schooling with basic skills acquired at home," whereas *skills-based* programs are "especially effective with students who come from disadvantaged backgrounds, have limited proficiency in English, or have special needs."[17]

This is not a debate between whole language and phonics; no one argues that phonics is not part of the reading process. But it *is* a debate about language and literacy learning. Within a whole language framework, "reading (or writing or oral language) is not something that can be segmented into component parts and still remain reading," explain Carole Edelsky and colleagues.[18] There is an emphasis on becoming "skilled language learners" rather than learning "language skills."[19] Students become skilled language learners when they are provided with rich literature and learning experiences, building upon the "funds of knowledge" they bring from home, and when attention to language conventions occurs through strategy lessons or the publishing process.[20]

Whole Language in Action

Ken Goodman summarizes "what's whole about whole language" as follows: language learning involves "whole situations"; the focus is on meaning making; learners use language for their own purposes, to pose their own questions; learners are encouraged to take risks; and "all the varied functions of oral and written language are appropriate and encouraged." In addition, "whole language assumes respect for learning, for the learner, and for the teacher."[21] Whole language classrooms often look more different than alike, reflecting teachers and learners in particular communities.

In the fifth-grade classroom I taught in Detroit in the late 1980s, "Utopia Town" included a post office, library, publishing house, museum, and general store, with each town area run by a committee. There was a cozy reading loft built by a dad who worked in construction. Cassie's mom built a storefront where students sold items such as stickers and envelopes, with profits used to purchase games or puzzles. We used a ledger book rather than money, and students balanced their own accounts at the end of each month. The day started with a class meeting for social studies discussions, literature sharing, learning strategies, or planning. A workshop time engaged students in writing, small group teaching, conferences, literature discussion, library browsing, and inquiry projects. The workshop structure supported independent and collaborative learning, while I worked closely with learners in small groups or conferences. We had daily time for quiet reading and for students to share their in-school and out-of-school experiences.

Throughout the year, there were extended opportunities for meaning making. We read with first-grade buddies, wrote to pen pals, shared favorite books, and published anthologies. Content and materials reflected varied cultural backgrounds so that students' histories were visible within the curriculum. We explored broad themes—such as "Childhood in America"— through oral histories, small-group inquiry, and thematic book clubs that included a range of children's historic fiction novels. Music, art, drama, and folk dance (an interest of mine) extended learning while creating a classroom community and particularly supporting English language learners. Within these experiences, students were *learning to be learners* and developing proficiency across a range of reading and writing genres. My fifth graders and I negotiated learning experiences and class procedures. Decisions were made by consensus rather than majority rule, requiring that kids speak persuasively and listen to each other.

Whole language teachers exploit every opportunity to engage students in firsthand meaning-making experiences. Students write letters to classmates, interview family members about their childhood, visit the local gas station, follow a recipe to make vegetable soup, or read articles about a current event. Simulations extend firsthand learning: reading historic fiction, watching a documentary, or turning the school into The Underground Railroad. The possibilities are endless, but the goal is to engage students in studying science like scientists, history like historians, and language like linguists. Teachers are learners along with their students, and students participate in the creative aspects of teaching such as selecting topics and materials.

Although "critical literacy" and "whole language" are distinct threads within the tapestry of progressive education, they are interwoven within what Edelsky calls "critical, whole language practice."[22] In the late 1980s, Toby Curry[23] and her seventh graders were disturbed that the largest incinerator in North America was being built near our school in Detroit. They sent out postcards in helium balloons from the school roof to track where the smoke (and pollution) would travel.[24] When the postcards were returned (from as far away as New York!), the students recorded locations on a map, shared findings in letters to local newspapers, and spoke with a mayor's office representative. These seventh graders engaged in what Paulo Freire calls "problem posing" around a significant community issue. Working collaboratively, they gained understandings of geography, environmental science, civics, and economics while using language and literacy in complex ways. Toby recalls that one student became pen pals with her postcard correspondent and "actually went to visit the following summer."[25]

Bob Peterson distinguishes critical pedagogy from other perspectives with an example of a child bringing canned food to school for a food drive. The traditional teacher compliments the child's initiative, but does not see a teaching opportunity. The progressive teacher encourages children to bring in cans of food, and to "count them, weigh them, categorize them, and write about how they feel." The critical teacher does all of these things, but also engages students in a discussion of poverty and hunger, not simply as problems faced by individuals, but as part of the systemic nature of inequality.[26] Some but not all whole language teachers operated from that critical perspective.

Whole language teachers assessed student learning continually through observation, conferences, descriptive evaluations, work samples, and portfolios; they rejected tests that reduce reading to skills and children to numbers. Children in whole language classrooms performed as well as their peers on standardized measures, but they also loved reading, considered themselves authors, and were passionate about learning. During one year, I worked as a literacy specialist with twelve first and second graders who were "not progressing" within the school reading program. While their classmates went through the basal reader, we wrote "All About Me" books, explored nursery rhymes, shared stories, and studied plants. At the end of the year, ten of the twelve children tested on grade level within the reading program. In my fifth-grade classroom, my students kept a reading log that included number of pages read. During a typical school year, my fifth graders read between two thousand and ten thousand pages. By contrast, the fifth-grade basal anthology was five hundred pages, if teachers managed to complete it.

History of the Whole Language Movement

Whole language pedagogy evolved within a professional movement with teachers in the forefront.[27] The term *whole language* came into use in the 1980s as teachers wanted to identify themselves as a community with shared beliefs and practices. Bess Altwerger and Elizabeth Saavedra write:

The whole language movement began as a grassroots effort by teachers and teacher educators to develop a pedagogical framework that would adequately reflect the enormous paradigmatic shifts occurring in the fields of literacy, linguistics, and language development. Together, they studied theory and interrogated classroom practice in a variety of scholarly contexts including university seminars, teacher study groups, and extended workshops.[28]

During the 1980s and 1990s, whole language conversations were widespread across the United States, Canada, Australia, and later in Latin America and Taiwan. In the United Kingdom and New Zealand, the term *whole language* did not become popular, perhaps because the beliefs underlying whole language were simply considered "good teaching." Connie Weaver traces whole language in the United States "to the mid-to-late 1970s, when Kenneth Goodman and others' insights into reading as a psycholinguistic process gained increasing recognition."[29]

Between 1965 and 1975, Ken Goodman—working with Yetta Goodman, doctoral students, and Detroit teachers—established a reading research center at Wayne State University.[30] Edelsky points out that the early "theoretical roots" of whole language "grew from the soil of the civil rights movement."[31] She adds, "Ken's research was based on the idea that written language is language and that *all* people learn language—no matter how standard or non-standard the dialect." Early studies included readers from Detroit's largely African American community, and subsequent studies included a wide range of languages and dialects. Yetta Goodman collected play party songs in order to illustrate the rich culture of inner-city children, often labeled "culturally deprived."[32] Together with Brooks Smith, a Deweyan scholar at Wayne, these educators envisioned a democratic curriculum informed by new insights into literacy.[33]

The social nature of research and practice in this community foregrounded the collaborative development of whole language. Research discussions involving teacher educators, graduate students, teachers, and linguists occurred over potluck lunches and frequent social gatherings. Visitors included Marie Clay, prominent New Zealand educator, and Brian Cambourne from Australia. In 1972, this expanding group of educators formed the Center for Expansion of Language and Thinking (CELT) and worked to build the national conversation around literacy learning. Whole language pedagogy developed within conversation and practice—in classrooms and professional organizations, teacher education programs, and research projects.

Teachers embracing whole language in the 1980s built upon earlier practices such as "read alouds," creative writing, classroom libraries, dramatic play stations, music and art, integrated thematic units, and project-based learning. They were familiar with *individualized reading* (also known as sustained silent reading); and the *language experience approach,* in which young children learned to read through their own dictated stories.[34] Teachers were inspired by teacher-authors such as Sylvia Ashton-Warner, who used Maori children's own words and stories for reading instruction in New Zealand; and Vivian Paley, who explored learning, imagination, storytelling, inclusion, and cultural diversity as an early childhood teacher in Chicago.[35]

Within progressive education, teachers have a critical role in theoretical conversations and curriculum development.[36] Whole language research methodologies allow teachers to see for themselves rather than trusting "what the research says." The Reading Miscue Inventory was adapted for classroom evaluation, providing teachers with insights into readers' strengths and proficiencies, as well as firsthand understandings of reading as a transactional process.[37] Marie Clay, Yetta Goodman, and others developed tools for documenting young children's early reading and writing. Denny Taylor engaged teachers in ethnographic evaluations leading to "biographic literacy profiles" of learners.[38]

As whole language captured the imagination of classroom teachers, ideas and practices were shared in book clubs, writing groups, and teacher study groups. Within these supportive communities, teachers shifted from basal reading programs to authentic texts; from segmented subject areas to thematic learning; and from whole-class, direct instruction to learning centers and student-led inquiry. Teachers' roles shifted as they abandoned red ink and comprehension quizzes in favor of reading conferences and student publications. A colleague, Mary Jo Regnier, told me, "I've been teaching since 1959 and these are the memorable years. Because the program is child-centered, each experience is new" and "learning occurs through conversation and exchange of ideas." In her previous years of teaching, she says, "everything was out of a manual. Social studies textbooks, basal readers. Everything was narrow. Now I have freedom." In addition, "There's more enthusiasm, and I think the kids learn more too."[39]

TAWL Groups

Whole language teachers faced many challenges including school or district mandates (for example, commercial programs required texts, testing, and grading policies), lack of support, and outright attacks. In my first years of teaching (1978 to 1981), I faced charges of "unsatisfactory teaching" on three occasions when administrators did not see quiet rows and rote learning. Altwerger and Saavedra write that "whole language teachers quickly learned that creating more collaborative, inquiry-based, meaning-centered classrooms and valuing students' experiences and knowledge constituted an enormous threat to the existing power structure and hierarchy of schools." Whole language teachers "formed local support networks, later known as TAWL

(Teachers Applying Whole Language) . . . to continue learning and agitating for change."[40]

The first TAWL groups, formed in the late 1970s, continue to thrive today. According to Dorothy Watson, the mid-Missouri TAWL started when Kitty Copeland and other teachers lingered in her office doorway at the University of Missouri, wondering how they might continue conversations begun in courses. Tucson TAWL was founded by teachers working with Yetta and Ken Goodman. Sarah Costello, one of the founders, reports feeling alienated and disenfranchised because "we were told what to teach, when to teach it, and how to determine what had been taught." At the same time, "we were excited, enthusiastic and full of possibility as we learned about research that was being conducted all over the world related to reading, writing, and thinking." Tucson TAWL has held an annual conference since 1980, and has had a large influence on the Tucson schools.[41] Although often supported by university educators and resources, TAWL groups were teacher-led and involved teacher-to-teacher learning.

By 1990, there were over seventy whole language support groups in the United States and Canada. They varied from five people sitting around a kitchen table to the Nova Scotia Reading Association or Winnipeg's Child-Centered, Experience-Based Learning group, which hosted a winter conference drawing thousands from across Canada. At that time, teachers in Canada and Australia enjoyed more agency and support, and shared inspiring stories of becoming whole language teachers in settings where professional learning and holistic education were valued. Lorraine Wilson describes the role of teachers' groups in Australia: "Through the 1970s, language experience was big in many of our schools, and out of this grew holistic education programs [aided] by the school-based curriculum movement where individual schools together with their local communities were free to develop their preferred school curricula." Throughout the 1980s and 1990s, in a climate where curriculum "was not being imposed from the top," local teachers shared their work at district meetings and "the Australian Literacy Educators' Association included many local councils to which teachers belonged."[42]

At this time, teacher study groups were models for democratic professional learning. The North Dakota Study Group, for example, was "concerned about the narrowness of the visions of accountability and assessment ... popular with policymakers and reformers" and met to share "more useful, fair and democratic ways to document and assess children's learning."[43] Margaret Stevenson, director of language arts in the Edmonton, Alberta, school district, organized teacher study groups across the district, limiting each group to twenty teachers for the sake of collaborative learning. In Tucson, school-based study groups became a common vehicle for professional learning and there was a principals' group of whole language administrators.[44]

While structures and topics varied, TAWL groups were friendly spaces for conversations about learning and teaching. Detroit TAWL met each month on Sunday mornings with coffee and bagels. We shared the latest children's books and addressed focused topics, sometimes with a common reading or invited guest. We wrote with local poets and talked with math educators about holistic math. We refined our understandings of literature discussion, student research, publication of children's work, equity and access to literacy, and collaborative and experiential learning. We shared curricular projects. For example, concerns about playground fighting prompted Jeanine Archey to have third graders write their grandparents about World War experiences. Grandparents' responses touched on every Second World War story: horrors of war, separation of families, women in the workforce, and Japanese internment camps. Detroit TAWL—spanning a large regional area and including kindergarten through community college and adult education teachers—later spawned five district TAWL groups. With teachers in our sister city, Windsor, Ontario, we sponsored the 1995 Whole Language Umbrella conference.

In the late 1980s, representatives from TAWL groups in the United States, Canada, and Australia formed the Whole Language Umbrella (WLU), a "confederation of whole language groups and individuals." There was a leadership meeting in Tucson over Labor Day weekend, 1988, and a constitutional convention in Winnipeg in February 1989—braving Arizona summer and Manitoba winter, an indication of whole language teachers' determination. When the first conference was held in St. Louis, Missouri, in 1990, there were two thousand participants. It was quite a long way from small living room meetings, although Dorothy Watson, the first WLU president, managed to make everyone feel at home.

Teacher Researchers and Scholars

While building on literacy research, whole language teachers were pushing learning and teaching in unimagined directions. With few publications describing whole language classrooms, teachers began to share reflective practice in a refreshing (and deliberate) departure from the didactic and directive writing of teachers' manuals. They studied literacy and learning as teacher researchers and wrote newsletters, articles, chapters, and books. During the 1980s, whole language teachers were in the forefront of teacher research—including doctoral dissertations—focusing on topics such as children's writing and learning in bilingual communities.[45]

At whole language conferences, teachers were respected for their expertise, whether as presenters or participants. Annual conferences in the Catskills and Vermont had a rejuvenating, summer camp flavor. Bill Martin Jr. and Richard C. Owen organized traveling conferences featuring whole language teachers and teacher educators. I participated as a teacher consultant in district, local, and state conferences, including a week-long university conference in Denver and another sponsored by the state of Alaska. At these interactive meetings, participants explored multicultural and social justice themes, looked closely at student work, talked informally with well-known researchers, engaged in writing workshops, worked closely with experienced teacher consultants, and met new authors and books. And there were *always* sing-alongs.

Becoming Whole Language Teachers in Whole Language Schools

The whole language movement was influenced by—and influenced—a national climate encouraging school empowerment and local, community-based schools. Rather than required training sessions led by commercial representatives, district or university teacher centers tailored professional development to teaching teams. Schools were offered a menu of professional development options and teachers were supported in attending local and national conferences. There was a visible shift in teachers' agency in their own classrooms, reflected in a graduate class on whole language that Toby Curry and I taught each spring for Wayne State. In 1989, teachers argued that whole language would not work in their setting, and worried about mandates and constraints. By 1992, teachers were making dramatic shifts in teaching that valued student learning and literacy development.

Supported by the school empowerment climate, teachers and principals developed whole language schools. La Escuela Fratney was one of ten whole language schools in Milwaukee, Wisconsin. Teachers in this community initiated *Rethinking Schools*, a journal that has had national impact as a venue for progressive and critical thinking about teaching. In New York City, principal Shelley Harwayne and a group of teachers created Manhattan New

School, where walls were decorated with children's artwork, small libraries were tucked in every corner, and classrooms had the feel of a cozy living room. At the Borton Primary School in Tucson, the entire community met at the flagpole to start the day with song and celebration. Classrooms had mascot names, such as The Tree Room, highlighting the learning community. Reading lofts, couches, floor rugs, and outdoor corridors provided creative spaces for children to learn collaboratively.[46] The Wildcat Room at Borton housed an on-site University of Arizona interdisciplinary "whole language block," blending coursework and practice for pre-service teachers.

The Dewey Center was a public school of choice with a whole language philosophy in the heart of Detroit. Hearing that the district was opening new magnet schools, Toby Curry and a group of teachers (myself included) proposed a P-8 school with a whole language theme. The process of writing the proposal was empowering as we envisioned a dream school where everyone, from principal to custodian, was engaged in children's literacy development. We named the school after John Dewey to emphasize that whole language was not an experimental program (as often occurs in inner-city settings) but built upon a long history of research and practice. The community came together—in the first evening meeting in many years—and adopted the proposal, embracing John Dewey's ideals for democratic education. A three-year state restructuring grant supported the change process (at a fraction of the cost now funneled into private charter schools), providing ongoing professional development, a leadership team, collaborative planning, artists in residence programs, and other innovations.[47]

In 1990, teachers in Indianapolis, working with Jerome Harste and Chris Leland from Indiana University, created the Center for Inquiry, a "multiage, public, K-8, inner-city school featuring children's literature, inquiry-based learning, critical literacy, and multiple ways of knowing curriculum." CFI is a professional development school focusing on "the preparation of urban elementary and middle school teachers."[48] In 2000, the school was identified by the International Reading Association as one of the best national teacher education programs. Today, five CFIs in the Indianapolis Public Schools serve students from kindergarten to twelfth grade.

Inspired by Indianapolis, South Carolina educators designed a Center for Inquiry as a "social action project from monthly TAWL group meetings." With grant support, the group visited Manhattan New School and wrote a proposal for a school where students, parents, and staff are "responsible for developing ourselves as more thoughtful, caring and intelligent people who delight in learning and are committed to creating a more compassionate, equitable, knowledgeable and democratic world!" Since 1996, the school has been a "genuine collaboration" between the University of South Carolina and Richland School District II.[49]

Becoming a whole language teacher can't be mandated or hurried. Gloria Norton describes ten years of "working at becoming a whole language school" at the Fair Oaks School in Redwood City, California. She says: "We always talk about trusting the child—we need to trust ourselves as well. We can't close off and think, 'Now I'm a whole language teacher.' Instead we must think of ourselves as *whole language thinkers*, always open to new ideas, always thinking, always questioning, always studying, and *always learning*" (emphases in original).[50]

Becoming a whole language teacher requires shifts in perspective and typically involves three to five years of investigating literacy learning and teaching through reflective practice. Most of the examples above are public schools with the same school budgets and resources available to other district schools. The whole language schools that continue today have managed to overcome the pressures of high-stakes tests and district-imposed curriculum.[51] The critical element is teacher expertise and support of teachers as learners.

Bandwagon and Backlash

By 1990, when two thousand teachers attended the first WLU conference, discussions within literacy education reflected the influence of literacy research, as well as critiques of commercial reading programs and standardized tests. Many teachers were exploring ideas and practices informed by whole language research. State and local school boards began to move away from required programs or instructional sequences. Meaning-centered language arts frameworks were adopted by districts and by states such as California and Kentucky. Typically, these were flexible frameworks that allowed for whole language, among other approaches, bolstering community control of local schools and the professional role of teachers.

At the same time, "whole language" had become a buzzword adopted by many teachers or schools more interested in keeping up with the latest fashion in education rather than seriously studying this "theory-in-practice."[52] Some districts even mandated "whole language" without acknowledging it required a major shift in perspective and not just the addition of packaged practices. Publishers decided almost overnight that they would have whole language materials; unfortunately their materials often contradicted whole language principles.[53] Frustrated teachers were sent to a one-week summer workshop with the expectation that they would "do whole language" in September. Of course, whole language curriculum can't be packaged or scripted; it develops as teachers and learners work together, using language to learn about (and act upon) their community and their world.

In response to the bandwagon, whole language conferences prohibited the commercial publisher circus prevalent at other literacy conferences. In publications and presentations, teachers shared reflective whole language practice through case studies of learners and classrooms with a focus on supporting literacy development and learning (rather than the "best way" to teach reading). Newcomers were offered introductory workshops and connected with TAWL groups. Whole language educators resisted "Do this Monday" professional development and pushed for focused teacher study over extended time. Ken Goodman pointed out: "Being a whole language teacher raises the level of professional authority and responsibility. It means accepting the responsibility of staying informed, of developing a sound base for classroom planning, practice, and decision making. It is important, therefore, that support be continuous and long-term."[54]

At the 1994 Whole Language Umbrella conference in San Diego, keynoters Carol Burke and Kathy Short distinguished between initial small changes of adopting whole language "window dressing" such as centers and fun activities, and the substantial shifts in belief to "curriculum as inquiry," where students, teachers, and families work to create democratic classrooms.[55] These discussions pushed our thinking forward, but some participants walked out, perhaps insulted by this critique. For the whole language community, "the existence of a nameable movement gave some legitimacy to those who had tried for years to oppose oppressive traditional education and also to those newly interested in experimenting with a different viewpoint."[56] However, Carole Edelsky and others argued that whole language educators "too often refrained from policing or drawing lines" with "those who opportunistically appropriated the label as well as those who did not identify as whole language educators at all but wrote about it."[57]

The backlash against whole language began in complaints. Those who initiated surface changes—without the necessary paradigm shift that is essential to whole language—did not see significant results. They said, "We tried whole language and it didn't work." Others who complained removed the "structure" from their classrooms because they misunderstood whole language as simply "fun." (Of course, coordinating varied and meaningful literacy experiences for twenty-five or thirty-five students requires extensive structure.) Still others complained that whole language required exemplary teachers to implement a curriculum too complex for most schools. While whole language does not require "super teachers" or special student populations, it does require support, for both children and teachers. However, the necessary "continuous and long-term" supports for this pedagogical shift were rare—particularly in U.S. schools.

In addition to those who were disappointed in whole language because they misunderstood its theoretical essence, there were significant assaults from institutions—distant at first and then closer and intensified. Throughout the 1980s and 90s, whole language educators experienced multiple attacks from district administrators, the religious right, policymakers, and from the business community, which wielded growing influence in educational policy. Traditionalists expected to see straight rows and whole class instruction. In coordinated efforts, the religious right attacked individual teachers and took over school boards.[58]

But the most powerful backlash came from a long-standing campaign instigated by corporate reformers intent on discrediting public education and reconstructing it to meet the needs of the business community. This campaign can be traced to Reagan's *A Nation at Risk* report of 1983, when American education first became "the scapegoat for a host of bad business decisions" in this case a decline of U.S. competitiveness in the global economy during the 1970s.[59] In the 1990s, the U.S. Business Roundtable laid out an explicit agenda to "reform the entire system of public education."[60] The Business Roundtable agenda, calling for standards and accountability (enforced by high-stakes tests), viewed schools as a pipeline for the workforce and students as products within a business model of productivity.[61]

One tactic of this corporate campaign was to show that public education was failing and "to blame that failure on whole language."[62] (Never mind that relatively few teachers and schools had actually made the paradigm shift described above.) Here's how this campaign worked. In trying to show failure, corporate reformers pushed reading tests, so that the inevitably disappointing scores could be used to show that schools and teachers were failing. Of course, those scores have been and continue to be notoriously linked to income levels and familiarity with standard English and mainstream "ways with words."[63] Nevertheless, politicians and the public believed in those scores and bought the claim that schools and teachers were failing.

The reformers then blamed the low test scores on whole language, a convenient target given its growingly faddish nature in the nineties. A coalition of policymakers and business leaders began to narrowly define "scientific" reading research and promote systematic phonics approaches. The Bush administration took up the call for "scientific" phonics instruction, while whole language approaches were denigrated. Referring to the followers of whole language, Bush education secretary Margaret Spellings remarked, "It's crazy. It's a religion."[64] The corporate/conservative offensive against whole language became politically embodied in the National Reading Panel (NRP) commissioned by the Bush administration.

The NRP report, issued in 2000, would lay the groundwork for the Reading First initiative, a critical component of Bush's No Child Left Behind Act of 2001. As Gerald Coles argues, the NRP was not a politically or instructionally neutral body but was geared to demonstrate that "systematic phonics beats whole language."[65] Elaborating, Constance Weaver observes that members of the panel were handpicked "precisely because they subscribed to the view that reading occurs from part to whole." Disregarding forty years of literacy research, the panel "defined reading as using a set of separate skills to process texts" and adopted a tunnel approach to its research, says Weaver:

> The panel did not investigate the effects of whole programs, comparing one approach with others in real classrooms. Nor did the panel even investigate research on differing views of what is involved in the reading process or the research on emergent literacy—the processes of learning to read and write. . . ."[66]

Rather, the NRP's investigation focused on discrete skills— phonemic awareness, phonics, fluency, vocabulary, and comprehension; used only statistical studies that rely on achievement test scores; and completely ignored writing, literature, and cultural issues.[67] The Reading First initiative, in turn, offered federal grants to school districts that adopted approved commercial programs that taught reading as a series of discrete skills.

Gerald Coles explains that the NRP report and Reading First were motivated by an effort to destroy any professional "wiggle room" or scholarly critique allowed by earlier reports and policies. One earlier report, *Preventing Reading Difficulties in Young Children,* included educational scholars and "a modicum of compromise," while professional responses to the report underscored the responsibility of teachers to evaluate students' needs and determine what they should be taught.[68] In this light, argues Coles, the attack on whole language was not really about reading, but was an effort by corporate and publishing interests to squash "a grassroots effort that emphasized teacher decision making in the classroom" and that valued students' experience and cultural backgrounds.[69]

Weaver notes that, in follow-up impact studies, Reading First was found to be unsuccessful in increasing students' abilities to comprehend reading, and that the U.S. Department of Education Inspector General found flagrant conflicts of interest and corruption in the program's administration.[70] While federal funding for Reading First was discontinued after 2009, the program played an important national role in shifting teaching away from whole language and toward programs preferred by mega-publishers such as McGraw-Hill.

The vitriolic attacks on whole language—in contrast to scholarly debate among literacy researchers—underline political and economic motives rather than a concern about learning to read. Margaret Spellings even blamed whole language for poverty and crime: "People don't understand how profoundly our country is being harmed by this. . . . Our poverty, our crime stem basically from these kids' inability to access society. It's crazy."[71] Regressive literacy policies were mandated through an atmosphere of censorship and fear that "bore a frightening resemblance to McCarthyism."[72] Applicants for Reading First funds were careful to omit the practices and educational researchers they knew to be "blacklisted from the realm of 'scientific' reading instruction."[73] California, for example, began striking down anything resembling whole language practice, and adopted scripted programs, blaming whole language for declines in state rankings, rather than reduced public education funding as an outcome of the 1978 tax reform law, Proposition 13. Books and libraries were removed from classrooms, good principals left in droves, teacher education programs were required to submit syllabi for review by phonics proponents, and whole language researchers and consultants were "banned" from California schools.[74]

Many prominent researchers were personally attacked. Spellings said, "I don't know why Ken Goodman is on this planet, but I don't think it's to teach kids to read."[75] In response, whole language activists and allies held forums and wrote books in defense of public education, urging American parents and teachers to "take action now— before time runs out."[76] Bess Altwerger exposed the Business Roundtable agenda to privatize schools and the use of standards and standardized curricula, high-stakes testing, and punitive accountability in the early 2000s.[77]

Since the late 1990s, publishers and educational opportunists have jumped from the whole language bandwagon. However, as Edelsky writes, "The movement labeled as whole language did not survive the corporatist assault." But "genuine whole language theory-in-practice" has indeed survived.[78] The political backlash against whole language is an indicator of the potential of whole language as a democratic pedagogy that creates spaces for learners to address issues in their community, ask critical questions, and take action.

Transformative Promise of Critical, Whole Language Classrooms

In writing this chapter, I was struck by the brilliant teaching and learning reflected in the accounts of whole language teachers, and the reflection and constructive critique within the whole language community. Whole language classrooms "brought greater access to rich, complex curriculum for all students; diminished hierarchies in the classroom; promoted greater respect for varied literacy and language practices; and increased the likelihood that more students would try on academic literacies and see that they fit."[79] Whole language was explored through classroom practice, and evolved as teachers shared observations and refined understandings in seminars and conferences, and during hurried lunches and Sunday bagels. At times, when we were part of a leadership team in a whole language school, we even engaged in difficult conversations about race and class.[80] Critical conversations occur when teachers and students are subjects of their own teaching and when teachers and families have agency in classroom and school decisions.

Today, creating curriculum that values all learners can seem like an impossible dream, even irrelevant, when teachers are required to follow commercial programs "with fidelity" and punitive evaluations motivate through fear of poor ratings and loss of their jobs. Melinda Smith, a sixth-grade teacher, writes, "My classroom is not mine anymore. It has been co-opted and the students and I are being taken along for the wild ride." Melinda mourns the loss of "valuing of all voices … as harmful policies weave their way into classrooms even at the elementary level."[81]

These dark times are reminiscent of my first years in the classroom in the 1980s, when cries of "back to the basics" constrained learning and teaching. As a fifth-grade teacher in 1989, I wrote: "My students are always surprised that I give credit for reading…. I am waiting for the day when teachers will get credit for helping learners to become independent literates who read and write purposefully, confidently, effectively, and joyfully."[82] Yet, while the scope and reach of today's corporate reformers is vastly more influential, I find hope in Melinda's willingness to speak up when so many teachers have been silenced. I am encouraged that teachers like Melinda *know* that reading and writing are meaning-making processes. They have experienced the power of wide reading and rich literature discussion, and how students become engaged when using literacy for important purposes.

Over the past years, the corporate campaign to destroy public education has become more overt, with school closings, district takeovers, and constant test prep, particularly in low-income communities. Alternative routes to teacher certification threaten to eliminate literacy research, teacher education, and ensure that teachers will become simply technicians and not professionals. On the bright side, the corporate agenda has become clear to the broader community, as even superintendents and school boards are disregarded in the corporate rush for public education dollars. It has become clear that NCLB, Reading First, Race to the Top, and high-stakes testing have had no positive impact on student learning or literacy development. In New York, where high-stakes tests are used for teacher evaluation and the Pearson company reaps huge shares of public school dollars, thousands of parents are opting out of state tests that they can see have no value for their children's learning.

In addition to addressing the implementation of current policies and the misuse of standardized tests, whole language perspectives provide critiques of the regressive content and mistaken theories underlying standards and tests; and the imposition of know-nothing views of reading learners and their teachers.[83] Whole language educators have been in the forefront of anti-reform protests, particularly in coalition groups such as Save Our Schools where guiding principles for public education include "curriculum responsive to and inclusive of local school communities" and "teacher, family and community leadership," in addition to demands for equitable funding and an end to high-stakes testing.[84] Edelsky writes:

> In the current context of assaults on education as well as on necessary conditions for education (e.g., access to ideas, tolerance of dissent, freedom to teach and to learn), whole language, though diminished in number and strength, remains committed to education for greater justice and equity. It deserves respect—for its increasingly politically aware classroom work; its activist struggles against high-stakes testing, scripted reading, and commissioned reports on reading; and its openness to criticism, self-criticism, and subsequent change. And it deserves allies.[85]

When writing this chapter, I found many current examples consistent with whole language and with what Edelsky calls critical, whole language practice,[86] although the term *whole language* is rarely used. However, whether or not the term *whole language* is used, the discussion of language pedagogy remains extremely critical today, in an era when reading—evaluated through high-stakes tests—is a focal point in corporate attacks on teachers and public schools. The struggle to protect public education *requires* that teachers have agency in classroom decision making, and support in gaining and refining their understandings and expertise. If we are to return to joyful learning and democratic classrooms, we must fight against the corporate reformers' agenda. But we must also fight for spaces for teachers to be professionals—and for teachers and students to be learners.

7

Teacher Solidarity Beats Scripted Instruction

Soto Street Elementary School, Los Angeles

Howard Ryan

We were like-minded teachers coming together to build our own integrity in classrooms, and we were accountable to each other and to what we believed in.

— LIBBI SWANSON, elementary school teacher

A SEVEN-YEAR THIRD-GRADE TEACHER, Rodette Doreza was ready to leave the profession—she just wasn't feeling effective in the classroom.[1] The problem was Open Court, the intensely scripted reading program that was a core curriculum in Los Angeles elementary schools for more than a decade. "The stories in the anthology assume that all the kids are on grade level—it's one size fits all," Doreza explains. "I mean, you innovate and differentiate. But it's so hard with that program. We have English language learners, and the kids are at different levels." Doreza teaches at Soto Street Elementary, a small school perched next to a tangle of freeways in the low-income Latino neighborhood of Boyle Heights, just east of downtown Los Angeles. Many of Doreza's colleagues found Open Court equally frustrating, while teachers nationally are struggling with the scripted or prepackaged programs that dominate America's reading instruction. What distinguished the teachers at Soto is that they stood together and, despite a resistant principal, created the space for something different.

Trouble with a Scripted Reading Program

"Students would be making growth in fluency, reading a hundred words a minute," recollects Iliana Panduro, who taught Open Court to her Soto kindergarten class. "But when it came down to retelling or explaining, comprehending the actual text, it wasn't there." Libbi Swanson, a former writing coach and teacher at Soto, notes the constraints of Open Court's strict pacing: "If one day you were teaching long-vowel *a* sounds, and you had thirteen children that really couldn't get the spelling patterns down, you still had to move on. There wasn't a lot of re-teach time built in." Enforcement of the program script (see box on page 189 for a sample) by Los Angeles Unified School District (LAUSD) varied depending on the administrator and the political winds from year to year. Swanson recalls the director of instruction for Soto's area being "very militant" about teachers following the script. "She made it very clear that at 9:15 you needed to be on this part of the lesson, and at 9:45 you should be wrapping that up and moving into the next part. Her expectation was that every teacher would be on the same page, literally." Second- and third-grade teacher Gabriela Spilman elaborates on the challenges posed by Open Court for Soto's English learners. "Open Court always gears toward students who are English speakers. I mean, they have an ELL [English language learner] component, but it's not quite as scaffolded as it needs to be. The vocabulary was extremely high. The readability level was middle school. Some of our students don't have the background experiences to help them make sense of the stories."

The problems experienced by teachers and students at Soto are inherent to any scripted curriculum that strips teachers of professional discretion. Critics also believe that the commercial reading programs—known in the language arts field as basal readers—are shortchanging kids, whether the programs are scripted or not.[2] As Debra Goodman points out in chapter 6, growing numbers of teachers were moving in a different direction in the 1980s and 90s, giving students a wide selection of literature to choose from, guiding them in the use of literacy to pursue their own purposes and interests. But the whole language movement suffered a conservative/corporate backlash, capped in 2002 with the launch of President Bush's Reading First initiative, which offered school districts federal grants for reading programs that were "scientifically based." Basal programs such as Open Court and SRA Reading Mastery, both sold by publishing giant McGraw-Hill, were designated as scientific under the Bush guidelines, whereas whole language and other innovative approaches did not qualify.[3] Reading First lost credibility and its funding was discontinued after a federally sponsored study in 2008 found that the program was having negligible impact on students' reading comprehension.[4] By then, however, the whole language movement had been effectively suppressed, with most states and school districts emphasizing traditional basal programs. A 2011 national survey found 84 percent of K-5 teachers using basal or "core" readers, half of whom followed the program "very closely."[5]

In LAUSD, Open Court made its entrée in 1999 as part of a "comprehensive district reading plan." All "low-performing" elementary schools were required to select one of three scripted reading programs, and 92 percent picked Open Court.[6] LAUSD also hired Open Court coaches (some teachers called them Open Court police) and, by 2002, had over four hundred coaches underwritten by the Packard Foundation, which put up $45 million to promote the reading program across California.[7] Teachers across LAUSD complained of Open Court's fast-paced scripting, but most saw no alternative to going along with the program. For teachers at Soto, that started to change with the arrival of fifth-grade teacher Kate Beaudet in fall 2006.

A Teacher's Script from Open Court Reading Program
Spelling: *Word Building*

- Say the word, use it in a sentence, and repeat the word.
- Have students say the word.
- Have students say the first sound.
- Have students check the *Sound/Spelling Cards* and pull down the correct letter card. (Early in the process, physically point to and touch the appropriate card.)
- Students pull down the correct letter card.
- Continue until word is spelled.
- Write the word on the board.
- Students compare their spelling to the model—proofread. Make changes if necessary.
- Say the next word and repeat the procedure.

Source: Routine Card, Level 1, Units 1–6, in *Open Court Reading: Let's Read!* Teacher's Edition, level 1, unit 1 (Columbus, OH: SRA/McGraw-Hill, 2002).

Literacy Advocate Comes to Soto

Beaudet, a reading specialist, came to Soto with a master's degree in language arts; clear, theoretically grounded ideas about teaching; and the passion of a social justice organizer. Prior to her Soto appointment, she had worked as a writing workshop coordinator at nearby Breed Street Elementary School, which had a successful program funded by the Annenberg Foundation and which was based on a balanced literacy model. Beaudet's position ended when the five-year Annenberg grant ended, but she maintained a strong belief in balanced literacy. Beaudet also brought community organizing experience as a member of the Coalition for Educational Justice, a citywide Los Angeles group committed to "improving the learning and working conditions of students, parents, and teachers" and bringing "equity and justice to the public educational system."[8]

Balanced literacy has been defined in various ways;[9] for Beaudet, it means the teacher gradually releasing responsibility and control to the students, and finding the right balance for each individual student. In practical terms, Beaudet's approach has much in common with the whole language model described by Goodman. Instruction is highly differentiated within a reading/ writing workshop environment. The emphasis is on students choosing what to read and write; and, to facilitate that, Beaudet maintains a large classroom library including a selection of "leveled books," involving a letter system (A, B, C, D, etc.) to help students find material at their reading level. Beaudet is also influenced by the critical pedagogy of Brazilian educator Paulo Freire, and she sees the student agency in balanced literacy from a social justice perspective:

This kind of work on curriculum *is* social justice work. Choice—having power over one's life and the power to make change—is a central aspect of being free. But our schools do not reflect this fundamental belief. Children have few choices about the direction or content of their learning. So how can we, from the time children are just beginning school, communicate to them that we honor their ability to make choices, that we consider their self-determination as crucial to their humanity and happiness?

One way to convey these vital messages is through reading and writing workshop. In a reading workshop, everyone is reading their own self-selected book. The teacher teaches short lessons, such as helping students choose a book at their "just right" level. In a writing workshop, the teacher may engage children in a genre study, but the children are deciding what to write about and the direction of their piece. The idea is that the child is in charge of how they're spending their literacy time. We are constantly communicating to our students: "Your choices matter. Your choices make all the difference in the world!"

Balanced literacy, the mainstay pedagogy at Columbia University's Teachers College in New York City under the leadership of Lucy Calkins, has also been at the center of controversy. Diane Ravitch describes how a heavy-handed implementation of balanced literacy in New York City and in San Diego, California, alienated many teachers, including those who agreed with its methods.[10] Ravitch's critique of the New York program is echoed by Julie Cavanagh, who teaches special education at a Brooklyn elementary school. Administration made no effort to build consensus with teachers before making the change, says Cavanagh, and there was inadequate staff training. "You left in June teaching one way, and when you came back in September you were expected to teach another way. People were just thrown into the fire." Worse, in order to fast-track the new methodology, the city's education department had Teachers College create a *scripted* version of balanced literacy—dictating how to teach it, and how much time to devote to each component.[11] Says Cavanagh: "You had, say, ten to fifteen minutes for your mini-lesson, then thirty minutes for independent reading, then twenty-five minutes for guided reading, then shared reading for thirty minutes." The writers workshop had a similar scheme, and math and other subjects also engaged a workshop format. The change wasn't dramatic at Cavanagh's own school, where balanced literacy—simply called the workshop model—was the practice well before it became mandated citywide. "I think it's a superior approach," Cavanagh comments. "Unfortunately, when things are implemented top-down, the intention is often perverted."

Another pitfall that can come into play in balanced literacy is the rigid use of leveled books. It is not uncommon for teachers with leveled book systems to require students to read books *only* at their assessed reading level. Reading researchers Kath Glasswell and Michael Ford give an example from a graduate student whose son hungered to read a book he saw in the "D basket" in his classroom. Instead of allowing the boy to choose the book, his teacher told him that he had to stick with the books in the C basket, matching his assessed level. When the boy was reassessed, he was jumped past D to the E level books. But his interest in the D book never waned, and his mother had to go out and buy it for him.[12]

Soto Street Elementary seemed to avoid such misfires. Unlike in New York City, balanced literacy was brought to Soto by the teachers themselves. With respect to leveled books, the Soto teachers saw the levels as a guide, not as a way to lock students into narrow reading choices. Beaudet, who doesn't like students to overfocus on the levels, stocks only a portion of her classroom library (30–40 percent) with leveled books. On the other hand, Beaudet will assign students to specific book levels when she believes their development requires it. She explains: "For some kids, like my little guy Edison who always chose books for the interesting cover rather than whether he could understand them, I had to give a range—'You can only choose books from this basket.'" The basket would contain H, I, and J books, for example.

Family Writing Workshops

What became a four-year struggle to bring balanced literacy to Soto began as a solo initiative in Beaudet's classroom. She devoted 10 percent of her language arts time to Open Court, "just enough to get something on the walls" in case any district administrators entered her classroom, she explains. But primarily, she taught reading/writing workshop. Soto principal Alma Ortiz (not her real name) allowed Beaudet to veer from the official program.

"She liked me in the beginning," Beaudet remembers, "and she knew that good stuff was happening in my classroom." Beaudet also launched a parent outreach project. Her family writing workshops, which she conducted in Spanish and held periodically over two years, brought together parents and students after school for food and then a shared writing activity. For Valentine's Day, for example, the parent and child would write each other a poem that went on a heart. "These were cute little writing activities," says Beaudet, "but it was really meant to let the parents see what I was doing in the classroom." She elaborates:

> I think that is so key in any kind of organizing that you do. Your first conversation with somebody is not going to be "I want you to come to a demonstration" or "I want you to come to a meeting," right? You have to build relationships. And family writing workshops really opened that door, because then parents got to know me at the school. I think that reaching out to parents in a way that puts your passions out there, and in a way that is not expecting anything from them, is crucial. I want them to know who I am, that I care about their children and the community, and that I also care very much about that kind of curriculum. If you lay this kind of foundation, then you can build on it.

Beaudet, who learned about the family workshop approach through the UCLA Writing Project, involved two Soto colleagues in the endeavor—writing coach Swanson, who helped plan the sessions, and fifth-grade teacher Carmen Orozco, who co-taught some sessions and invited parents as well.

Beaudet also built productive relationships with other faculty during her first year. Several teachers had questions about balanced literacy. She invited them into her classroom, offered informal coaching and demonstration lessons. She shared writing lessons and unit plans with Swanson, who in turn passed

them along to all the teachers, which earned Beaudet a reputation as a resource person. Beaudet notes: "Every piece of paper
that I construct, I always put my name on the bottom of it. Then
people would see my name on things, make associations about
who I am, and seek me out if they're like-minded."

Book Battle

In spring 2007, Beaudet saw a great opportunity to broaden the
school's exposure to balanced literacy and the children's exposure
to richer, more accessible literature. Soto received a three-year
grant as part of California's High Priority School Grant (HPSG)
program for underperforming schools. Decision making on how
to spend the grant falls to the recipient's School Site Council
(SSC), a body made up equally of school staff and parents and
mandated by the state education code. Beaudet wrote a proposal
asking the SSC to spend $50,000 to create a book room with a
large supply of leveled books. Beaudet also offered to train staff
in balanced literacy techniques as part of the package. The proposal would not eliminate Open Court but supplement it with
classroom libraries and professional literature to help teachers bring independent reading into the classroom. "Half of our
classrooms at the time didn't have classroom libraries," Beaudet
notes, "so students had little access to books." Beaudet also put
copies of the proposal in staff mailboxes, helping foster a school-
wide conversation.

The SSC received the proposal well, approving a scaled-down
version for $15,000. But the following September, they learned
that Principal Ortiz, who had spoken neither for nor against the
proposed book room, had quietly allocated the HPSG funds
for other purposes. "What happened to this money?" Beaudet
asked at an SSC meeting. Ortiz responded, "Things happen and I
needed to make a decision." Undermining the SSC's decision was
not in keeping with the education code, but council members

were unclear about the principal's authority on such matters. Beaudet sums up what happened: "The proposal got approved, but the money got hijacked."

The principal's opposition to a popular proposal drew new battle lines at Soto. On the one hand, it made many teachers and SSC members question the administrator and her intentions. "People were saying, 'I don't understand. We passed that,'" Beaudet recalls. "They were really upset." On the other hand, four teachers (out of about twenty at the school) lined up with Ortiz and became hostile to Beaudet's ideas. The book room was too much work, they would say. "We have kids. We've gotta get home." The bottom line was that some teachers, albeit a minority, did like Open Court and saw the new pedagogy as a threat. The SSC didn't give up on the book room idea. Twice more—in the second and third years of the state grant—the body proposed moving ahead with the $15,000 allocation, and Ortiz undermined them each time. Nevertheless, the SSC became one of the venues where parents and teachers expressed their new literacy vision and challenged the administration.

Through the book room proposal and other initiatives, Soto teachers came to recognize they had a leader in Beaudet. At the end of her first year at Soto, the teachers elected her as the union chapter chair (that is, building rep) and also voted her onto the SSC. Yet there was no smooth sailing, and political developments the following school year complicated Soto organizing. Ortiz, who had admired Beaudet's work, turned hostile when Beaudet supported a proposal by the Partnership for Los Angeles Schools (PLAS) to take over Soto. One of Mayor Antonio Villaraigosa's first moves upon his election in 2005 was to seek mayoral control of LAUSD. When that failed, the mayor created PLAS, a nonprofit organization that would come to operate twenty-two LAUSD schools. The teachers union, United Teachers Los Angeles (UTLA), initially supported PLAS as an opportunity for members to enjoy curricular and operational autonomy at participating school sites; the union later pulled back its support, as problems in PLAS emerged. For Beaudet and other Soto teachers who were looking for a richer curriculum, becoming a PLAS school, which would require a vote by teachers and parents, appeared to be a promising option. What Beaudet did not know at the time was that the principal is almost always replaced when PLAS takes over a school. Ortiz very likely knew this, however, because she took immediate retaliatory action. She assigned Araceli Silva, the school's new assistant principal (AP) and a former Open Court coach, to evaluate Beaudet's teaching. Beaudet recounts: "The AP was constantly in my classroom, challenging what I was doing, insisting I adhere to the Open Court program—which I refused to do. They never put anything in writing, but the constant meetings were draining." When the harassment continued into the fall of her third year at Soto, Beaudet found a remedy. She had attended a UTLA meeting at which LAUSD's new chief academic officer, Judy Elliott, stated: "Open Court is a tool. That's it. We all want to get to the second floor. I don't care how you get there." That flexible posture hadn't filtered down to the school sites, but it gave Beaudet an avenue for redress. She secured the help of a union official, who called LAUSD senior administration; LAUSD, in turn, called Ortiz and advised her to leave Beaudet alone. PLAS later dropped its pursuit of Soto, but the discussions around PLAS wound up hardening lines at the school between supporters and opponents of balanced literacy.

Doors Open, Teachers Unify

Despite several bumps in the road—Ortiz undermining the SSC's book room decision; divisions between teachers, exacerbated by the PLAS controversy; harassment of Beaudet—certain stars aligned during the 2007–8 and 2008–9 school years that would support Beaudet's organizing and help Soto teachers unify behind balanced literacy. First, in fall 2007, after the book room proposal fell through, Beaudet happened to mention to Lester Garcia, director of the Boyle Heights Learning Collaborative, that she needed more materials for her classroom. The collaborative, established through an Annenberg grant, had its building at Breed Street Elementary, and Beaudet's office had been housed there during her tenure at Breed. "Well, if you write up a proposal, I'll see what I can do," said Garcia. The result was a $2,500 grant, enough for Beaudet to buy "a ton of leveled readers" for her classroom, as well as a large selection of individual, non-leveled children's books. The collection included a strong multicultural emphasis. "Children can identify with the material," Beaudet explains, "because they see themselves in the illustrations."

Second, in 2008–9, LAUSD was ordered by the state to better support its "program improvement" (PI) schools, which were the schools with low test scores. In response, the district directed all its PI schools to establish campus learning centers for English learners and to implement a Response to Intervention (RTI) program, the latter being "a multi-tier approach to the early identification and support of students with learning and behavior needs."[13] Details for the learning centers and RTI program were left for each school site to work out. At Soto, the responsibility initially fell to the two instructors who were outside the classroom: Libbi Swanson and English learner coordinator Amanda Doerkson. "They were very bright women," Beaudet observes, "but they didn't really have experience with intervention." So Beaudet offered, "Let's work together on this." She proposed a structure for the learning center; trained Swanson, Doerkson, and two teaching assistants in intervention strategies; and loaned to the new learning center all the leveled readers she had obtained through the Boyle Heights Learning Collaborative.

Beaudet's new level of collaboration with the two coordinators was powerful from an organizing standpoint. Swanson and

Doerkson were respected opinion makers among the teachers, and they aligned politically with Ortiz. But they were also professionals, and their disagreements with Beaudet regarding the Soto principal did not prevent them from collaborating with and learning from Beaudet. Swanson recalls that her work with Beaudet created "a little bit of tension" between herself and Ortiz. Whereas the two had had "a really great professional working relationship" before, now Ortiz saw Swanson and Doerkson "taking sides with Kate," and "Kate was seen as this person that was trying to infiltrate our staff and make our staff follow her rules." At the same time, Swanson was intrigued by balanced literacy: "What the administrator was asking me to do kind of went against the grain of what I believed was best for kids."

While the staff was gravitating to balanced literacy as a teaching approach, they were still reluctant to speak out or fight for change. What they needed was an appropriate opportunity to unite. This presented itself in the school's selection process to fill a new RTI coordinator position, whose duties—overseeing the training of teachers, ensuring that students were receiving proper support—would commence in fall 2009. With two competing visions of teaching at play in the school, the person filling that position could clearly impact the school's direction. The UTLA contract gives teachers a voice in the appointment of coordinators; though not a direct election, it provides for a confirmation process. First, interested faculty members submit their names to the principal for consideration. Then the principal presents his/her choice to the faculty. The principal's choice requires a majority yes vote of the faculty in order to be confirmed. Also, if the principal's selection gets less than 40 percent of the vote, then that person may not re-apply. Hence, the faculty could defeat the principal's candidate through a strong no vote. In the Soto vote, which took place in February 2008, the principal's choice was Araceli Silva, the Open Court enforcer whose AP job was ending because of budget cuts. If more than 60 percent of faculty voted no on Silva, then the principal would have to put forward Beaudet for consideration, since she was the only other candidate. Beaudet explained this all to the faculty, and made her case for the vote's significance: "Look, if I have this position, this is how *we* can use it. This is not only about servicing children who are struggling; it's about augmenting teachers' skills."

The teachers agreed and defied their principal. Only three voted in favor of Silva, and then a strong majority supported Beaudet in the re-vote. Lining up with the balanced literacy advocate were the two influential coordinators, Swanson and Doerkson. "That vote really coalesced the teachers," Beaudet observes. "It took a lot for them to vote no. A couple of the teachers said, 'I don't know if that's disrespectful to the principal.' But they stood firm."

"Team Read"

With little district guidance regarding the duties of an RTI coordinator, Beaudet was essentially allowed to create her own position. One of her aims, when the staff gathered for a few days of professional development before students arrived for the 2009–10 school year, was to help ground the staff in a common understanding of reading research; another aim was to work with the teachers to plan a "professional learning community" (PLC) at Soto. Part of a larger movement identified with such terms as *teacher research, action research,* and *practitioner inquiry,* PLCs can take the form of an authentic collaboration that empowers teachers professionally; or they can manifest as a team model through which school management binds teachers to test-driven instruction.[14] The PLC created by Beaudet and her colleagues—which they called Team Read—was a democratic and empowering initiative, focused on building their capacity to teach balanced literacy. Their plan was to meet monthly through the school year as a PLC; that is, every fourth week, their regular weekly professional development (PD) periods would be devoted to Team Read.

Not surprisingly, Principal Ortiz did not support Team Read; she tried to stop it from forming and meeting. "Typically PLCs involve the admin. It's where the admin and teachers really work together," says Beaudet. "But it didn't happen that way at our school—not that we didn't want it to. We actually had invited the principal to come." One way Ortiz tried to block Team Read was by proposing that the PD meetings only occur through grade-level teams; that is, the teachers would meet in six different groups, together with others who teach the same grade—a format that wasn't conducive to Team Read. Fortunately for the teachers, the UTLA contract gives LAUSD teachers a voice in the use of PD time. Specifically, half of the school year's twenty-six PD slots are to be determined by the Local School Leadership Council (LSLC) which, at Soto, consisted of the principal, three teachers, a support staff member, and a parent. The three teachers, by voting as a block, could generally have their way in the body. When Ortiz proposed, "I just need fifteen minutes on the PD meeting agenda," the teachers would push back: "No, let's have a vote."

At many LAUSD schools, according to Beaudet, administrators "fill up all of the PDs with their own agendas" because teachers do not know their rights under the contract. The teachers insisted on their rights at Soto, however. There were still months of wrangling and negotiation on the LSLC. The three LSLC teachers were careful to stay in communication with other members of Team Read to ensure that what they were bringing to LSLC meetings was representative of the majority of teachers. On three separate occasions, they submitted petitions signed by 80 percent of the teachers in support of Team Read. One compromise that the teachers made with Ortiz was that participation in Team Read would be optional, rather than mandatory for all teachers. "We naturally wanted everybody to participate,"

Beaudet says. "But then, when there was resistance, we thought it best to let people opt out, which validated their own professional discretion." The four teachers who were hostile to balanced literacy chose not to participate.

For the sixteen teachers who did participate, Team Read was like emerging from the desert for a cold drink of water. Though the PLC did not gain official standing with administration until late fall, they had been meeting unofficially since the beginning of the school year. Some sessions were devoted to reading and discussing professional texts, such as excerpts from Richard Allington's *What Really Matters in Response to Intervention*.[15] They discussed their classroom practice, sometimes reviewing videotapes of team members giving lessons. Swanson, who left her writing coach position to return to regular classroom teaching in 2009–10, describes what Team Read meant to her: "We were like-minded teachers coming together to build our own integrity in classrooms, and we were accountable to each other and to what we believed in. We were able to hear ideas and talk about things that were frustrating us in terms of pedagogy, or just in terms of how certain lessons went. I felt like I grew so much just being around other educators that were dealing with the same kinds of things that I was." Gabriela Spilman was similarly inspired: "A lot of times teachers are treated like crap, like we're not really professionals. Having two hours to sit with other people who want to learn to help students felt really good." She recalls that Iliana Panduro was videotaped conferring with a student. "We would watch it and discuss it and everybody felt safe. I mean, she felt safe enough to be recorded and broadcast, and to talk about it and say: 'Oh, this was great. Well, maybe we can change this—I was a little too long.' LAUSD doesn't really have a lot of that."

Beaudet talks about the Soto teachers standing up to the district's Open Court mandates, trusting their own classroom decisions, and how this made a difference for the kids:

People were really putting their heart into it and taking a lot of risks. Simply doing independent reading every day was risky for them, because that wasn't the Open Court program. And when you start empowering people to make professional decisions— "I am the teacher in this room, and I think that that part is not very valuable, but this part is"—I think that's huge, especially for people who have never deviated from the program. I remember one teacher whispering to me, "I'm not even going to do those fluency packets." Then she was surprised by the results. She said, "Every one of my kids went up in fluency, and I didn't even spend one iota on it. It was just independent reading." And that was this huge revelation for her.

UCLA Training Grant

Balanced literacy was making great progress at Soto, but Beaudet knew that much more was needed. In late fall 2009, she learned of another opportunity: UCLA Center X, a project within the university's school of education that promotes school transformation and social justice, was accepting applications for Teacher-Initiated Inquiry Project (TIIP) grants. Why not apply for funding to provide fuller and more formal training in balanced literacy for Soto teachers? So, Beaudet and four other members of Team Read (Doreza, Spilman, Swanson, and Isabel Najera) wrote a grant proposal for $30,000, which, over the course of two years, would send several Soto teachers to New York for a one-week summer institute at the Teachers College Reading and Writing Project. Those attending the institute could share information with their colleagues through Team Read, analyze data from classrooms, and review and plan curriculum. The grant would also pay for substitute teachers so that the trained teachers could be released to give demonstration lessons in their colleagues' classrooms. Beaudet hoped that the TIIP would "solidify our working together," while also developing other teachers' leadership: "My plan was not to be the person who was always leading the PD, but that others would take over, and I would just be a participant. Now they'd be getting training from the master, Lucy Calkins. Plus, you're surrounded by five hundred like-minded people from all over the country. It leads one to think: 'Wait a minute. It's not just me at Soto Street Elementary. Everybody's doing this!'" She also saw the TIIP as a way to professionally validate the teachers, who are rarely funded to support their learning: "It could inspire feelings as in, 'Wow, someone is willing to pay for me to attend this? Somebody else validates my learning trajectory enough that they're actually going to pay for my education?'"

Beaudet distributed the draft proposal to members of Team Read and incorporated feedback from her colleagues. She was pleased when she learned from Center X that they wanted to offer the Soto team the award; the project would commence the following school year. Just one small formality remained: Center X needed the school principal to sign off on accepting the grant. But Ortiz refused to do so. Swanson comments:

> It was clearly an amazing opportunity for our school and our students. We were going to use the grant to facilitate learning for every classroom on campus. However, the administration argued that they should have been part of the development and writing of the grant. And they didn't like the way that it was worded, in terms of coming from a social justice point of view. They saw that as being antagonistic. But it was really more of a power struggle.

The teachers lobbied Ortiz in multiple small meetings, and signed a petition as well. Things came to a head when Swanson and Spilman requested a large meeting with the principal and the AP, where all concerned teachers could attend and make their case. Fourteen teachers came together to collectively confront their boss. Beaudet found the meeting particularly inspiring, because other teachers were finding their voices and she didn't have to speak at all: "Even people who were always quiet, who would never say anything, said: 'But Ms. Ortiz, I don't understand. It's going be good for our kids. It's thirty thousand dollars to learn.'" Another said: "For God's sake, this is about children. It's not about individuals here." Swanson, who was very outspoken at the meeting, describes it as a personal turning point: "I actually had to leave the room because I was very angry. And prior to that, like I said, I had a really amenable professional and personal relationship with my administrator." Ortiz, meanwhile, remained adamant: "No. And you can't have it without my signature."

But the teachers would prevail. In lieu of the principal's signature, Beaudet sent an explanatory letter to Center X, accompanied by a statement of support signed by the members of Team Read. A few weeks later, TIIP director Emma Hipolito called Beaudet to say that the Soto proposal would indeed be accepted and that Ortiz had signed off on it. "Let's just say you have friends," was the director's explanation. Five teachers wound up attending the institute at Teachers College that summer, including one teacher not covered by the grant but who attended at her own expense. (Team Read and its Teacher-Initiated Inquiry Project are showcased with photos at the UCLA Center X website.)[16]

Parent Literacy Workshops

After the teachers began collaborating through the PLC, Spilman recalls, parents who were on the school's three councils—SSC, Compensatory Education Advisory Council (CEAC), and English Learner Advisory Committee (ELAC)—began to ask questions. What is this reading thing going on in class? What are they doing in the learning center? "Maybe we should let the parents know," Spilman suggested to Beaudet, who hadn't done her family writing workshops in some time. The two organized a workshop series in the spring of 2010, with a focus on reading instruction. Their goal was both to share with parents the new teaching model that was being practiced at Soto, and to engage parents in helping their children become effective readers. Many of the parents were monolingual Spanish speakers, and many were not literate in their own language, Spilman notes. Parents were nevertheless eager to participate. "We had the multipurpose room full of parents who were so excited to come to the workshops." Spilman adds that Ortiz was supportive of the workshops as well. The five sessions addressed the following topics:

- How we learn.
- Reading strategies.
- Independent reading.
- Finding "just right" books.
- Reading comprehension through vocabulary development.

Beaudet described the "how we learn" workshop. It begins with parents telling the group something they learned to do well. The parents suggest cooking, swimming, and dancing, for example. They are then walked through a series of questions, with their answers charted on the board. How did you get interested in learning that? Did somebody help you learn? How so? What made you get better? The parents share their skills, experiences, and memories. Then Beaudet connects parents' learning to what the Soto kids are doing every day in reading workshops, in an approach guided by Australian educator Brian Cambourne's "conditions of learning."[17] She told the parents:

Oh, somebody you knew was passionate about cooking? Somebody showed you? Well, that's what the teacher does when they do that little mini-lesson at the beginning of reading workshop.

You said you got better by practicing, by cooking every day alongside your mom? That's what the kids are doing. They're going to practice by doing lots and lots of reading, every day without fail, for thirty minutes to an hour.

Oh, you shared what you baked with a friend? That's what the kids are going to do at the end. They're going to share their thoughts about what they read with a reading buddy.

Through the workshops, parents learned how important it is for their children to have books available at home or through trips to the library; or why it's valuable to read with their children; or how to help their children find books that are "just right" for their reading level. The workshops also offered teaching strategies, even if the parents couldn't speak English or didn't know how to read. "You don't have to know the words," Spilman would explain. "You can just look at the illustration and make up your own story. You are reading with your children." Or a parent would ask, "If I read to my child in Spanish, will that help them learn to read English?" "Yes," Spilman would encourage them, "because your child is learning concepts of print. They're learning that we read from left to right and from top to bottom. They're learning the concept of word boundaries, that the word starts here and ends there." (Researchers confirm that reading skills transfer well across languages.)[18] Spilman and Beaudet made sure that a few students attended each workshop, so that parents and students could practice working together and modeling whatever methods were being taught. They also took photos at the workshops and posted them prominently in the school lobby, which pleased the parents and helped promote the series.

Beaudet points out that several of the parents who attended the workshops became passionate advocates—at the SSC, CEAC, and ELAC meetings—for purchasing more books at the school. Two parents who were "very tight with Ms. Ortiz" challenged her by voting yes on buying more books, says Beaudet. Although the three-year High Priority School Grant had ended by the 2009–10 school year, the SSC approved a $2,500 book expenditure for that school year, and Ortiz did not block it this time.

The Soto Project and Education Organizing Strategy

Sadly, Team Read and the balanced literacy movement at Soto would not sustain beyond 2009–10. Beaudet accepted a position at the UCLA Community School, an LAUSD pilot school. Most of the other teachers who made up Team Read would, for varied reasons, soon leave as well. In fall 2011, Doreza and Panduro advised me that they were the only two Soto teachers who were following a balanced literacy model. The remainder built their language arts around *Treasures,* the new Macmillan–McGraw-Hill program adopted by LAUSD that year and which is also highly scripted.

The teachers who participated in the collective process at Soto nevertheless remain enriched by the experience and remain dedicated to balanced literacy teaching. Doreza, who had been on the verge of quitting teaching before Beaudet's arrival at Soto, was among the five who had partnered in the Teacher-Initiated Inquiry Project, including attending the balanced literacy summer institute in New York. "It was that project that actually made me stay in teaching," she says. "It was a commitment for two years. So I said okay, I'm going to see this project through and see how it can help me to be more effective." Spilman speaks to the professional empowerment that she and others gained by uniting around Team Read: "A lot of the time teaching feels like, 'Okay, this is what I have to do because the principal said we have to do it.' But with Team Read, it felt like, 'No, we want to be professionals. We want to have this team and we want to learn this. They're our students and we want to help them. So you're not going to tell me what to do this time, because it's not your school. It's our school.'"

The Soto project has several implications for education organizing strategy and resistance to the corporate takeover of schools. First, the movement for public education needs living alternatives showing that a better education and better world are possible. The corporate approach that came under challenge at Soto—with its scripted lessons, paltry libraries, little space for independent reading or for student choice and control in their own learning—fits what Gloria Ladson-Billings calls a "pedagogy of poverty." Poor children are seen as "a different breed of human being," she observes, who cannot benefit from expansive curricula or innovative pedagogical strategies but rather require regimentation and drills.[19] The Soto teachers rallied for an alternative to the pedagogy of poverty, insisting that their students deserve resources, differentiation, and choices, and that students have the right to discover the joy of reading. At the same time, the Soto teachers resisted the corporate job description for themselves: they would not be followers of scripts in a test-score factory but would be empowered professionals, building their craft with colleagues.

Second, the Soto teachers pursued their alternative through an organizing model, asserting their collective will against the boss while engaging the parents as well. When considered historically, Soto's democratic pedagogy and culture of teacher-led research were both inherited from the whole language movement. Yet Soto added an organizing dimension that was largely missing in the prior movement, whose orientation was more professional and pedagogical than political. (Carole Edelsky remarked in 2006 that whole language "Should Have Been" an explicitly political and social justice movement, "But It Wasn't." She insisted, "It Still Can Become One.")[20]

Third, the largest potentials of Soto as an organizing and social justice project were not realized but would be conceivable through connection to a larger movement. Trajectories that might expand the parent-community organizing in a Soto-style project would include demands for well-stocked and diverse classroom and school libraries, greater access to literature in the children's home language, and strengthening of the school's bilingual programs. Of course, the pursuit of democratic and culturally responsive pedagogy fits well with other social justice school demands such as for lower class size, expanded health and counseling services, and arts and sports programs.

Similar to what Edelsky observed in the whole language movement, most of the Soto teachers did not view their balanced literacy work in explicit social justice terms. Whereas Beaudet's own outlook and teaching emphasized social justice, most of her colleagues were drawn to balanced literacy simply because they believed it would help their teaching of reading and writing. They were "sold by the research," as Beaudet puts it. On the other hand, through the balanced literacy campaign, Beaudet was able to engage her colleagues in a series of hands-on social justice lessons, derived from their own collective action and from ongoing conversations about literacy, equity, and student empowerment. (A more explicit social justice curriculum can be found in chapter 8's Crenshaw High School case study.)

One question I had about the Soto campaign was whether its particular tools and circumstances were so unique as to be hard to replicate. It certainly helped that LAUSD was, by 2008, easing its enforcement of the Open Court script; that RTI coordinators and learning centers were being added to the PI schools; that the UTLA contract provided for a teacher voice in the selection of coordinators; that UCLA Center X was offering grants under its Teacher-Initiated Inquiry Project. But Beaudet's answer is simple: "The particulars are unimportant. What counts is that the teachers were resourceful and found a way."

8

A Transformational Curriculum
in South L.A.

CRENSHAW HIGH SCHOOL, LOS ANGELES

Howard Ryan and *Joseph Zeccola*

Teaching the skills and perspectives needed for real participation
in a democratic society is one of the most revolutionary tasks
that an educator committed to social justice can undertake.

—LISA DELPIT[1]

CHAPTER 7 DESCRIBED A GROUP of teachers who organized
for democratic pedagogy and appropriate literary resources and
professional development in their school. Here we examine an
even more ambitious project that committed explicitly to social
justice and community-connected education.[2]

Crenshaw High School, situated in the heart of the predominantly black Crenshaw district in South Los Angeles, has a long
history of neglect at the hands of Los Angeles Unified School
District (LAUSD). It also has a history of organizing. In the early
2000s, Crenshaw teachers, parents, students, and community
members formed the Crenshaw Cougar Coalition to demand
more resources for the school. In 2005, the school nearly lost
its accreditation with the Western Association of Schools and
Colleges (WASC). Among the problems cited by WASC was the
school administration's failure to properly submit the school's

yearly improvement plan. In response, the Cougar Coalition decided to fashion and implement its own school plan. Aided by the Rossier School of Education at the University of Southern California, and the Tom and Ethel Bradley Foundation, the coalition implemented various innovations to promote student-centered teaching at Crenshaw, including a "small learning community" (SLC) structure, block scheduling, and a community garden.

In 2011–12, Crenshaw's school improvement efforts culminated in the Extended Learning Cultural Model (ELCM), a curricular reform plan based on social justice and school-community partnership , and backed by an initial $200,000 grant from the Ford Foundation. The first year would involve two of the school's SLCs: the Social Justice and Law Academy (SJLA), led by history teacher Alex Caputo-Pearl; and the Business Management and Entrepreneurship Academy (BME), led by business teacher Maynard Brown. If the pilot year was successful, the aim was to expand ELCM throughout Crenshaw High, and also to engage other schools, starting with Crenshaw's feeder elementary and middle schools.

After a highly successful pilot year, ELCM suffered a tragic reversal. The district superintendent, a graduate of the academy of billionaire school reformer Eli Broad, imposed a hostile reconstitution of Crenshaw with most of the school staff dismissed. Despite that outcome, the Crenshaw experiment would have lasting impact in the school district and community, and its unique vision of school transformation deserves study.

This chapter outlines the guiding framework of ELCM and describes the collaborative work of four SJLA teachers who introduced ELCM in their tenth-grade English, math, history, and chemistry classes. The chapter also covers two components of ELCM's "extended learning" during the same pilot year: a community research project with South Los Angeles's Community

Health Councils, in which ten students participated, and a parent organizing and training program.

Extended Learning Cultural Model

As explained in the Ford grant's executive summary (appended at the end of this chapter), ELCM would make "stronger connections between learning and the contexts of the school and community through a problem-based approach." Teachers would collaborate to build culturally relevant, interdisciplinary curricula. Students would investigate, analyze, and craft solutions to problems in their community. Partnerships with community organizations, university programs, and businesses would provide students opportunities for field research and work experience. Parents would engage in leadership development and adopt active roles in the planning and implementation of instruction. Lewis King, a UCLA psychiatry professor and resident scholar of the Tom and Ethel Bradley Foundation, played a vital role in the parent component with a "Parent Academy"—a workshop series on family, culture, education politics, and parent/community organizing. King was one of two academics who brought theoretical breadth and institutional know-how to Crenshaw's ongoing transformation efforts. The other was Sylvia Rousseau, an education professor at the University of Southern California who would serve as Crenshaw's interim principal in 2011–12 and who also served as the principal investigator for the Ford grant— that is, she was responsible for ELCM's oversight.

Cathy Garcia, former math teacher and union chapter chair at Crenshaw, remarks on the "extended learning" in ELCM, and distinguishes Crenshaw's approach from the term's more common definition:

> Often when folks talk about extended learning, they literally mean making the school day an hour longer or having

Saturday school, and that's not the way we understand the term. Crenshaw's extended learning is based on the premise that whatever we do inside the classroom needs to be extended beyond the walls, taken out to the community. It therefore required the active engagement of parents and community organizations. If the SJLA partners with the Community Health Councils, and they say, "Well, we want interns who are going to be canvassing the neighborhood and collecting surveys and then number-crunching some data," that means students are going to be interfacing with people. So we have to make sure the way they present themselves is professional. Maybe the English teacher can practice oral presentations. They're going to be crunching data. So if they're going to need to know percentages and decimals, then how are we scaffolding our students into those tasks? Then finally, there's the idea that we're creating better citizens, with students contributing something back to their community. That is how we understand extended learning.

ELCM seeks to help students discover how they can become agents of change to transform their world. Caputo-Pearl—past union chapter chair at Crenshaw and now president of the city-wide union, United Teachers Los Angeles (UTLA)—distinguishes the Crenshaw model of social justice teaching from other types of politically conscious education:

Progressive classroom teaching typically relies on a lot of stand-alone lessons—about how to view the U.S.-Mexico war or whatever. Then there tends to be a lot of things that help students express their own cultural identities, which is great and necessary. What there tends not to be are coherent activities across a bunch of disciplines that carry forward over a number of weeks or months, that merge work on cultural identity with critical analysis of things going on in the world—collaborative teaching that explicitly tries to help develop analytical skills in social studies, science, English, math. And when you think about what makes a leader, what makes someone believe they have a little bit of control over the world, it has to be that combination. So you can walk into a situation—a Starbucks, for example—and say: "Hmm. I wonder how Starbucks got off the ground as a business. I wonder where their coffee comes from. I wonder what the management and corporate structure is." That's what makes an agent of change. And to do that you've got to explicitly focus on analytical skills across different disciplines the way that we try to do.

ELCM, and the larger Crenshaw school transformation, also sought to replace a *deficit* view—of the students, their families, the community—with a more positive conception. The deficit outlook, which has long guided education and social programs in low-income communities of color, attributes poverty not to systemic sources such as job scarcity or racism but rather to the impoverished individuals and communities themselves.[3] The outlook is expressed in the influential "culture of poverty" theory developed by anthropologist Oscar Lewis in the 1960s. "The individual who grows up in this culture has a strong feeling of fatalism, helplessness, dependence and inferiority," wrote Lewis, and "little disposition to defer gratification and plan for the future."[4] In today's education field, a deficit orientation is reflected in the notion of the "at-risk" student, in which the child or their family must be "fixed" in some way.[5]

An alternative to the deficit model has been called the *assets-based* approach, which focuses on a community's resources, capacities, and abilities.[6] In the case of Crenshaw High, school activists engaged the ingenuity and creativity of parents, students, and teachers, as well as local institutional resources, to demand adequate funding from the school district and to lead the school's systemic redesign. ELCM extended upon and deepened that redesign.

Extended Learning Time for Teachers

Schools must create a passion for learning not only among children but also among their teachers. . . . We will change American education only insofar as we make all our schools educationally inspiring and intellectually challenging for teachers.

—DEBORAH MEIER [7]

Teachers' professional collaboration was built into the Ford Foundation grant through extended time—including paid hours—to learn, plan, and put the ELCM to work in their classrooms. The four teachers featured here—Caputo-Pearl in history, Garcia in math, Jeff Ponferrada in English, and Susana Rafael in chemistry—began their joint planning during spring break of 2011, in order to have a shared curriculum ready for rollout the coming fall. The teachers saw their planning process as an opportunity to rediscover their own teaching identities, creating an environment of inquiry and reflection, as Garcia explains:

We actually went back, like we were graduate students again, pulled up all those articles from our books and readings that we all had, back to the philosophy that really motivated us when we first started. We read Paulo Freire. And we said, "This is exactly what I want to do." Back in graduate school, we had read bell hooks. And then we had said, "Yes! That is what I want to do in my classroom." And then we got into our classroom, and we're like, "Oh no! I gotta do this standard. I gotta do the SPA [Secondary Periodic Assessment]. I gotta do the CAHSEE [California High School Exit Exam]." We took the time to actually go back and reread and ask, "Are we living up to the ideal of our philosophies which we crafted so long ago?" We gave ourselves the space to have these conversations.

While re-exploring their teaching fundamentals, the teachers agreed that, in the coming year, each would teach at least one unit supporting the objective of ELCM—that is, to prepare students to analyze and act upon issues in their community. Plus, selected students would participate in an internship that extends their learning into the community. The team's vision of community-connected teaching drew strong inspiration from an English unit that Ponferrada had been teaching for some years based on the book, *Our America: Life and Death on the South Side of Chicago.*[8] Written by two youngsters, the book had its genesis when National Public Radio journalist David Isay offered thirteen-year-old LeAlan Jones and fourteen-year-old Lloyd Newman a microphone and tape recorder, and asked them to interview the residents of Chicago's Ida B. Wells housing project. The boys tell of a treacherous field behind the housing project, where bullets are often flying, and about kids whose parents fear letting them outside because of all of the drug dealers in the vicinity. Isay turned the boys' recordings into an award-winning radio documentary. The book takes a powerful turn when a five-year-old boy in Ida B. Wells is pushed to his death from a twelfth-story window by two other boys, aged ten and eleven. The incident drew national news, prompting Isay to return to his young reporters. Jones and Newman would re-interview the people in Ida B. Wells and ask their thoughts about the killing—"Why do you think this happened? How could it have been prevented?" After reading *Our America,* Ponferrada's students conducted their own local investigation or "community ethnography." Equipped with interviewing guidelines and disposable cameras, the students created portraits of their America through posters or PowerPoint presentations.

The teachers also sought to connect students' learning across subject areas. At one meeting, Garcia recalls, the four quizzed each other about their teaching and their lessons. "What do you teach?" she asked science teacher Rafael. "I get chemistry, but what does that mean exactly? What kinds of skills are you giving them?" The two noticed a commonality immediately. "Suzy had this whole thing on density and volume, and I have to do that in geometry—maybe not density per se, but I'm giving them volume formulas and area formulas, talking about units squared and cubed." They found a similar link with Caputo-Pearl, who explained how one of the history standards requires students to analyze data and reach conclusions based on tables, graphs, and charts. Such conversations helped build the teachers' day-to-day collaboration, and made them more attuned to students' learning needs across the curriculum.

One area of common practice for the team—and for all the SJLA teachers—was "habits of mind," a nationally influential model for promoting students' scholarly thinking. Deborah Meier outlined five essential habits in her 1995 book, *The Power of Their Ideas,* while Arthur Costa and Bena Kallick later identified sixteen of them.[9] The SJLA teachers adapted the model and added a series of positive identities—for teachers as well as students (illustrated in the "Our America" unit that follows). Says Caputo-Pearl: "Across the curriculum and classes, we focus on identities and habits of mind—cultural, ethnic, and language identities, background identities of students, but also introducing and supporting students to develop more academic identities, and identities as agents of change in their community."

The Collaborative Units of Study
Our America: The Collaborative Unit in English

Prior to introducing *Our America,* Ponferrada takes his students through a series of lessons that prepare them for the reading and orient them to the academy's justice-based concepts. In an icebreaker unit called "All Eyes on Me," each student tells the class a bit about themselves. Then each produces a small booklet composed of photos, drawings, poetry, or other creative entries telling much more about their lives, families, and interests. These are also shared with the class, building community while communicating to the students that they are each important in the class.

Next comes a stereotypes exercise. Ponferrada writes four words on the board: "immigrant," "terrorist," "homosexual," and "teenage mom." On Post-its, the students write their first thoughts in response to each word, and put these on the board. "The majority of responses were examples of stereotypes connected to each of those social groups," Ponferrada explains. "Some responses for 'immigrant' included 'Mexican,' 'border hoppers,' and 'illegal.'" The class discusses students' responses (Are they ideas that they personally believe? Where did the ideas come from?), followed by the writing of essays.

With the discussion of stereotypes, Ponferrada begins introducing vocabulary relevant to *Our America* and to justice studies generally. Students learn about *marginalization* and two types of responses to stereotyping. A *self-fulfilling prophecy* is when a person gives in to stereotypes, allowing them to come true; an *anomaly* is when a person resists stereotypes, proving them wrong. Other terms include *oppression, dominant culture, poverty, privilege, segregation,* and *class.*

Our America is read in class—sometimes aloud in the group, sometimes quietly. Students learn to annotate while reading. They write chapter summaries. They pick out passages from the book that illustrate terms and concepts studied in class. They do skits and role plays. A classroom poster lists the habits of mind and identities that Ponferrada considers important objectives for the unit:

IDENTITY	HABIT OF MIND
Powerful and purposeful reader	Reading and examining with purpose, while assessing evidence
Observer and empathizer	Understanding point of view
Connector and agent of change	Understanding cause and effect, and making connections
Intellectual and scholar	Questioning and building intellectual curiosity

"A lot of what I focused on were the identities of 'connector' and 'agent of change,'" says Ponferrada. "So, once you see yourself in the book, and once you connect your community with what LeAlan and Lloyd were going through in the community of *Our America*, what can you do to enact change?" In this vein, Ponferrada introduced students to three contrasting approaches to resistance—*conforming resistance,* in which members of marginalized groups attempt to assimilate and become part of the dominant culture; *self-defeating resistance,* which results in a negative outcome; and *transformational resistance,* in which resisters create change for themselves, their education, or their community in a positive way.

In the unit's culminating task, consisting of an essay and a visual presentation, students elaborate on the connections between *Our America* and their own community. The key questions are:

• In what ways do LeAlan and Lloyd act out transformative resistance in spite of their experiences in the marginalized community of the Ida B. Wells?

- In what ways do people in your neighborhoods, schools, etc. act out transformative resistance in spite of their experiences in the marginalized Crenshaw community?

"One of the main reasons I chose *Our America*," comments Ponferrada, "is because the stories and the two characters parallel a lot of what I've seen my students go through, talk about, share in the classroom." Tenth grader Fabiola Leyva describes how she connected to *Our America*, and how it made her think about herself possibly being an agent of change:

> I don't like reading books; I think they're boring. But that book really caught my eye, because it shows the struggle not only for those kids but for a lot of people in different parts of the world. For those two little kids to try to change their community, it was impressive. Now that I've read *Our America*, it makes me believe. Because a lot of what happens around my community—the shots and the killing—it made me want to help change that. I won't just do something and everything is going to change, but little by little it can happen if more people do this.

Ponferrada's class exemplified an assets-based approach in multiple ways. The "All Eyes on Me" unit elevated the students, their lives, and the things they value. The study of systems that stereotype and oppress marginalized communities, along with strategies for resistance, similarly affirmed the students and their communities. But the assets-based centerpiece was *Our America*, in which two boys living in circumstances comparable to that of the Crenshaw students displayed capacities as investigators, community analysts, writers, and even comedians. The clear message of the course was that the students had similar capacities that could be tapped and honed.

For the future, Ponferrada proposed to make better use of technology in the community ethnography portion of the unit: "I was made aware at the end of last year how the Media Academy at our school has video cameras, and the media teacher could teach students to record and how to conduct interviews. So I want to see if I can work closely with them to bring that project to life." He also envisioned the next step in developing students as scholars or agents of change, by "taking those projects outside of my classroom to present to the academy, the school, or at a community event."

Community Mapping: The Collaborative Unit in Math[10]

"Something I struggle with as a math teacher," observes Cathy Garcia, "is how do you create a social justice-based lesson in mathematics. It's not just, 'Hey, you gotta pass math so that you can get into college.' It's gotta be more than that." Garcia discovered that collaborating with other teachers and doing so across the curriculum helped her to develop social justice-based lessons, and also helped get students excited about learning math. Her discovery began the year before the Ford-funded ELCM project was launched. Students were coming to her with math questions related to their *Our America* projects in Ponferrada's class. They would say: "Ms. Garcia, I really want to turn this into a pie chart. But I don't know how." Or: "I really need to learn how to turn these raw numbers into percentages. How do I do that?" Garcia notes, "Now the kids themselves were realizing math does not exist in a vacuum."

ELCM gave Garcia a fitting opportunity to plan a cross-curricular unit by using a shared data set—from LAUSD's "school report cards"—with Caputo-Pearl from history and Rafael from science. In her math class, the students worked with that data to do some community mapping, as Garcia explains:

The report cards show things like test scores and graduation and attendance rates. We took report cards from Crenshaw, Fremont, the Kennedy Schools, the Palisades School of Art—random ones from all over the city—and printed them out for the students. Then we looked at a map of the city and tried to identify where those schools are in relationship to the map. The kids easily made connections just based on that.

What the students could see was that the schools in the more affluent and white areas of Los Angeles, such as the Westside, consistently produced better report cards than schools in the south and east parts of Los Angeles, which are predominantly poor and black or Latino. The data patterns generated lively student discussions about race, class, and educational equity in the city.

Garcia also found that the community mapping exercise led to students generating their own questions about their city: "Ms. Garcia, why isn't Beverly Hills part of L.A.?" "How come Santa Monica isn't a part of L.A.?" "Why do we have this strange little strip going down through the center of L.A., all the way down to the beach?"

The "little strip" is the Alameda Corridor, a railway line that moves cargo from the ports of Los Angeles and Long Beach to national rail connections near downtown Los Angeles. Garcia points out: "There was absolutely no guiding question that said, 'Tell me why you think L.A. looks the way it does.' My simply putting the map in front of them made them ask that question." She responded to their questions by suggesting resources: "You know, that sounds like a history question. Maybe you should go ask Mr. Caputo-Pearl." "Why don't you go onto Google? Why don't you use that computer over there?" Says Garcia: "It started them on that journey of 'How do I find out?' And the kids went and they started finding out."

Finally, Garcia used the city map to teach other math skills, and the students brought their heightened engagement and curiosity to those lessons as well:

We talked about how to read the map and use the scale, and how that connects to similarity and congruence.* If I taught similarity and congruence any other way, it wouldn't have engaged them like this. I then put a transparent grid over the map and said, "Let's make an estimate of the area of Los Angeles. Let's convert square centimeters into square miles using proportions and ratios." And the students loved doing it. I know from past experience that, had I given them a worksheet on proportions and ratios, many would have not done it. Only 50 percent of my students would have turned it in. But this time, almost everyone finished it. I even had students who were absent come in and say, "I know I missed yesterday, but I really need to make it up." Teachers, and especially math teachers, almost never hear that. But they were telling me, "Ms. Garcia, can I finish it at nutrition?" I'd say, "You can take it home." And they'd say, "I want to finish it now!" It was amazing to me. They were engaged.

Integrating Reading Instruction: The Collaborative Unit in History

Alex Caputo-Pearl's history unit featured the same data set of school report cards used in Garcia's class, but he combined it with reading and analytical work. Students were given multiple articles reflecting Republican and "progressive caucus Democratic" viewpoints on school reform.[11] From those articles, Caputo-Pearl explains, students had to make some choices for their culminating task.

---

* In geometry, *congruence* refers to figures with the same shape and size, while *similarity* refers to figures with the same shape but which may be different in size.

The assignment is to read the articles, then look at the data from the school report cards, and then merge the articles and data to assess policy positions—that is, to assess whether the Republican position or the progressive caucus Democrat position is one that would seem to work in school reform. Then they write a well-structured essay that includes articulating some of the policy perspectives and incorporating data.

This was a challenging assignment for these tenth graders on multiple levels. Students are launched into the complex and tricky terrain of education policy. The assigned readings are authentic documents from the field; they have not been watered down for easier reading, as are many high school textbooks. The assignment integrates reading, writing, policy analysis, and data analysis. Departing from the traditional mode of history instruction which focuses on subject content, Caputo-Pearl's approach gives as much attention to helping students master a range of academic skills, as it does to the course content itself. His students work on the skills from the beginning of the school year and well before tackling the ambitious assignment on school reform.

Caputo-Pearl's guiding framework for the teaching of reading and text analysis is the Reading Apprenticeship program from WestEd, an education consulting firm. Students learn how to "talk to the text," reinforcing what Ponferrada teaches in English class. They write notes in the margins of documents or on a separate sheet—asking questions, commenting, summarizing, and explaining what they do or don't understand. Caputo-Pearl introduces a "reading assessment rubric" that helps both student and teacher monitor students' progress as they struggle to engage with difficult texts. The rubric, excerpted on page 225, identifies three levels of progress in students' reading and reading engagement.[12]

We can see Reading Apprenticeship at work in a unit on African history, which precedes the school reform assignment. In

RUBRIC FOR CURRICULUM-EMBEDDED READING ASSESSMENT

Noticing Reading	Few or no marks on the page along with vague responses to process questions and confused answers to comprehension questions.
Focusing on Reading	Marks on the page and responses to questions give insight into student's reading process and comprehension.
Taking Control of Reading	Substantial marking on the page and elaborated answers to questions give detailed information about student's reading process and comprehension.

the sample below, a student responds to lines from "A Morning in the Heart of Africa," a poem by Congolese independence leader Patrice Lumumba. Caputo-Pearl then adds his own remarks, lending guidance and encouragement (see page 226).

Another student underlined the poem in several places, but only wrote two small responses in the margin—"their strong bodies" and "they only had their fists to fight." Caputo-Pearl marked a comment using language from the rubric: "OK, I can tell you focused on reading, but I need to see more to see you are taking control of reading!"

Caputo-Pearl's class emphasizes collaborative learning, including co-authored essays. But he is very deliberate in how students are grouped, and he strikes a careful balance between individual and group work. "I give them some choice, but I basically choose the groups. Then if they really have some issue or

Lumumba Poem Lines	Student Response	Teacher Comment
Your tyrants built the lustrous, magic temples to preserve your soul, preserve your suffering.	This sentence needs clarification. I didn't understand the text.	Very good that you noticed this.
Then they put a treacherous big viper on your chest, on your neck they laid the yoke of fire-water, they took your sweet wife for the flitter of cheap pearls, your incredible riches that nobody could measure.	This sentence was clear to me. It clearly states they stole African goods and sold them in their country for more money.	Very good to note *this*.
From your hut, the tom-toms sounded into the dark of night carrying cruel laments up mighty black rivers, abused girls, streams of tears and blood, about ships that sailed to the country where the little man wallows in an ant-hill and where dollar is king, to that damned land which they called a motherland.	The paragraph here is trying to state how they round up the Africans on a boat and took them to the "motherland" / slave plantation.	Good summary.

want to pair off in a different way, I'll bend to certain things. But I have to make sure that there are students at different skill levels in each group." While the education reform essays were jointly written by each group, much of the groundwork was handled individually. For example, each student completed a graphic organizer that helped "pull out main points" and "organize some thoughts" generated by the readings. Then the group pulled from these notes three points of interest to be developed in their essays, with each member drafting a paragraph on one of the key points. Once the papers were drafted, the students made small presentations to the class.

Caputo-Pearl reflects back on the unit and the work of his students: "Overall, I was happy with it. I think it was constructed well, in the sense that students had to use certain reading strategies to get into the articles, and certain interpretation skills to get into the data. Because Crenshaw was in the data, there was definitely a higher degree of interest than you might get in doing other historical stuff. And I was happy that there weren't a lot of kids who failed. You want to give every opportunity you can for kids to pass an important assignment. I was happy that there was participation and engagement for almost all of the students."

The Scientific Method: The Collaborative Unit in Chemistry

The SJLA tenth-grade science teacher Susana Rafael had an interesting challenge. She had to try to complete a collaborative unit in chemistry, while at the same time teaching chemistry content standards that didn't exactly lend themselves to a community project. Rafael decided to focus on teaching students how to use science as a tool to solve problems—in this case, a possible societal problem. Rafael explains the theory behind her collaborative unit:

Chemistry wasn't as easy to tie in. But we have these investigation/experimentation standards which, for every single science class, are the same. The students are able to collect data, analyze data, form hypotheses, and these types of things. So it was a chance to do that. I think that's really important because there's a big misconception. Most of our students associate science only with facts and memorization; they don't see science as a tool for discovery and learning. So showing how you can apply it is important.

Rafael connected with the collaborative unit by having her students develop a potential experiment using the same school report card data set that Garcia and Caputo-Pearl used in their classes. The students wouldn't actually do the experiment, but they'd use the scientific method to document a problem, propose a solution, and identify how they'd go about testing their hypothesis to see if their proposed solution would solve their problem. Rafael explains: "We focused on attendance or graduation rates. The idea was to create a procedure for how they would test certain variables and see what it is about Crenshaw and the students here, why they're not graduating at the same rates as at other schools."

The students brainstormed the various factors that interfere with student achievement and graduation. If students aren't coming to school on time, why is that? If they aren't keeping up with their classwork, then why? Students also proposed solutions such as incentives: if students are rewarded with some prize at the end of the four years, would this motivate more students to graduate? Rafael continues: "Then I told them to just focus on one factor and how you can improve that. The point was to show that problems are complex—it's not just one thing such as students like to sleep late. There's a bunch of variables affecting these outcomes. They chose one of the problems to focus on and how to test their potential solution."

The students worked in groups. After each group agreed on a framing of the problem and a proposed solution as the basis for an experiment, each group would write a grant proposal to fund their experiment. What materials would they need? How would they approach it? Also, each group produced a lab report as their final product, describing the information, materials, and procedures. Rafael adds:

I have them record the group roles: what did each group member do? There was some accountability so that I could verify and credit the work of each student. The report included an analysis: what do these numbers mean? And lastly, it had a conclusion where I asked them to answer these questions: What did you learn? What are some errors you could have made?

A big part of science, Rafael points out, is being able to identify things that go wrong. "Science isn't necessarily about the right answer, because a lot of times you don't know what the right answer is. You're trying to eliminate the wrong answers."

As a result of Rafael's piece of the collaborative unit, the SJLA students learned that they can use scientific tools to help solve societal problems—enhancing their proficiency with science while furthering the belief that all of their schooling can help them become agents of change in their community.

The work on education policy issues—in math, history, and chemistry class—incorporated an assets-based approach on various levels. The students were seen not simply as learners in a low-income community needing skills—though they certainly did need skills. They were also viewed as citizens who had the capacity to critique the education system and to organize for its betterment. In Caputo Pearl's class, we saw an additional assets component: he consciously designed the small groups to include a mix of skills, thereby engaging the more advanced students as tutors and resources for the struggling students.

Internships: Extending Learning into the Community

In ECLM's pilot year, more than thirty SJLA students participated in community internships, which allowed them to take skills they'd begun to develop in the classroom and apply them in real-world situations. One very promising internship project grew out of the school's relationship with a local health advocacy organization, as Garcia recounts:

> We originally approached the Community Health Councils after we lost our school nurse due to budget cuts. We no longer had anyone to provide basic nursing care, let alone address the wider problems of sexually transmitted disease, teen pregnancy, access to healthy food, diabetes, lack of exercise. We asked them, "How can we work with you to bring this kind of service to our school?"

At the same time, Garcia recalls, the teacher leaders of SJLA also used the opportunity to approach CHC about becoming a part of the school curriculum, in what would eventually become ELCM. After a series of discussions regarding Crenshaw's goal of engaging students in the community, CHC proposed: "Why don't we start employing some of your students through internships? We'll train them in our office, and they can learn how to survey the issue of access to healthy food in the Crenshaw community." Garcia observes: "That sounded very much like what our students were already doing in ELCM—talking to community, analyzing data. We'd apprenticed them and now they're going into a workplace situation—with other adults and professionals who share a social justice agenda."

CHC saw the high school as a worthy partner to collaborate with on community health uplift. One of the Councils' objectives is to identify alternative sources of food in communities—both from the standpoint of nutrition and economic development, explains CHC executive director and founder Lark Galloway-Gilliam: "And the high school has that wonderful garden that fell into disservice. We're trying to work with them to resurrect it, help them to find some partners, look at how to open it up to the community." Another objective, notes Galloway-Gilliam, is to enhance access to health care services. "In communities like South Los Angeles, there are few hospitals or doctors. We did some advocacy with the county to get more community clinics into the area, and we're working with Crenshaw with the idea of bringing in a school-based clinic."

The internships that CHC fashioned with Crenshaw were part of a wider ten-year study. "We are trying to change the community resources, so there's more support for healthful living," says CHC policy director Gwendolyn Flynn.

We focus on food, nutrition, grocery stores, restaurants, and physical activity. We also look at health disparities, especially comparing South L.A. with communities on the Westside— which have better health outcomes than we do here. We are talking about diet-related chronic illnesses that can be prevented, such as diabetes, heart disease, and high blood pressure. There's like an eight-year difference in life expectancy between this neighborhood and those five miles west. We were approaching the end of our study, and we wanted to assess whether change has happened where food is concerned. It was almost serendipity when we learned about the Crenshaw extended learning project, because we were thinking about who we could enlist to help conduct these studies.

CHC policy analyst Breanna Morrison, who coordinated the internships, recalls the meeting where CHC formalized a plan with Rousseau and Caputo-Pearl from Crenshaw:

We talked about compensation for the students because, of course, you want to provide incentive to participate. But we also talked about finding a way to really incorporate the program and research into the curriculum of the students. We wanted to increase education about nutrition. We wanted to increase students' capacity in community advocacy and the policymaking process—by showing that if you conduct research and provide academically substantiated knowledge that can be conveyed to decision makers, it can impact policy change.

After a robust training conducted by a University of Southern California professor, the selected interns went out into the community to survey the quality of food available at various stores and markets around South Los Angeles. Morrison explains how this worked:

We identified all of the grocery stores defined by the Department of Public Health through their environmental health rating. The stores are all in a database online. We then did a random sampling. We tried to assign students to survey the stores that were closest to the school. We also required their parents or a guardian to participate in the training and the surveys, because we didn't want the students to go out and conduct the analysis by themselves.

It was learning for the parents as well and really got them engaged. They would have the dialogue about, "Oh, this is how you read expiration dates, and this is how you check the calories." After that—once I did the quality control for the first two surveys—most of the students obtained the knowledge that we conveyed in the trainings very well.

Ten SJLA tenth graders were selected for the CHC program from among a large pool of applicants. Students saw the internships as a chance to learn and grow, and to get involved in their communities in productive ways. Tenth grader Allen Harris made some discoveries about how people in low-income areas are almost forced to eat less-healthy foods:

I saw this white rice and this brown rice, and the white rice was like two dollars and the brown rice was like two fifty. So, the problem that you get to is that most whole grain foods are more expensive than processed food, and that's why people will buy a quick burger or candy. Nobody wants to drive to a rich neighborhood where they have healthier food. It's expensive and people don't have the money these days to afford something fresh or good.

Classmate Kateryn Salazar adds, "I like to help my community and I would know more about the foods—if it is healthy or not, how many types of foods I have to eat, or if it's expired." For Fabiola Leyva, the surveys really connected with the idea of being an agent of change:

I felt good because I thought I was making a change in my community. If you want to change anything you have to start with yourself. There was a man and his son at one of the stores, and they asked, "Why are you doing this?" I explained to them and they said, "Oh, okay. Good." That's happened to me a lot of times, and some people said they were going to check labels more to see if food was expired, and I felt good about that.

Another participating student, Alejandro Dias, liked the opportunity to work on his communication skills: "I felt like I got more public speaking skills, because usually I'm not really good with speaking with people or confronting them. I felt good about myself for doing this."

For the SJLA teachers, the CHC project offered an exciting model for Crenshaw internships in years to come. Says Caputo-Pearl: "We're trying to build these partnerships where, eventually, the vast majority of students can get involved in some activity like that." Garcia adds that the internships are really at the heart of what the SJLA is trying to accomplish at Crenshaw: "It is our goal that our students, as juniors and seniors over the next two years, will start to work with community organizations and actually begin solving the problems that they identify. We've got a list of community organizations that want to work with the Social Justice Academy."

Extended Learning for Parents

The final piece of the puzzle for Crenshaw's Extended Learning Cultural Model is the parents. Without a genuine and explicit buy-in from the parents, Crenshaw's model would never take true root in the community. The Ford grant specifically provided for parent training, leadership, and mentoring, as well as capacity building—that is, recruiting more parents to get involved in Crenshaw's model. Caputo-Pearl explains how parents were engaged at Crenshaw by Kahllid Al-Alim, the parent organizer at Crenshaw whose work was funded by the grant:

> Kahllid works with us specifically on parent outreach. If the kids are taking on all this stuff after school or during the school day, their parents need to be aware of it. Because their parents might think, "You know what? I don't think I want my kid to have a job." Or "I think I need my kid at home," for whatever reason. So we need to engage the parents. We need to talk with them, let them know what our philosophy is.
>
> It's a conversation about why we need to be doing this for the betterment of the child. Because that parent, and myself as teacher, we have the same end goal in mind: How do we take that child and turn them into a productive member of society as an adult? How do we work together to make that student reach his/her full potential?
>
> We use organizations like Kahllid's [Coalition for Educational Justice] to help us engage the parents at large. We also use

existing parent groups. At Crenshaw, we have a history of organizing. We already have the Crenshaw Cougar Coalition. We already have parents engaged because of the School Site Council. So we said, "How do we take those existing avenues and now just expand them a little bit more, and motivate them a little bit more?"

Al-Alim is also a parent organizer with the Coalition for Educational Justice (CEJ)—a parent/teacher/student alliance with chapters in several Los Angeles schools—and an elected member of the Park Mesa Heights Neighborhood Council, whose area includes Crenshaw. His role in ELCM was to recruit and develop parents, and to make parents in Crenshaw's feeder elementary and middle schools aware of the reform going on at the high school. Al-Alim has a son and a daughter in one of Crenshaw's feeder elementary schools, as well as an older daughter who completed her teaching credential at the University of Texas and is now a special education teacher. Regarding his older daughter, he remarks: "She is an inspiration for me to keep doing this parent component and talking to other parents who have been really crying out for quality schools for their children."

Through the Parent Academy (the workshop series led by Lewis King) and through one-on-one engagement, parents learn about ELCM and such classroom concepts as habits of mind, positive identities, and metacognitive work such as "talking to the text." King's "intentional civility" model challenges parents to rethink their relationship to their children's academic work and to view it as a shared project. "Parent engagement," says Al-Alim, "is about rethinking what education is. It's not just about your children getting a textbook, coming home with it, doing their homework, and going back to school. It's a new way." He adds that the parents were receptive. "They got a chance to ask questions, to demonstrate it to each other. And then we would ask,

'Can they talk to another parent about it and see if they would like to get involved?'" He describes some of his success stories:

> One parent works with LAUSD in the parent recruitment aspect. His son is in the Social Justice Academy, and he brought to our attention things that are going on in other districts. So that was an excellent collaboration because it helped formulate ideas about what we were going to do at Crenshaw through our Parent Academy.
>
> It was also good to see a balance of attendees: we had some Latino parents; we had some African-American male and female parents; and I was particularly happy about other black men showing up. They would sit there and listen to Dr. King, express their agreement, and then say, "Well, this is what I'm having trouble with at home." Dr. King would take that and give them another way of thinking about how they approach not getting homework done—issues like that.

Achievement of the Extended Learning Cultural Model

The Crenshaw teachers and community attempted a groundbreaking, all-encompassing education reform model that extended learning into multiple environments. Was it a success? Though implementing a model of this magnitude takes years to fully realize, there were some immediate results by spring 2012. Lewis King saw an impact on classroom learning as well as school culture:

> For the first time, we got people—parents, teachers, and a significant group of community members—united and focused around education of the child in the Crenshaw community. We began to see very significant progress in the classrooms in which we were working. We were not unaware of the need to create a research and development model, to create a laboratory. We

paid careful attention to professional development as well as results in the classroom. As far as school culture, we've seen an enormous jump in kids wanting to be in the classroom. They are more eager to participate and show more affinity for learning.

King also saw ELCM moving productively beyond the pilot phase toward full implementation: "We're absolutely optimistic about the possibilities of bringing this model to scale throughout the entire school. The two SLCs have dramatically turned themselves around. We've begun to engage the rest of the faculty about the model, and we are making some movement."

Jeff Ponferrada likewise considered Crenshaw at a critical point in its turnaround, and saw ELCM at the center of that transformation.

I'm still new here—it's only my fourth year. But this year out of all the years, there's been a lot of work outside of the classroom to improve teaching practices, and to improve education as a whole for every student on campus. A big part of that is with Principal Rousseau. Another part is the Ford Foundation grant, where we really delve into our teaching and how we envision it moving forward. We had a lot of time over the summer to reflect on what we were each doing in our individual classes, and how we as teachers can work together to create a cohesive academy identity, and how that identity would push our students to the next level. I see a lot of promise at Crenshaw right now.

The school showed promise as well in that year's state standardized test results, though not in every category. Black students exceeded their 2011–12 growth target by 38 percent; special needs students, by a striking 271 percent. On the other hand, English learners fell 29 percent short of their target, while Latinos showed no growth from the prior year.[13] The school turnaround was, of course, a work in progress; as King notes, the plan was to expand ELCM schoolwide in the years ahead. Perhaps the most telling indicator that Crenshaw was on the right path lay in a March 27, 2012, report sent to LAUSD by a visiting committee from WASC, the school accrediting agency. The committee observed that Principal Rousseau had "captured the loyalty, support and respect of every student, teacher, staff member and parent that the VC [visiting committee] met during the visit. The entire school is now working together as a team."[14]

All that was needed was for LAUSD to embrace Crenshaw's work and give it full support. Indeed, Crenshaw leaders had reached out to LAUSD superintendent John Deasy on multiple occasions, inviting his involvement in ELCM and the school's transformation. Their invitations received no response. Instead, as the 2012–13 school year opened, and more Crenshaw teachers were receiving ELCM-related training—through a faculty workshop on multicultural teaching—the superintendent moved promptly to crush Crenshaw's reform movement.

LAUSD Dismantles Crenshaw Reforms, Dismisses Staff

On October 24, 2012, Crenshaw staff received a chilling letter from John Deasy. "A review of four years of performance data indicate less than adequate progress in the achievement of Crenshaw's students," said the Los Angeles schools chief. The school would therefore be "transformed" and "redesigned." The new operation, scheduled to launch on July 1, 2013, would feature three magnet schools with "a full complement" of Advanced Placement courses and an "immediate exploration of IB pathways"—referring to the International Baccalaureate, an acclaimed college preparatory program.[15]

Deasy's interest in Crenshaw reform hardly seemed genuine, however. No one at the school was consulted in the making of his plan, and his letter did not acknowledge the school's current reform work or accomplishments. Moreover, Crenshaw's decade-long school improvement work had not attracted much support from LAUSD. On the contrary, the district had contributed to the school's continuing difficulties since the 2005 accreditation debacle, in part by imposing a perpetual turnover of school leadership. As the WASC visitors noted with disappointment in their March 2012 report, five principals and twenty-one assistant principals had passed through Crenshaw since 2005; the school had seen four head counselors in the past four years; and its current principal, Rousseau, was only interim. "How can a school function properly with this level of administrative instability?" the visitors remarked. "It is evident that the school is in desperate need of 'consistent quality leadership.'"[16]

But Deasy's letter contained another announcement that made the superintendent's intentions even more clear: "All current staff members at Crenshaw will be invited to apply for positions in the transformed school." That is, in a school that WASC had observed "working together as a team," everyone's jobs would now be up for grabs. Crenshaw would suffer another period of destabilization. And the school's activist teachers—such as those in the Social Justice Academy or who engaged in the union—recognized that they were going to be targeted. Significantly too, the school's highly respected interim principal, Rousseau, was not reappointed in 2012–13.

Deasy was no fan of ELCM or the community-connected vision of education that Rousseau, King, and the activist teachers and parents had embraced at Crenshaw. His was the top-down business model favored by the Broad Academy.[17] A high-profile challenge to that model at Crenshaw, and spreading to its feeder schools and beyond, could not be allowed. As Caputo-Pearl observes:

> The ELCM is based on education as a tool for critical thinking and contribution to social justice—not education as a market

and business, as Deasy promotes. It had the support of prominent academics of color, with whom Deasy could not stand
toe-to-toe. It was led by progressive unionists, not district hacks.
The ELCM was, pure and simple, a direct threat to Deasy, and
he knew he had to destroy it.

The Crenshaw community protested, held press conferences, packed LAUSD hearings. One student told the school
board at its December 2012 meeting: "There are students at our
school that are affected by foster care and have to change all
the time, and changing the school like this is just wrong in so
many ways and on so many levels." A Crenshaw parent added:
"You wouldn't do this in Beverly Hills. You wouldn't do this in
the Valley"—a more affluent area in the north of Los Angeles.
"But because this is the last predominantly black school in L.A.,
you think that it's okay? Look at these people behind me. It's
not okay. You reconstitute Crenshaw, we're gonna reconstitute
you."[18] But the school board voted unanimously to endorse
Deasy's plans, and ELCM was halted in its tracks. The Ford
Foundation regretfully stopped ELCM's funding, as Ford program director Jeannie Oakes explained to Deasy and others in
a December letter:

> The Ford Foundation has a history of investment at Crenshaw,
> and we think the Extended Learning Cultural Model holds
> promise as an approach to deepen and expand the opportunities
> available to students and the quality of their learning experiences
> to support their success. However, the recently announced plans
> by LAUSD to substantially reorganize Crenshaw's structure and
> staffing, in combination with the likely community response,
> leads us to believe that we need to hold off on future financial
> support to Crenshaw until it has a better sense of what its future
> holds.[19]

Most Crenshaw staff reapplied for their jobs in the spring of 2013. But of sixty-two teachers reapplying, only twenty-nine were selected for the revamped school.[20] Caputo-Pearl, Garcia, and many others who had given lead in the school's transformational work—and some who had received outstanding teacher awards from the district—were among those dismissed. UTLA charged Deasy with unfair labor practices over the alleged targeting of twelve union activists who were not rehired. As of this writing, the state's Public Employment Relations Board has yet to rule on the UTLA charge. Meanwhile, many of the displaced teachers secured positions at other schools in the district.

Reflections

"We got into teaching because we believed it was a socially revolutionary act, that you change the world through education," observes Garcia. "I form a ripple and I affect all these people, and they now form their own set of ripples." The Crenshaw teachers engaged their community, tapped university and foundation resources, and started a ripple with extraordinary potentials. Yet the Crenshaw movement could not prevent the district's hostile reconstitution—a move that has also been visited upon other South Los Angeles high schools.[21] We are forced to ask, What role *can* school transformation play in the fight for public education? Won't the most effective democratic models be regarded as a threat and ultimately face dismantling by corporate interests?

Caputo-Pearl reflected on such questions during a May 2015 interview. He had taught at another high school the year following Crenshaw's reconstitution. But in UTLA's 2014 election, he headed up a slate that swept all seven top officer positions. He has since been working with the members to transform their union into a militant, democratic, community-connected organization in the mold trailblazed by the Chicago Teachers Union. "We should all be driving toward standards based on a quality, culturally relevant curriculum in schools," he says. "And such efforts must include community, parents, and students, like we did at Crenshaw. That kind of organizing not only provides a model of what we want to be providing to students, but it engages the right people who need to be part of the broader movement to protect and expand public education."

While acknowledging that "the heart of the Crenshaw program was destroyed," Caputo-Pearl sees significant organizing victories emerging from Crenshaw and which are still unfolding in LAUSD and beyond. First, a cohort of leaders were developed in the project—and in the struggle to protect the project—who continue to organize around similar issues. One of these is Tauheedah Shakur, a Crenshaw student leader who, after graduating, became a staff organizer with Youth Justice Coalition in South Los Angeles.[22] Some of the dismissed Crenshaw teachers went on to implement progressive, ethnic studies-type curricula at other schools, Caputo-Pearl adds, while others "have now stepped up into greater roles within the union." In another organizing trajectory: graduate student Lena Jackson produced a documentary film about the Crenshaw reconstitution and has been showing it to audiences around the country, contributing to a national discussion about corporate-driven attacks that target schools in communities of color.[23]

Second, Caputo-Pearl believes that the Crenshaw work contributed to his union electoral victory. "The new leader's battle scars are a selling point for many teachers," reported the *Los Angeles Times*, with one teacher commenting, "I respect a man who has been stomped on and still has the stamina and courage to speak truth to power."[24] Caputo-Pearl and his team would promptly shift UTLA toward social-movement unionism. At the union's 2014 summer leadership conference, Caputo-Pearl rolled out a "Schools LA Students Deserve Contract and Community Campaign." This began with a "school blitz" in which the new union officers visited over four hundred campuses to discuss union contract demands. By the following April, escalating mobilizations had won what UTLA called "round one" in the campaign: a contract settlement with enhanced health benefits and job security, caps on class size and counselor student loads, and creation of a health services task force that "will allow us to better organize for more social, emotional, and nursing support for students."[25]

The transformational work at Crenshaw had always missed a vital ingredient: it lacked a teachers union equally committed to school transformation and to broad public education organizing. Caputo-Pearl remarks: "To sustain that kind of organizing model, you need a strong labor component and a strong community component. I think we built a reasonably strong community movement side, given the historical period that we live in. But we had a union that was not flexing its muscles in the way that we needed." Yet the union is now recreating itself, and the Crenshaw experience would inform the union's new community-connected organizing vision.

In October 2014, Los Angeles public education advocates secured a welcome victory when Superintendent Deasy resigned amid several scandals. One scandal involved a $1.3 billion deal to provide every LAUSD student with an Apple iPad, including instructional software from Pearson. The contract had provoked parent and student protest over its use of bond moneys that were supposed to target badly needed school infrastructure improvements. But Deasy suffered much greater scrutiny when emails revealed that he had been in close communication with Pearson and Apple before the contract was opened for competitive bidding.[26] That same fall, LAUSD was beset by a technological crisis with MISIS (My Integrated Student Information System), a new student tracking and scheduling software that was overwhelmed with glitches. At South Los Angeles's Jefferson High School, students were packed into the auditorium for weeks waiting to be assigned their classes.[27] For Caputo-Pearl, the Crenshaw struggle played a contributing role in Deasy's fall from grace: "It was part of a narrative that we helped develop in the early months of the new UTLA leadership. Rather than Deasy being a savior of South L.A. schools, as he put himself forward as, he destroyed South L.A. schools. He crushed the Crenshaw program; he brought disaster to Jefferson with the MISIS crisis." Indeed, such a narrative also appeared in the major media. For example, in its story on Caputo-Pearl's election as union president, the *Los Angeles Times* noted that he had helped develop "a homegrown improvement plan" at Crenshaw that had won foundation and university support. Yet, the *Times* reports, Caputo-Pearl was "on the receiving end" when Deasy cited low achievement and replaced the school staff. Deasy, following his departure from LAUSD, would take a position as "superintendent-in-residence" with the Broad Academy.[28]

The Crenshaw struggle and its aftermath illuminate how the strands of a public education organizing strategy—transforming schools, transforming teachers unions, and challenging the forces of corporate school reform—can intersect. With the city teachers union now under progressive leadership, the possibilities extend further, and we hope to see more organizing lessons emanating from Los Angeles.

Problem-Based, Community-Connected Extended Learning

CRENSHAW HIGH SCHOOL

Executive Summary

TIME FRAME FOR FUNDED WORK:
March 2011–March 2012, with subsequent consideration
for multi-year grant

FUNDING AMOUNT:
$200,000

FUNDED INSTITUTIONS:
Initiates with Social Justice and Law Academy (SJLA) and Business
Management and Entrepreneurship Academy (BME)
at Crenshaw High

GRANTING INSTITUTION:
Ford Foundation

FISCAL AGENT:
University of Southern California

PRINCIPAL INVESTIGATOR:
Sylvia Rousseau, continuing to work in close collaboration
with the faculty project leads, Alex Caputo-Pearl and
Maynard Brown, and with the principal, Carrie Allen
and the GCEP executive director, Beverly Ryder

This project seeks to extend learning time and enhance learning experiences by making stronger connections between learning and the contexts of the school and community through a problem-based approach. The organizing idea is one of co-constructing knowledge at every juncture in the ecosystems that surround the student: parent-to-child, student-to-teacher, teacher-to-parent, student-to-community, community-to-school.

The project is school-initiated and grows out of a history of movement at Crenshaw High School (CHS) towards reform, pioneered by the parent/faculty/administration/student collaboration in the Crenshaw Cougar Coalition, which contributed to the initiation of the partnership with the Greater Crenshaw Educational Partnership (GCEP). Project implementation will build on recent reforms at CHS, including wall-to-wall SLCs, block scheduling, a resource coordinating team, structured professional development, and new partnerships that bring relevance to the educational enterprise. Moreover, the project will build on broader community initiatives, such as the Los Angeles Urban League's Neighborhoods@Work program. In these ways, the project seeks to address graduation rates, class passing rates, provision of effective instruction, API scores, program improvement status, and other school indicators, as well as assist in reversing CHS's recent declines in enrollment.

The first 12 months of the project will be a planning and initiation period, piloted by the two small learning communities. The first 12 months will include:

Extended Time for Teachers

Teachers in the two pilot academies will work collaboratively for 8–14 additional planning hours per month. In this extended learning time for teachers, they will:

- Work with the USC Rossier School of Education and the Tom and Ethel Bradley Foundation to extend capacity for facilitating students' proficiencies in literacy and math in a culturally relevant context
- Engage professional development provided by USC Rossier School faculty to implement problem-based learning focused on California Content standards, 21st Century Skills, and research-based pedagogy
- Produce two collaborative standards-based units of study
- Demonstrate proficiency, through observations, in teaching literacy and mathematics in a culturally-relevant context
- Develop a peer observation and feedback system, resulting in identification of model classrooms to be used for school-wide teaching and learning
- Create interdisciplinary problem-based culminating tasks for 12th, 11th, and 10th graders, respectively
- Collaboratively create formative assessments, and accompanying rubrics, that help to scaffold students into the problem-based culminating tasks

- Collaboratively assess student work and make instructional adjustments accordingly
- Build relationships with existing and new organizational partners and parents in the context of bringing additional support to the problem-based, community-connected extended learning model
- Experience internships with community and business institutions to increase teacher awareness of social action efforts and 21st-century workplace skills.

Student Activities

In addition to benefiting from during-the-school-day implementation of the new units created by teachers during their extended planning time, students will be involved in pilot efforts in extended learning time through both existing programs, and through new efforts to provide academic support. Student activities will include:

- Extensive engagement with expository text and mathematic/scientific critical thinking, with resulting increased literacy and mathematics proficiency rates
- Targeting tutoring, based on individual student data analysis, that supports students who have not achieved proficiency in reading comprehension and mathematics, with resulting increased scores on the CST and CAHSEE
- Extensive engagement with cultural histories and structured learning experiences to cultivate autonomous learners
- Through work with UCLA IDEA (Institute for Democracy, Education, and Access), extensive student-led research on the development and implementation of the problem-based, community-connected extended learning model.

Parent Activities

Parents will recruit other parents to get involved in and shape the problem-based, community-connected extended learning model. Parents will engage in training, leadership development, and mentoring. Parent activities will include:

- Through work with the Bradley Foundation, extensive engagement with intentional civility training sessions and structured dialogue sessions with teachers and administrators on the role of culture, family, and community experiences in informing instruction

- Adopting roles in the planning and implementation of the problem-based model
- Through work with the Coalition for Educational Justice (CEJ), extensive engagement with trainings on the broader school reform context and parent/community organizing
- Mentoring other parents in intentional civility, the role of culture in shaping instruction, the problem-based model, the school reform context, and community organizing
- Increasing involvement in school governance and decision making
- Bringing their cultural, historical, community, and ethnic knowledge into the school to shape instruction and other policies and practices at the site

Afterword

Where Do We Go from Here?

THIS CONCLUDING PIECE OFFERS SOME general thoughts on organizing strategy and next steps for the educational justice movement. Questions of immediate strategy (Where do we go from here?) are best framed within a long-term strategy (How will our aims ultimately be achieved?). Public education advocates and progressive movements don't typically take up the long-term questions, although our opponents very likely do. Remember Lewis Powell's 1971 call to corporate leaders, discussed in chapter 1: "Strength lies in organization, in careful long-range planning and implementation, in consistency of action over an indefinite period of years, in the scale of financing available only through joint effort."[1]

In the current milieu of U.S. education organizing, perhaps the most concrete long-term proposal comes from the opt-out movement, with its focus on high-stakes testing. Because corporate school reform relies so pivotally on the tests, some activists reason that, if we can grow opt-outs to a critical mass, it would not only undermine the tests but could end corporate reform altogether. Denisha Jones, co-administrator for the national United Opt Out, proposes that a mass boycott could force the "testing industrial complex" to grind to a halt: "Once it became apparent how much profit could be made off of testing all children in public schools all the time, the beast was unleashed, and now the only way we can stop it is to starve the beast, deny it the data it needs to survive."[2]

The mass opt-out thesis, however, is too narrow as a vision for change. It underestimates the drivers of corporate reform, whose capacity to dictate education policy owes not so much to the tests as to the reformers' concentrated wealth and political power. If one mechanism for implementing their control of schools (i.e., testing) is thwarted, the reformers will surely devise others.[3] From an organizing standpoint: a focus on testing—or any other singular aspect of the education arena—cannot match a more diversified approach. Every manifestation of the corporate assault on schools provides potentially rich organizing opportunity, be it privatization, race/class inequities and under-resourcing, militaristic discipline regimes, or the marginalization of multicultural and bilingual education. Such is not to minimize the achievements of the opt-out movement, which has done so much to build public awareness of the harms of high-stakes testing and the corporate takeover of schools. And it is important to note that United Opt Out has been shifting toward a broader organizing platform beyond the tests.[4]

One alternative long-term framework starts with the assumption that quality public education for all can only be achieved as one component of a broader social justice movement. My own embrace of that perspective owes both to an assessment of the powerful forces behind reform and an understanding that the corporate takeover of schools is integrally linked to broader aims of neoliberal capitalism. Joel Jordan develops a similar outlook in chapter 5, and he also envisions one avenue whereby single-issue education organizing can advance into multi-issue organizing, with the schools serving as centers for community social justice organizing. The Chicago Teachers Union pushes toward a multi-issue perspective in its 2015 report *A Just Chicago: Fighting for the City Our Students Deserve* (http://ajustchicago.org). The report links school quality with wider conditions and policies in the city, calling for action in such areas as jobs, housing and homelessness, criminal justice and policing, healthcare, and school funding equity.

Let's give Jordan's long-term trajectory a name: *school-based community organizing.* Where would it begin and how would it proceed? Before school-based community organizing could become an option, we must have an organized *base* at the school. Perhaps our trajectory would unfold in two stages. In stage one, the teachers reach out to the community—first and foremost, to the parents—to talk about making a better school or addressing an urgent need or crisis at the school. The focus, in any case, is toward the school or school district. In stage two, the school committee has matured, with a campaign or two under its belt, and is ready to embark on a social justice project beyond the school. In chapter 8, we could see that the Crenshaw High School movement progressed in this manner. Its initial focus was to demand more resources for the school. After the accreditation crisis, it turned to transforming the school with small learning communities. Finally, in the Extended Learning Cultural Model, it fashioned a curriculum that engaged students in study and action around community problems.

Of course, there are no guarantees. With an aggressive district administration, the school organizing project may not even sustain through stage one. Its sustainability increases if the project can move beyond a single school to engage "safety in numbers." Teachers networked through their union or social justice teachers group can help make this possible. If the teachers have transformed their union, then they have far more resources and support available. Larger strategic initiatives, such as the California statewide project described by Jordan, also become possible.

Organizing on Curricular Issues

When I began research for this book, my view of education organizing covered the familiar ground of teachers union contract campaigns and protests of budget cuts, school closures, and high-stakes tests. I hadn't pictured the curriculum as a terrain for anti-corporate organizing in schools. (Although the opt-out movement does address an important aspect of the curriculum in terms of testing, it doesn't typically organize for specific curriculum.) My thinking changed when I discovered the projects at Crenshaw High and Soto Street Elementary.

Soto's balanced literacy campaign especially intrigued me as an organizing project. While it hadn't the breadth or sophistication of Crenshaw, the simplicity of Soto made it compelling. If education activists wanted to try the Soto model, it could more readily be attempted as a starter project than could a project like Crenshaw, which requires a deeper organizing foundation. Even with relative simplicity, the Soto project challenged multiple parts of corporate schooling. On the one hand, it said that teachers are professionals, not followers of scripts; on the other hand, it said that low-income kids deserve the same access to rich literature, and to learning as an engaged discovery process, that affluent kids enjoy. I wanted to buttress the Soto study with a pedagogical background chapter, and reached out to Ken Goodman, the "father" of whole language, from where balanced literacy had its genesis. Ken introduced me to his daughter Debra Goodman and, to my delight, she agreed to write a chapter on the whole language movement of the 1980s and 90s.

Although whole language never coalesced as a political movement to challenge the corporate takeover of schools, the tradition nonetheless offers a huge body of knowledge and experience that can inform education organizing and resistance to corporate reform. The practice of grassroots teacher research groups collaboratively building their craft was a vital part of the whole language movement, and provides an empowering alternative to the corporate model of teachers as low-skilled and low-paid test-prep technicians. Equally vital to whole language (and to balanced literacy) are quality classroom libraries and school libraries. The demand for such, stocked with authentic children's and adolescent literature, and reflecting racial and language diversity, could enliven and deepen education organizing, particularly in low-income communities of color.[5] The Soto experience also suggests that a literacy justice approach can be a powerful way to engage parents.

In today's hostile climate, teachers who embrace learner-centered and social justice approaches to their work must often do so under the radar with the classroom door closed. An organized community is needed to open the doors and ensure that all students have access to democratic and justice-driven teaching, backed with appropriate resources. Moreover, if pursued within a larger strategy, organizing for curricular transformation—or for other school improvements, or for the defense of schools against privatization and defunding—can develop leaders and build grassroots power toward wider educational and social justice.

Notes

INTRODUCTION

1.   Doug Smith and Max Brantley, "Conservative Think-Tanker to Head UA School-Reform Operation," *Arkansas Times*, July 28, 2005.
2.   Lyndsey Layton, "How Bill Gates Pulled Off the Swift Common Core Revolution," *Washington Post*, June 7, 2014.
3.   See Steven Brill, *Class Warfare: Inside the Fight to Fix America's Schools* (New York: Simon & Schuster, 2011), 254–64.
4.   Howard Ryan, "D.C. Teachers Hold Union Election While City Watches," *Labor Notes*, October 18, 2010.
5.   Howard Ryan, "'Superman' Tugs Heartstrings by Thumping Teachers," *Labor Notes*, October 25, 2010.
6.   According to Joanne Barkan, in "Got Dough? How Billionaires Rule Our Schools," *Dissent* (winter 2011).
7.   Alexandra Bradbury et al., *How to Jump-Start Your Union: Lessons from the Chicago Teachers* (Detroit: Labor Notes, 2014).
8.   Chicago Teachers Union community board members are listed at http://ctunet.com/community.
9.   Blocks Together is at http://btchicago.org; Dignity in Schools is at http://dignityinschools.org.
10.   See Chicago Teachers Union, *The Schools Chicago's Students Deserve: Research-Based Proposals to Strengthen Elementary and Secondary Education in the Chicago Public Schools* (Chicago: CTU, 2012), available at http://ctunet.com. This aspect of the 2012 contract campaign is also covered in Bradbury, *How to Jump-Start Your Union*, 107–9.
11.   Chicago Teachers Union, *Highlights of 2012–2015 Tentative Agreement Between the Chicago Teachers Union and the Chicago Board of Education* (Chicago: CTU, September 2012), retrieved from http://ctunet.com.
12.   On the St. Paul campaign, see Eric S. Fought, *Power of Community: Organizing for the Schools St. Paul Children Deserve* (St. Paul, MN: Saint Paul Federation of Teachers, 2014), retrieved from Alliance to Reclaim Our Schools, http://reclaimourschools.org. On Portland, see Elizabeth Thiel, "Portland Teachers Nearly Strike, Win 150 New Jobs," *Labor Notes*, February 25, 2014; and Portland Association of Teachers, "PAT Initial Bargaining Proposal: Summary of Proposals Designed to Create the Schools Portland Students Deserve," 2013, http://media.oregonlive.com/nielsen_impact/other/PATpreamble2013.pdf. On Los Angeles, see United Teachers Los Angeles, "Contract Summary: We Won Round One in the Fight for the Schools LA Students Deserve," April 2015, retrieved from http://utla.net.
13.   Arne Duncan, "Secretary Arne Duncan's Remarks at 'For Democracy's Future' Forum

at the White House" (Washington: U.S. Department of Education, January 10, 2012), retrieved from http://ed.gov.

1. The Hidden Aims of School Reform

1. Bill Gates, "Remarks of Bill Gates, Harvard Commencement 2007," *Harvard Gazette*, June 7, 2007; retrieved from http://news.harvard.edu.
2. Peter Brimelow, "What to Do About America's Schools," *Fortune* (September 19, 1983): 64.
3. Dennis A. Williams, "Can the Schools Be Saved?," *Newsweek* (May 9, 1983): 50–58.
4. John E. Chubb and Terry M. Moe, *Politics, Markets, and America's Schools* (Washington: Brookings, 1990), 47, 38.
5. Diane Ravitch, *The Death and Life of the Great American School System: How Testing and Choice Are Undermining Education* (New York: Basic Books, 2010), 195–222.
6. From list of Achieve contributors at http://achieve.org/contributors.
7. White House, "President Obama Calls for New Steps to Prepare America's Children for Success in College and Careers," press release, February 22, 2010, retrieved from http://whitehouse.gov; Bill Gates, speech to National Conference of State Legislatures, July 21, 2009, retrieved from http://gatesfoundation.org; and Eli Broad, statement at Senator Barack Obama American Competitiveness Summit, Pittsburgh, June 26, 2008, retrieved from http://broadeducation.org.
8. See Jennifer Washburn, *University, Inc.: The Corporate Corruption of American Higher Education* (Cambridge, MA: Basic Books, 2005); and Rudy Fichtenbaum, "Corporatization of Higher Education and the Attack on American Workers," PowerPoint presentation, n.d., retrieved from the American Association of University Professors Collective Bargaining Congress at http://aaupcbc.org. For European perspectives, see Stavros Moutsios, "The De-Europeanization of the University under the Balogna Process," *Thesis Eleven* 199, no. 1 (2013): 22–46; and Ilkka Kauppinen, "European Round Table of Industrialists and the Restructuring of European Higher Education," *Globalisation, Societies and Education* 12, no. 4 (2014): 498–519.
9. David Sirota, "Getting Rich Off of Schoolchildren," *Salon*, March 11, 2013.
10. Michelle Fine and Michael Fabricant, *The Changing Politics of Education: Privatization and the Dispossessed Lives Left Behind* (Boulder, CO: Paradigm, 2013), 27.
11. For KIPP, see "Doris and Donald Fisher Fund Gives $60 Million to Charter Schools," *Jewish Business News,* January 20, 2015, retrieved from http://jewishbusinessnews.com. For the Charter School Growth Fund, I relied on the Growth Fund's IRS Forms 990-PF for 2004 through 2013. For Teach for America, I relied on Ken Libby, *Doris and Donald Fisher Education Giving, 2003–2011* (Boulder, CO: National Education Policy Center, July 5, 2012), retrieved from http://nepc.colorado.edu, plus the Fisher Fund's IRS Form 990-PF for 2012.
12. Elizabeth Bloom, "Introduction: Forewarned Is Forearmed," in *Resisting Reform: Reclaiming Public Education Through Grassroots Activism*, ed. Kjersti VanSlyke-Briggs, Elizabeth Bloom, and Danielle Boudet (Charlotte, NC: Information Age, 2015), 7.
13. Brian Jones, "Keys to the Schoolhouse: Black Teachers, Privatization, and the Future of Teacher Unions," in *What's Race Got to Do With It? How Current School Reform Policy Maintains Racial and Economic Inequality*, ed. Bree Picower and Edwin Mayorga (New York: Peter Lang, 2015), 82, 86.
14. Bree Picower and Edwin Mayorga, introduction to *What's Race Got to Do With It?*, 6. The authors quote from Louise Derman-Sparks and Carol Brunson Phillips, *Teaching/Learning Anti-Racism: A Developmental Approach* (New York: Teachers College Press, 1997), 10.

15. Picower and Mayorga, *What's Race Got to Do With It?*, 8, 6.

16. For extensive evidence, see Eduardo Bonilla-Silva, *Racism without Racists: Color-Blind Racism and the Persistence of Racial Inequality in America*, 4th ed. (Lanham, MD: Rowman & Littlefield, 2014).

17. Picower and Mayorga, *What's Race Got to Do With It?*, 8.

18. A sampling is Margaret L. Andersen and Patricia Hill Collins, eds., *Race, Class and Gender: An Anthology*, 9th ed. (Boston: Cengage Learning, 2015); Edward Taylor, David Gillborn, and Gloria Ladson-Billings, eds., *Foundations of Critical Race Theory in Education*, 2nd ed. (New York: Routledge, 2015); Mike Cole, *Critical Race Theory and Education: A Marxist Response* (New York: Palgrave Macmillan, 2009); and Manning Marable, "Beyond Racial Identity Politics: Toward a Liberation Theory for Multicultural Democracy," *Race and Class* 35, no. 1 (July-September 1993): 113–30.

19. See Alfredo Saad-Filho and Deborah Johnston, *Neoliberalism: A Critical Reader* (Ann Arbor, MI: Pluto Press, 2005).

20. Peter B. Evans and William H. Sewell, Jr., "Neoliberalism: Policy Regimes, International Regimes, and Social Effects," in *Social Resilience in the Neoliberal Era*, ed. Peter A. Hall and Michèle Lamont (New York: Cambridge University Press, 2014), 36–37.

21. See Robert Brenner, *The Economics of Global Turbulence: The Advanced Capitalist Economies from Long Boom to Long Downturn, 1945–2005* (New York: Verso, 2006).

22. Ron Miller, *Free Schools, Free People: Education and Democracy after the 1960s* (Albany, NY: State University of New York Press, 2002).

23. Ted Nace, *Gangs of America: The Rise of Corporate Power and the Disabling of Democracy* (San Francisco: Berrett-Koehler Publishers, 2003), 137–52.

24. Hedrick Smith, *Who Stole the American Dream?* (New York: Random House, 2012), 5–12.

25. Lewis F. Powell, "Attack on American Free Enterprise System," August 23, 1971, www.law.wlu.edu/powellarchives/page.asp?pageid=1251.

26. Smith, *Who Stole the American Dream?*, 12.

27. Kim Moody, *An Injury to All: The Decline of American Unionism* (New York: Verso, 1988), 130.

28. This calculation is based on Emmanuel Saez's March 2012 data update to Thomas Piketty and Emmanuel Saez, "Income Inequality in the United States, 1913–1998," *Quarterly Journal of Economics* 118, no. 1 (2003): 1–39, http://elsa.berkeley.edu/~saez/#income.

29. National Commission on Excellence in Education, *A Nation at Risk: The Imperative for Educational Reform* (Washington: U.S. Department of Education, April 1983); the report's recommendations are at http://ed.gov/pubs/NatAtRisk/recomm.html.

30. Ira Shor, *Culture Wars: School and Society in the Conservative Restoration 1969–1984* (New York: Routledge, 1986), 89.

31. See Jane Agee, "Negotiating a Teaching Identity: An African American Teacher's Struggle to Teach in Test-Driven Contexts," *Teachers College Record* 106, no. 4 (2004): 747–74.

32. The "No Excuses" model is praised in Jay Mathews, *Work Hard. Be Nice: How Two Inspired Teachers Created the Most Promising Schools in America* (New York: Workman Publishing, 2009); and David Whitman, *Sweating the Small Stuff: Inner-City Schools and the New Paternalism* (Washington: Fordham Institute, 2008). Critiques are Joan F. Goodman, "Charter Management Organizations and the Regulated Environment: Is It Worth the Price?" *Educational Researcher* 42, no. 89 (March 2013): 89–96; Beth Sondel and Joseph L. Boselovic, "'No Excuses' in New Orleans," *Jacobin*, July 24, 2014; and Jim Horn, *Work Hard, Be Hard: Journeys Through "No Excuses" Teaching* (New York: Rowman & Littlefield, 2016).

33. White House, "Reform for the Future," position statement, accessed July 25, 2015 at http://whitehouse.gov.

34. National Commission on Excellence in Education, *A Nation at Risk: The Imperative for Educational* Reform (Washington: U.S. Department of Education, April 1983), 9.

35. Gary S. Becker, *Human Capital: A Theoretical and Empirical Analysis, with Special Reference to Education* (New York: National Bureau of Economic Research, 1964); and Theodore Schultz, *The Economic Value of Education* (New York: Columbia University Press, 1963).

36. Donna Cooper, Adam Hersh, and Ann O'Leary, *The Competition that Really Matters: Comparing U.S., Chinese, and Indian Investments in the Next-Generation Workforce* (Washington: Center for American Progress, September 2012), 19; retrieved from http://americanprogress.org.

37. Business Roundtable, *Business Leader's Guide to Setting Academic Standards* (Washington: BRT, June 1996), 2; retrieved from http://eric.ed.gov.

38. Confederation of British Industry, *Towards a Skills Revolution: Report of the Vocational Education and Training Task Force* (London: CBI, 1990), 9; retrieved from http://vital.new.voced.edu.au.

39. George P. Shultz and Eric A. Hanushek, "Education Is the Key to a Healthy Economy," *Wall Street Journal,* April 30, 2012.

40. See Steve Klees's synopsis in "Business, as Usual, Distorts Education," October 16, 2014, Global Campaign for Education, http://campaignforeducationusa.org; and Santosh Mehrotra, "Human Capital or Human Development? Search for a Knowledge Paradigm for Education and Development," *Economic and Political Weekly* 40, no. 4 (January 22–28, 2005): 300–06.

41. Gerald Friedman, "Collapsing Investment and the Great Recession," *Dollars and Sense* (July/August 2013), 24, figure 1.

42. From 1980 to 2011, according to data from the National Center for Education Statistics, http://nces.ed.gov.

43. Regarding financialization, see Kristian Weise, "Sustainability Requires the End of Financialisation," November 29, 2011; from *Social Europe* at http://socialeurope.eu.

44. Eric A. Hanushek, Paul E. Peterson, and Ludger Woessmann, *Endangering Prosperity: A Global View of the American School* (Washington: Brookings, 2013), Kindle edition, chap. 1.

45. Marc V. Levine, *The Skills Gap and Unemployment in Wisconsin: Separating Fact from Fiction,* working paper (Milwaukee, WI: Center for Economic Development, University of Wisconsin-Milwaukee, February 2013), 4; retrieved from http://uwm.edu/ced.

46. Richard Vedder, Christopher Denhart, and Jonathan Robe, *Why Are Recent College Graduates Underemployed? University Enrollments and Labor Market Realities* (Washington: Center For College Affordability and Productivity, January 2013), 24, figure 10; retrieved from http://centerforcollegeaffordability.org.

47. Michael S. Teitelbaum, "Is the U.S. Losing the Tech Race?" *Los Angeles Times,* April 20, 2014.

48. Cited in Michael Anft, "The STEM Crisis: Reality or Myth?" *Chronicle of Higher Education,* November 11, 2013.

49. Quoted in ibid.

50. For Michigan, see Amy Lane, "Snyder Tax Break for Business: 60%," *Crain's Detroit Business,* March 18, 2011; and Gary Olson, *Governor Rick Snyder's Fiscal Year 2011–12 State Budget Recommendation: Charting a New Fiscal Future for Michigan* (Lansing, MI: Public Sector Consultants, February 2011), retrieved from http://pscinc.com. For New Jersey, see Jon Whiten, *New Jersey's Subsidy Surge Has Not Subsided* (Trenton: New Jersey Policy Perspectives, April 2013), http://njpp.org.

51.   The falling public education expenditure in many developing countries, owing to austerity imposed by the World Bank and International Monetary Fund, is documented in Fernando Reimers and Luís Tiburcio, *Education, Adjustment and Reconstruction: Options for Change* (Paris: UNESCO, 1993), http://unesco.org. Regarding the impact of such lending policies on a wider range of economic and social issues, see SAPRIN, *Structural Adjustment: The SAPRI Report—The Policy Roots of Economic Crisis, Poverty and Inequality* (New York: Zed Books, 2013).

52.   Class Size Matters, "A Complete Guide to the Corporate Reform Movement," February 20, 2013, retrieved from http://classsizematters.org. Data on funders obtained from a linked spreadsheet. Business Roundtable members are listed at http://businessroundtable.org/about/members.

53.   See Pauline Lipman, *The New Political Economy of Urban Education: Neoliberalism, Race, and the Right to the City* (New York: Routledge, 2011); and Lipman, *Making Sense of Renaissance 2010 School Policy in Chicago: Race, Class, and the Cultural Politics of Neoliberal Urban Restructuring* (Chicago: Great Cities Institute, January 2009), retrieved from https://greatcities.uic.edu.

54.   Kathy Emery, "The Business Roundtable and Systemic Reform: How Corporate-Engineered High-Stakes Testing Has Eliminated Community Participation in Developing Educational Goals and Policies" (PhD diss., University of California at Davis, 2002), 45–46; retrieved from http://educationanddemocracy.org.

55.   Ibid., 50.

56.   Ibid., 51.

57.   Edward Rust, *No Turning Back: A Progress Report on the Business Roundtable Education Initiative* (Washington: Business Roundtable, 1999), quoted in Emery, "The Business Roundtable and Systemic Reform, 48.

58.   Several of the national summits are documented at http://www.achieve.org/summits.

59.   David J. Hoff, "Big Business Going to Bat for NCLB," *Education Week*, October 18, 2006.

60.   Massachusetts Business Alliance for Education, http://mbae.org.

61.   See Steven J. Klees, Joel Samoff, and Nelly P. Stromquist, eds., *The World Bank and Education: Critiques and Alternatives* (Rotterdam, Netherlands: Sense Publishers, 2012). A broader outlook on the World Bank and similar agencies is Richard Peet, *Unholy Trinity: The IMF, World Bank and WTO*, 2nd ed. (New York: Zed Books, 2009).

62.   Regarding school privatization, a 2012 OECD working paper on "choice and equity" acknowledges a wide debate but, at the same time, weighs in in favor of "market mechanisms" through "autonomous schools" and "government-dependent private schools." Pauline Musset, *School Choice and Equity: Current Policies in OECD Countries and a Literature Review* (Paris: OECD, February 2, 2012), 6, 20.

63.   Katerina Ananiadou and Magdalena Claro, *21st Century Skills and Competencies for New Millennium Learners in OECD Countries*, EDU Working Paper no. 41 (Paris: OECD, December 18, 2009), 5; retrieved from http://oecd.org.

64.   Terry Hyland, "Teaching, Learning and NVQs: Challenging Behaviourism and Competence in Adult Education Theory and Practice," paper presented at the 1994 Standing Conference on University Teaching and Research in the Education of Adults; held in Hull, England; retrieved at http://leeds.ac.uk/educol/documents/00002967.htm.

65.   Stefan Hopmann and Gertrude Brinek, introduction to *PISA zufolge PISA: Hält PISA, was es verspricht? (PISA According to PISA: Does PISA Keep What It Promises?)*, ed. Stefan Thomas Hopmann, Gertrude Brinek, and Martin Retzl (Berlin: LIT, 2007), 12. See also Martin Carnoy, *International Test Score Comparisons and Educational Policy: A Review of the Critiques* (Boulder, CO: National Education Policy Center, October 2015), retrieved from http://nepc.colorado.edu.

66. Simon Breakspear, *The Policy Impact of PISA: An Exploration of the Normative Effects of International Benchmarking in School System Performance* (Paris: OECD, 2012), 8, 9; retrieved from http://oecd.org.

67. OECD, *The High Cost of Low Educational Performance; The Long-Run Economic Impact of Improving PISA Outcomes* (Paris: OECD, 2010), 6; retrieved from http://oecd.org.

68. Quoted in Sam Dillon, "Top Test Scores from Shanghai Stun Educators," *New York Times*, December 7, 2010.

69. Quoted in Ben Packham, "Labor Billions Failed Students, Coalition Says," *The Australian*, December 4, 2013.

70. Michael Gove, "Secretary of State for Education Michael Gove's Statement in the House on the OECD's 2012 PISA Results," December 3, 2013, retrieved from http://gov.uk.

71. Jens Dolin, "PISA: An Example of the Use and Misuse of Large-Scale Comparative Tests," in *PISA According to PISA: Does PISA Keep What It Promises*, ed. Stefan Thomas Hopmann, Gergrude Brinek, and Martin Retzl (Vienna: LIT, 2007), 97.

72. Jens Dolin, "Science Education Standards and Their Assessment in Denmark," in *Making It Comparable: Standards in Science Education*, ed. David Waddington, Peter Nentwig, and Sascha Schanze (New York: Waxmann, 2007), 80, 81.

73. Laura Figazzolo, *Testing, Ranking, Reforming: Impact of PISA 2006 on the Education Policy Debate* (Brussels: Education International, 2009), 14, 15, 16; retrieved from http://ei-ie.org.

74. OECD, *Improving Schools: Strategies for Action in Mexico* (Paris: OECD, 2010), retrieved from http://oecd.org.

75. An illustrative and World Bank-supported school autonomy program is described in Cheryl T. Desmond, "EDUCO Schools in El Salvador: A Democratic Tree in a Globalized Forest?" *International Education* 38, no. (2009), http://trace.tennessee.edu/internationaleducation/vol38/iss2/2. See also Felipe Barrera-Osorio, Tazeen Fasih, and Harry Anthony Patrinos, *Decentralized Decision-Making in Schools: The Theory and Evidence on School-Based Management* (Washington: World Bank, 2009).

76. Jane Slaughter, "Mexican Teachers Resist Their Own Brand of 'Education Reform,'" *Labor Notes*, February 17, 2015.

77. Hilda Vázquez Medina and Adam Goodman, "Mexican Education Reform from Below," *Boston Review*, September 16, 2013.

78. Richard Woodward, "Towards Complex Multilateralism? Civil Society and the OECD," in *The OECD and Transnational Governance*, ed. Rianne Mahon and Stephen McBride (Seattle: University of Washington Press, 2009), 91, 94.

79. OECD, *Boosting Jobs and Incomes: Policy Lessons from Reassessing the OECD Jobs Strategy* (Paris: OECD, 2006), 21, 22; retrieved from http://oecd.org.

80. Jean Anyon explores these differential pedagogies in "Social Class and the Hidden Curriculum of Work," *Journal of Education* 162, no. 1 (1980), http://generative.edb.utexas.edu/classes/2011CISpring/CIreadings/06Anyon1980.pdf.

81. On high-stakes testing, see Wayne Au, *Unequal by Design: High-Stakes Testing and the Standardization of Inequality* (New York: Routledge, 2009). On the scripting of reading instruction, see chap. 3 in Patrick Shannon, *Reading Against Democracy: The Broken Promises of Reading Instruction* (Portsmouth, NH: Heinemann, 2007), 36–68.

82. Business Roundtable, *Business Leader's Guide*, 22.

83. University of Chicago Laboratory Schools, *Kindergarten Program of Study 2013–2014* (Chicago: Laboratory Schools, 2013), 10; retrieved from http://ucls.uchicago.edu.

84. David Coleman and Susan Pimentel, *Revised Publishers' Criteria for the Common Core State Standards in English Language Arts and Literacy, Grades 3–12* (Washington: Common

Core State Standards Initiative, April 12, 2012), 4; retrieved from http://corestandards.org.

85. Quoted in Catherine Gewertz, "Teachers Reflect Standards in Basals," *Education Week,* May 9, 2012.

86. Daniel E. Ferguson, "Martin Luther King Jr. and the Common Core: A Critical Reading of 'Close Reading.'" *Rethinking Schools* 28, no. 2 (winter 2013–14): 18–21.

87. Relay's disciplinary routines are outlined in Lynn Kalinauskas, "DPS Embraces Relay Training," *Greater Park Hill News,* September 1, 2015, retrieved from http://greaterparkhill.org. See also Peggy Robertson, "Relay Graduate School Indoctrination," September 7, 2015; and "Understanding Teach Like a Champion," September 13, 2015, both at the author's blog, Peg with Pen, at http://pegwithpen.com.

88. Matthew Lynde Chesnut, "Teach for Ambivalence, Or How I Learned to Stop Worrying and Love to Teach," in *Teach for America Counter-Narratives: Alumni Speak Up and Speak Out,* ed. T. James Brewer and Kathleen de Marrais (New York: Peter Lang, 2015), 68.

89. Janese Daniels, Xiaming Liu, and Bess Altwerger, "'Zero Inch Voices': Imposing Silence in Primary Classrooms," in *Literacy Policies and Practice in Conflict: Reclaiming Classrooms in Networked Times,* ed. Nancy Rankie Shelton and Bess Altwerger (New York: Routledge, 2015), 94–95.

90. "Margaret Thatcher: A Life in Quotes," *The Guardian,* April 8, 2013.

91. Paul Tough, *How Children Succeed: Grit, Curiosity, and the Hidden Power of Character* (Boston: Houghton Mifflin, 2012).

92. "Work Relentlessly," from the TFA-sponsored Teaching As Leadership website, accessed October 23, 2015 at http://teachingasleadership.org.

93. As Eduardo Bonilla-Silva points out, the existence of discrimination and institutional/structural racism in the United States is widely denied today, with racial inequities instead attributed to the "lack of motivation" or "culture of poverty" within communities of color. In Bonilla-Silva, *Racism Without Racists: Color-Blind Racism and the Persistence of Racial Inequality in America,* 4th ed. (New York: Rowman & Littlefield, 2014), 73–99.

94. On the racial impact of corporate school reform, see Picower and Mayorga, *What's Race Got to Do With It?* On the language impact, see Patricia Gándara and Gabriel Baca, "NCLB and California's English Language Learners: The Perfect Storm," *Language Policy* 7, no. 3 (2008): 201–16; and Jeff Bale, "English-Only to the Core: What the Common Core Means for Emergent Bilingual Youth," *Rethinking Schools* 30, no. 1 (fall 2015): 20–27.

95. Gándara and Baca, "NCLB and California's English Language Learners."

96. Harold Berlak, "Cultural Politics, the Science of Assessment and Democratic Renewal of Public Education," in *Assessment: Social Practice and Social Product,* ed. Ann Filer (New York: Routledge, 2000), 195.

97. Civic Committee of the Commercial Club of Chicago, *Left Behind: A Report of the Education Committee* (Chicago: Commercial Club, July 2003), 3, http://civiccommittee.org/initiatives/education/left_behind.pdf.

98. Lipman, *New Political Economy of Urban Education;* and Lipman, *Making Sense of Rensaissance 2010.*

99. For New Orleans, see Kristen L. Buras, *Charter Schools, Race, and Urban Space: Where the Market Meets Grassroots Resistance* (New York: Routledge, 2015). For Philadelphia, see Maia Bloomfield Cucchiara, *Marketing Schools, Marketing Cities: Who Wins and Who Loses When Schools Become Urban Amenities* (Chicago: University of Chicago Press, 2013). For further examples, see Doug Martin, "Warren Buffett and Corporate School

Reformers to Gentrify/Charterize Indianapolis and Other Cities," Fire Dog Lake, September 19, 2011, at http://firedoglake.com.

100. G. William Domhoff, "Power at the Local Level: Growth Coalition Theory," at his website, Who Rules America?, n.d., http://www2.ucsc.edu/whorulesamerica.

101. See, for example, Alyssa Figueoa, "8 Things You Should Know About Corporations Like Pearson that Make Huge Profits from Standardized Tests," *Alternet*, August 6, 2013, retrieved from http://alternet.org.

102. Matthew M. Chingos, *Strength in Numbers: State Spending on K–12 Assessment Systems* (Washington: Brown Center on Education Policy, Brookings Institution: 2012), 1; retrieved from http://brookings.edu.

103. National Center for Education Statistics, *Digest of Education Statistics 2013* (Washington: U.S. Department of Education, May 2015), 358.

104. Charter schools tend to rely on inexperienced teachers with lower levels of education, which means lower pay and fewer health and retirement benefits, observe Bruce Baker and Gary Miron in *The Business of Charter Schooling: Understanding the Policies that Charter Operators Use for Financial Benefit* (Boulder, CO: National Education Policy Center, December 2015), 23; retrieved from http://nepc.colorado.edu.

105. Author's calculations using chain enrollment figures from Gary Miron and Charisse Gulosino, *Profiles of For-Profit and Nonprofit Education Management Organizations*, 14th ed., 2011–12 (Boulder, CO: National Education Policy Center, University of Colorado, November 2013), 13, 15; retrieved from http://nepc.colorado.edu; and total charter enrollment figures from the 2008 and 2013 editions of *Digest of Education Statistics*. The chain percentage for 2003 may be slightly higher than indicated. In their annual data collection for 2008, Miron and Gulosino uncovered thirty-one small chains, or "education management organizations," that "were in existence for several years, although they had not previously been profiled in our report" (page 4).

106. KIPP Infinity Charter School Financial Statements (years ended June 30, 2013 and 2012), 10, 12; retrieved from http://kippnyc.org.

107. Quoted in Robin Lake and Allison Demeritt, *Paying for Scale: Results of a Symposium on CMO Finance* (Seattle: Center on Reinventing Public Education, January 2011), 3; retrieved from http://crpe.org.

108. Scott Hiaasen and Kathleen McGrory, "Academica: Florida's Richest Charter School Management Firm," *Miami Herald*, December 14, 2011.

109. The national figure is from a 2014 fourteen-state survey, which found that charter schools occupying private, non-school district facilities paid a median facility expenditure of 5.8 percent of per pupil revenue. Cited in Safal Partners, *Finding Space: Charter Schools in District-Owned Facilities* (Houston: National School Resource Center, 2015), 4; retrieved from http://charterschoolcenter.org.

110. Catherine Candisky and Jim Siegel, "Charter School's Lease Deals Scrutinized," *Columbus Dispatch*, October 12, 2014.

111. Hiaasen and McGrory, "Academica: Florida's Richest Charter"; and Stephanie Strom, "For School Company, Issues of Money and Control," *New York Times*, April 23, 2010.

112. Figures are based on a 2014 survey cited in Safal Partners, *Finding Space*, 4.

113. Daniel Taub, "André Agassi Forms Charter-School Fund with Canyon Capital," *Bloomberg News*, June 2, 2011. The project is the Turner-Agassi Charter School Facilities Fund at http://turneragassi.com.

114. According to Kate Smith, "Record Charter-School Defaults Underscored by Albany Closings," *Bloomberg Business*, March 24, 2015.

115. Julian Vasquez Heilig, "Why Do Hedge Funds ADORE Charters?" October 23, 2012; and Heilig, "Why Do Hedge Funds ADORE Charters? Pt. II: 39%+ Return," December

7, 2012; both posted on Heilig's blog, Cloaking Inequity, at http://cloakingequity.com.

116. Heilig, "Why Do Hedge Funds ADORE Charters?"; and Juan Gonzalez, "Hedge Fund Executives Give 'Til It Hurts to Politicians, especially Cuomo, to Get More Charter Schools," *New York Daily News,* March 11, 2015.

117. Mike Cherney, "Investors Go to School on Charters," *Wall Street Journal,* June 11, 2012.

118. Local Initiatives Support Corporation, "Bonds & Blackboards: Investing in Charter Schools," March 10, 2015, symposium flyer, retrieved from http://lisc.org.

119. Katrina Stevens, "How Many Connections Can 18,000 Educators Make?," EdSurge website, July 1, 2014; retrieved from http://edsurge.com.

120. John Watson et al., *Keeping Pace with K–12 Digital Learning: An Annual Review of Policy and Practice,* 11th ed. (Durango, CO: Evergreen Education Group, 2014), 10; retrieved from http://evergreenedgroup.com.

121. The 55 percent figure is based on Maillie LLP, *Agora Cyber Charter School Annual Financial Report* (for year ended June 30, 2013), 16; retrieved from http://k12.com/agora/who-we-are/board. I also consulted with an Agora teacher (name withheld), email communication, June 6, 2014.

122. The elementary-level figure is cited in Stephanie Saul, "Profits and Questions at Online Charter Schools," *New York Times,* December 12, 2011. The secondary-level figure is from my interview with an Agora teacher (name withheld), December 11, 2012.

123. Bill Raden, "Cyber Charter School Revolt Against K12 Inc. Continues," *Capital & Main,* September 3, 2014; retrieved from http://capitalandmain.com.

124. Terry M. Moe and John E. Chubb, *Liberated Learning: Technology, Politics, and the Future of American Education* (San Francisco: Jossey-Bass, 2009), 7.

125. Gordon Lafer, *Do Poor Kids Deserve Lower-Quality Education Than Rich Kids? Evaluating School Privatization Proposals in Milwaukee, Wisconsin* (Washington: Economic Policy Institute, April 4, 2014), 8, 9, 12; retrieved from http://epi.org.

126. Michael B. Horn and Heather Staker, *The Rise of K–12 Blended Learning* (San Mateo, CA: Innosight Institute, 2011), 13; retrieved from http://christenseninstitute.org.

127. Howard Blume, "Backers Want Half of LAUSD Students in Charter Schools in Eight Years, Report Says," *Los Angeles Times,* September 21, 2015.

128. Eli Broad, *The Art of Being Unreasonable: Lessons in Unconventional Thinking* (Hoboken, NJ: Wiley, 2012), Kindle edition, chap. 12.

129. See Pablo Eisenberg, "'Strategic Philanthropy' Shifts Too Much Power to Donors," *Chronicle of Philanthropy,* August 20, 2013, retrieved from http://philanthropy.com; and Andrew Bowman, "The Flip Side to Bill Gates' Charity Billions," *New Internationalist,* April 2012, retrieved from http://newint.org.

130. Broad, *Art of Being Unreasonable,* chap. 19.

131. Eli Broad, "Charters' Competitive Edge," *Los Angeles Times,* February 5, 2008.

132. The March 14, 2014, interview of Gates, by *Washington Post* reporter Lyndsey Layton, is excerpted in Valerie Strauss, "How Microsoft Will Make Money from Common Core (Despite What Bill Gates Said)," *Washington Post,* July 12, 2014.

133. Stacy Skelly, "Global Leader Pearson Creates Leading Curriculum, Apps for Digital Learning Environments," February 20, 2014, Pearson company press release, retrieved from http://prweb.com.

134. Steve Clarke, "Fourth-Largest US School District Boots Up 1:1 Initiative with Microsoft Technology," February 6, 2014, Microsoft press release, retrieved from http://blogs.microsoft.com.

135. Gregg Keizer, "Bill Gates Sells $925M in Microsoft Stock, Still Owns $13.6B Worth," *Computer World,* November 11, 2014, retrieved from http://computerworld.com.

136. Anupreeta Das, "Breaking Down Bill Gates's Wealth," *Wall Street Journal,* September 19, 2014.
137. Bill Gates, "Work Hard. Be Nice." January 21, 2010, retrieved from http://gatesnotes. org.

2. TEACHERS UNIONS THAT PARTNER WITH BILLIONAIRES

1. Randi Weingarten, "Conflict Makes Good Stories, Collaboration Makes Good Schools," *Huffington Post,* January 5, 2011.
2. Quoted in Sarah Jaffe, "Massachusetts Teachers Aim to Knock Down 'Data Walls,'" *In These Times* (February 12, 2014): 5
3. Wayne Au, *Unequal by Design: High-Stakes Testing and the Standardization of Inequality* (New York: Routledge, 2009); Stephen Ball, *Global Education Inc.: New Policy Networks and the Neoliberal Imaginary* (New York: Routledge, 2012); Pauline Lipman, *The New Political Economy of Urban Education: Neoliberalism, Race, and the Right to the City* (New York: Routledge, 2011); Kenneth Saltman, *Capitalizing on Disaster: Taking and Breaking Public Schools* (Boulder, CO: Paradigm, 2007); and Kenneth Saltman, *The Gift of Education: Public Education and Venture Philanthropy* (New York: Palgrave Macmillan, 2010).
4. The CTU reports are available at http://ctunet/quest-center/research.
5. Bob Chase, "The New NEA: Reinventing the Teachers Unions for a New Era," address to the National Press Club, Washington, DC, February 5, 1997, retrieved from the Education Intelligence Agency blog at http://eiaonline.com/ ChaseNewUnionism1997.pdf.
6. Randi Weingarten, "Pushing Forward Together," *American Educator* (winter 2013–14): 1; retrieved from http://aft.org.
7. According to retired teacher and union activist Jack Gerson, "The Neoliberal Agenda and the Response of Teachers Unions," in William H. Watkins, ed., *The Assault on Public Education: Confronting the Politics of Corporate School Reform* (New York: Teachers College Press, 2012), 116–17. Broad's 2002 strategic retreat included Weingarten, who was then president of New York City's United Federation of Teachers; Adam Urbanski, president of the Rochester Teachers Association in New York; and Bob Chase, who had recently served as NEA president. The full participant list can be found in "2002 Eli Broad Foundation Retreat Has Education Bigs Meet," posted at the website of Parent Advocates, http://parentadvocates.org.
8. Mercedes Schneider, "The Gates Grant Addiction," February 24, 2014, retrieved from Schneider's blog at http://deutsch29.wordpress.com.
9. Wendy Kopp and Dennis Van Roekel, "3 Ways to Improve the USA's Teachers," *USA Today,* December 20, 2011. A helpful backgrounder on Teach for America is Barbara Miner, "Looking Past the Spin: Teach for America," *Rethinking Schools* 24, no. 3, spring 2010.
10. Caitlin Emma, "Exclusive: AFT Shuns Gates Funding," *Politico,* March 10, 2014.
11. National Council on Education Standards and Testing, *Raising Standards for American Education: A Report to Congress, the Secretary of Education, the National Education Goals Panel, and the American People* (Washington: Government Printing Office, January 24, 1992), 1, 3; retrieved from Education Resources Information Center at http://eric. ed.gov.
12. Ibid., 3.
13. Ibid., 5.
14. Ibid., 6.

15. Matthew Gandal, *Making Standards Matter, 1996: An Annual Fifty-State Report on Efforts to Raise Academic Standards* (Washington: American Federation of Teachers, 1996), 10, retrieved from Education Resources Information Center at http://eric.ed.gov.

16. Ibid., 37.

17. Ibid., 41.

18. Ibid., 37.

19. Sandra Feldman, letter to AFT vice presidents, February 18, 2004. Quoted in Julia E. Koppich, "A Tale of Two Approaches: The AFT, the NEA, and NCLB," *Peabody Journal of Education* 80, no. 2 (2005): 148.

20. Sandra Feldman, "AFT on Meeting the Challenges," in an AFT NCLB newsletter, n.d. Quoted in Koppich, "A Tale of Two Approaches," 149. Though the newsletter is undated, it appears to have been a follow-up to the above-cited letter to vice presidents; it was "distributed more widely to AFT leadership," according to Koppich.

21. The Achieve donors' list is at http://achieve.org/contributors.

22. Work group members are listed in a National Governors Association press release, "Common Core State Standards Development Work Group and Feedback Group announced," July 1, 2009, retrieved from http://nga.org.

23. Alliance for Childhood, *Joint Statement of Early Childhood Health and Education Professionals on the Common Core Standards Initiative* (New York: Alliance for Childhood, March 2, 2010), retrieved from http://allianceforchildhood.org.

24. Nancy Carlsson-Paige, Geralyn Bywater McLaughlin, and Joan Wolfsheimer Almon, *Reading Instruction in Kindergarten: Little to Gain and Much to Lose* (New York: Alliance for Childhood, January 2015), retrieved from http://allianceforchildhood.org.

25. Elfrieda H. Hiebert and Heidi Anne E. Mesmer, "Upping the Ante of Text Complexity in the Common Core State Standards: Examining Its Potential Impact on Young Readers," *Educational Researcher* 42, no. 1 (January–February 2013): 44–51.

26. Daniel E. Ferguson, "Martin Luther King Jr. and the Common Core: A Critical Reading of 'Close Reading,'" *Rethinking Schools* 28, no. 2 (winter 2013): 18–21.

27. Diane Ravitch, "The Inside Story of How Bill Gates Bought the Common Core Standards," June 8, 2014, retrieved from http://dianeravitch.net.

28. Chicago Teachers Union, *Arguments Against the Common Core: A Chicago Teachers Union Position Paper* (Chicago: CTU, July 2014), 5; retrieved from http://ctunet.com.

29. Tim Walker, "10 Things You Should Know about the Common Core," *NEA Today*, fall 2013, retrieved from http://nea.org.

30. Ibid., version with reader comments, http://neatoday.org/2013/10/16/10-things-you-should-know-about-the-common-core.

31. CReATE (Chicagoland Researchers and Advocates for Transformative Education), *Chicago School Reform: Myths, Realities, and New Visions*, revised (Chicago: CReATE, 2015); retrieved from http://createchicago.org.

32. International Reading Association and National Council of Teachers of English, *Standards for the English Language Arts* (Urbana, IL: IRA and NCTE, 1996), 3; retrieved from http://ncte.org.

33. See part 6 in Wayne Au and Melissa Bollow Tempel, eds., *Pencils Down: Rethinking High-Stakes Testing and Accountability in Public Schools* (Milwaukee, WI: Rethinking Schools, 2012), 217–83.

34. See the AFT report by Howard Nelson, *Testing More, Teaching Less: What America's Obsession with Student Testing Costs in Money and Lost Instructional Time* (Washington: American Federation of Teachers, 2013), retrieved from http://aft.org.

35. FairTest, *Common Core Assessments:More Tests, But Not Much Better* (Jamaica Plain, MA: FairTest, n.d.), retrieved from http://fairtest.org.

36. Katie Lapham, interview with the author, May 17, 2015.
37. Relevant state legislation is compiled by the Education Commission of the States at http://ecs.org.
38. Weingarten's speech was posted by Valerie Strauss in "Randi Weingarten Calls for 'New Approach to Unionism' and Support for Obama," *Washington Post*, July 27, 2012.
39. New Haven Public Schools, *NHPS Teacher Evaluation and Development Process: Teachers and Administrators Guide* (New Haven, CT: NHPS, August 2010), 9; retrieved from The New Teachers Project at http://tntp.org.
40. David Low, interview with the author, August 6, 2012.
41. David Cicarella, interview with the author, August 10, 2012.
42. Strauss, "Randi Weingarten Calls for 'New Approach.'"
43. New Haven teacher, interview with the author, August 5, 2012.
44. New Haven teacher, interview with the author, August 7, 2012.
45. Jane K. Marshall, letter posted in a blog by Diane Ravitch, "A Retired Teacher Reviews 'Reign of Error,'" December 21, 2013, retrieved from http://dianeravitch.net.
46. Abbe Smith, "New Haven Schools Remove 34 Teachers from Classrooms under New Evaluation System," *New Haven Register*, September 13, 2011.
47. Paul Abowd, "DC Teachers to Vote on Privately Funded Merit Pay Plan," *Labor Notes*, April 9, 2010; Bill Turque, "Celebration Glosses Over Fine Print on Bonuses," *Washington Post*, September 14, 2010; and Bill Turque, "Foundations Reserve Right to Pull Funding if D.C. Schools Chief Rhee Leaves," *Washington Post*, April 28, 2010.
48. George Parker, Michelle Rhee, and Randi Weingarten, "Joint Statement by Washington Teachers' Union President George Parker, DC Public Schools Chancellor Michelle Rhee and American Federation of Teachers President Randi Weingarten on Tentative Agreement Between TWU and DCPS," press release, April 7, 2010, retrieved from http://dcps.dc.gov.
49. Bill Turque, "Rhee Dismisses 241 D.C. Teachers; Union Vows to Contest Firings," *Washington Post*, July 24, 2010.
50. The survey was conducted at a 2011 education summit for WTU members, facilitated by a third-party organization, AmericaSpeaks. Among other survey findings: 71 percent of respondents thought the IMPACT score they received the prior year was "unfair" or "somewhat unfair"; 65 percent found themselves "significantly" or "somewhat" teaching to the test. *Education Transition Summit: Report to Mayor Vincent Gray and the Education Transition Team;* compiled by AmericaSpeaks on behalf of the Washington Teachers Union, January 25, 2011. Report obtained from the Washington Teachers Union.
51. Susan Headden, *Inside IMPACT: D.C.'s Model Teacher Evaluation System* (Washington: Education Sector, 2011), 2, 8; retrieved from http://educationsector.org.
52. District of Columbia Public Schools, "Key Changes to IMPACT for 2012–2013," press release, August 2012, retrieved from the National Council on Teacher Quality at http://nctq.org.
53. Education Trust and The New Teacher Project, "Building a Foundation for Equitable Access," webinar presentation (April 2, 2014), 15; retrieved from http://tntp.org.
54. District of Columbia Public Schools, *IMPACT: The District of Columbia Public Schools Effectiveness Assessment System for School-Based Personnel; Group 1: General Education Teachers with Individual Value-Added Student Achievement Data* (Washington: DCPS, 2014-2015), 61.
55. The IMPACT guidebook states that the "developing" teacher has *three* years to improve. But this actually translates into two years after the teacher receives his or her end-of-year, less-than-effective rating. Ibid., 62.

56. Elizabeth Davis, interview with the author, November 12, 2012.

57. Malvery Smith, interview with the author, October 2, 2012.

58. Nathan Saunders, interview with the author, September 4, 2010.

59. One exception is in New York City in the 1930s and 40s, when a left-wing union leadership joined teacher demands with a strong commitment to the fight for racial equality. See Clarence Taylor, *Reds at the Blackboard: Communism, Civil Rights, and the New York City Teachers Union* (New York: Columbia University Press, 2011).

60. Quoted in Sean Noonan, Stephanie Farmer, and Fran Huckaby, *A Sea of Red: Chicago Teachers Union Members Reflect on How the Social Organizing Model of Unionism Helped Win the Union's 2012 Contract Campaign* (Chicago: Chicago Teachers Union, February 2014), 7; retrieved from http://ctunet.com.

61. Two exemplary studies of social-movement unionism, both focused on Chicago teachers, are Huckaby, *A Sea of Red*; and Alexandra Bradbury et al., *How to Jump-Start Your Union: Lessons from the Chicago Teachers* (Detroit: Labor Notes, 2014). For a multi-sector perspective, the very best source is Jane Slaughter, ed., *A Troublemaker's Handbook 2: How to Fight Back Where You Work—and Win!* (Detroit: Labor Notes, 2005).

62. Noonan et al., *Sea of Red*, 9.

63. Quoted in ibid., 9.

64. Jerald E. Podair, *The Strike That Changed New York: Blacks, Whites, and the Ocean Hill-Brownsville Crisis* (New Haven, CT: Yale University Press, 2002); Steve Golin, *The Newark Teacher Strikes: Hopes on the Line* (New Brunswick, NJ: Rutgers Univesity Press, 2002). See also the fall 2014 issue of *Theory, Research, and Action in Urban Education* (from http://traue.commons.gc.cuny.edu), which is focused on community control and includes much coverage of the 1968–69 crisis in New York City's Ocean Hill-Brownsville neighborhood.

65. The CTU community board members are listed at http://ctunet.com/community.

66. Jackson Potter, interviews with the author, December 18, 2011; and October 28, 2012.

67. A summation of the referendum's provisions is in *The Springfield Teacher* (May 2012), newsletter of the Springfield Education Association, retrieved from http://seateachers.com.

68. Dan Clawson, "No More Backroom Deals: A Draconian Proposal Threatened Massachusetts Teachers. Here's How They Defeated It," *Jacobin* (November 17, 2014): 4, 5.

69. Ibid., 5.

70. Michael Winerip, "Move to Outsource Teacher Licensing Process Draws Protest," *New York Times*, May 6, 2012; Nini Hayes, "Stanford/Pearson Test for New Teachers Draws Fire," *Rethinking Schools* 27, no. 2 (winter 2012–13): 7–8.

71. Jamie Rinaldi, interview with the author, February 5, 2015.

72. Massachusetts Teachers Association, "MTA Position Statement on DESE's Performance-Based Licensure Plan" (Boston: MTA, October 22, 2014), retrieved from http://massteacher.org.

73. Clawson, "No More Backroom Deals," 5.

74. Ibid., 4, 5.

75. Laura Barrett, "MTA Supports RTTT Application: Union Cites Value of Having a Voice in Federal Process," *MTA Today* (June–July 2010): 3; retrieved from http://massteacher.org/mtatoday.

76. Barbara Madeloni, "Fighting for Our Vision of Public Education," *MTA Today* (summer 2014): 4; retrieved from http://massteacher.org/mtatoday.

3. A School Community Says No to Privatization

1. This chapter draws from the author's interviews as follows: Syreeta Epps, May 8, 2012. Shirley Ewing, August 28, 2012. Jolene Galpin, June 5, 2012. Tina Garner, May 8, 2012.

Jessie Hudson, October 27 and November 28, 2011; and May 7, 2012. Paul Jakes, June 11, 2012. Latina King, May 8 and June 9, 2012. Bettye Sherrod, June 2 and 7, 2012. Christel Williams, November 13, 2012.

2. Civic Committee of the Commercial Club of Chicago, *Left Behind: A Report of the Education Committee* (Chicago: Commercial Club of Chicago, July 2003), 3; http://civiccommittee.org/initiatives/education/left_behind.pdf.

3. Ibid., 52.

4. New Schools for Chicago discusses its aim to "expand the pipeline of quality operators" at http://newschoolsnow.org/about-us/next-phase; and its role in recommending charter schools to CPS at http://newschoolsnow.org/investors/our-investment-model.

5. Quoted in Rosalind Rossi, "Civic Leaders Donating $50 Million Want Accountability from Schools," *Chicago Sun-Times*, November 30, 2004.

6. For national perspectives, see Erica Frankenberg, Genevieve Siegel-Hawley, and Jia Wang, *Choice Without Equity: Charter School Segregation and the Need for Civil Rights Standards* (Los Angeles: The Civil Rights Project, January 2010), retrieved from http://civilrightsproject.ucla.edu; and Michael Fabricant and Michelle Fine, *Charter Schools and the Corporate Makeover of Public Education: What's at Stake?* (New York: Teachers College Press, 2012).

7. Carol Caref et al., *The Black and White of Education in Chicago's Public Schools/Class, Charters & Chaos: A Hard Look at Privatization Schemes Masquerading as Education Policy* (Chicago: Chicago Teachers Union, November 30, 2012), 9; retrieved from http://ctunet.com.

8. Ibid., 8.

9. Regarding the unimpressive performance of Chicago charter schools, see Joel Hood and Noreen S. Ahmed-Ullah, "Report Finds Charters Struggling Like Other CPS Schools," *Chicago Tribune*, November 30, 2011. While most Chicago charter schools are officially non-selective and open to all students, the application process winds up favoring high-achieving students and the more challenged students are often pushed out, according to Ben Joravsky, "Stacking the Odds in Favor of Charter Schools," *Chicago Reader*, April 13, 2011.

10. Pauline Lipman, *Making Sense of Renaissance 2010 School Policy in Chicago: Race, Class, and the Cultural Politics of Neoliberal Urban Restructuring* (Chicago: Great Cities Institute, University of Illinois at Chicago, January 2009), retrieved from http://uic.edu. See also Lipman's *The New Political Economy of Urban Education: Neoliberalism, Race, and the Right to the City* (New York: Routledge, 2011).

11. Maya Roney, "America's Next Hot Neighborhoods," *Business Week*, March 6, 2007.

12. Pauline Lipman and Alecia S. Person, *Students as Collateral Damage? A Preliminary Study of Renaissance 2010 School Closings in the Midsouth* (Chicago: Collaborative for Education and Justice in Education, University of Illinois at Chicago, January 2007), 6; http://uic.edu/educ/ceje/articles/midsouth%20initial%20report%201-31-07.pdf.

13. Jitu Brown, Eric (Rico) Gutstein, and Pauline Lipman, "Arne Duncan and the Chicago Success Story: Myth or Reality?" *Rethinking Schools* 23, no. 3 (spring 2009).

14. Quoted in "Derrion Albert's Death May Be Rooted in School Closures," *NBC Chicago*, October 7, 2009.

15. Karen Lewis's remarks to Chicago Board of Education, March 23, 2011, http://ctunet.com/blog?month=march-2011.

16. Rosalind Rossi, "Beidler Backers Fight Talk of Moving Elementary," *Chicago Sun-Times*, April 3, 2011.

17. Ibid.

18. Galpin made her calculations using data she obtained from Chicago Public Schools,

dividing each school's gross square footage by the number of students enrolled at each school. She also did a random sampling of utilization rates at schools that were not being targeted for closure and found that many of the non-targeted schools were utilized at 40 or 50 percent of the national norm, as compared to Beidler's 80 percent. National trends on school space utilization are tracked by *School Planning & Management* magazine. Its survey found that new elementary schools completed in 2012 had a median space per student of 137 square feet; the middle school median was 153 square feet; and the high school median was 172 square feet; Paul Abramson, "School Renovations Led Increase in Spending," in *School Construction Report*, 2013 (Dayton, OH: School Planning & Management, 2013), 6.

19. Figures are from the Chicago Teachers Union, *Twelve Months Later: The Impact of School Closings in Chicago* (Chicago: CTU, 2014), 1; retrieved from http://ctunet.

20. Noreen S. Ahmed-Ullah, "CPS Plans 60 More Charters in 5 Years," *Chicago Tribune*, May 16, 2012.

4. UNITING TO SERVE STUDENTS IN THE FACE OF A HOSTILE PRINCIPAL

1. This chapter draws from the author's interviews as follows: Hector Basave, February 16, 2013. Group interview with Kelvyn Park teachers Elaine Allen, Pat Peterson, Jerry Skinner, April Truhlar, Eric Wagner, and Jamie Yuhas, September 2, 2011. Joint interview with Mireya Dones and Maritza Rios, November 25, 2011. Adourthus McDowell, November 28, 2011. Jerry Skinner, July 29, 2011, and August 15, 2012. Eric Wagner, August 20, 2012. Jamie Yuhas, August 21, 2012. Except where otherwise indicated, all information on conditions and events at Kelvyn Park High School was obtained from the individual interviews with Jerry Skinner and Eric Wagner.

2. Cited by Jerry Skinner in his email communication to Kelvyn Park High School staff, February 15, 2010.

3. The courts have made varied rulings regarding LSC authority, says McDowell, with some favoring CPS's interpretation and others favoring that of community advocates. For more on the LSCs, see Designs for Change, *Chicago's Local School Councils: What the Research Says* (January 2002), retrieved from http://designsforchange.org; and Julie Woestehoff and Monty Neill, *Chicago School Reform: Lessons for the Nation* (January 2007), retrieved from http://fairtest.org.

5. HOW TO FIGHT BACK

1. See Jia Wang, *Choice Without Equity: Charter School Segregation and the Need for Civil Rights Standards* (Los Angeles: The Civil Rights Project, January 2010), retrieved from http://civilrightsproject.ucla.edu; and Michael Fabricant and Michelle Fine, *Charter Schools and the Corporate Makeover of Public Education: What's at Stake?* (New York: Teachers College Press, 2012).

2. See John Marsh, *Class Dismissed: Why We Cannot Teach or Learn Our Way Out of Inequality* (New York: Monthly Review, 2011).

6. CRITICAL LITERACY, DEMOCRATIC SCHOOLS, AND THE WHOLE LANGUAGE MOVEMENT

1. For a detailed discussion of the whole language research base, see Carole Edelsky, Bess Altwerger, and Barbara Flores, *Whole Language: What's the Difference?* (Portsmouth, NH: Heinemann, 1991).

2.   Although the Whole Language Umbrella is still alive and well. See http://ncte.org/wlu.

3.   Bess Altwerger, "Whole Language Teachers: Empowered Professionals," in *Whole Language: Empowerment at the Chalk Face*, ed. Janie Hydrick (New York: Scholastic, 1991), 15–29.

4.   On curriculum development in whole language classrooms, see Carolyn Burke and Kathy Short, *Creating Curriculum: Teachers and Students Creating Communities of Learners* (Portsmouth, NH: Heinemann, 1991).

5.   Debra Goodman, "Growing Up Whole Language," in *Reflections and Connections: Essays in Honor of Kenneth S. Goodman's Influence on Language Education*, ed. Ann M. Marek, Carole Edelsky, and Kenneth S. Goodman (Cresskill, NJ: Hampton Press, 1999), 187–210.

6.   Described in detail in Debra Goodman, "The Whole Language Movement in Detroit: A Teacher's Story—Part Two," in *Whole Language Teaching, Whole Hearted Practice: Looking Back, Looking Forward*, ed. Monica Taylor (New York: Peter Lang, 2007), 45–53.

7.   For a more nuanced discussion, see Bess Altwerger, ed., *Reading for Profit: How the Bottom Line Leaves Kids Behind* (Portsmouth, NH: Heinemann, 2005).

8.   Nancy Carlsson-Paige, Geralyn Bywater McLaughlin, and Joan Wolfsheimer Almon, *Reading Instruction in Kindergarten: Little to Gain and Much to Lose* (New York: Alliance for Childhood, January 2015); retrieved from Defending the Early Years at deyproject.org.

9.   Curt Dudley-Marling and Pat Paugh, "The Rich Get Richer, the Poor Get Direct Instruction," in Altwerger, *Reading for Profit*, 156–71.

10.   Patrick Shannon, *Reading Against Democracy: The Broken Promises of Reading Instruction* (Portsmouth, NH: Heinemann, 2007).

11.   The names in this anecdote are fictitious.

12.   In *Grand Conversations: Literature Groups in Action* (Richmond Hill, Ontario: Scholastic, 1990), Ralph Peterson and Maryann Eeds describe the need for both "extensive reading"—that is, sustained silent reading or "Drop Everything and Read" time—and "intensive reading" of literature discussion and inquiry study. The current focus on "close reading" ignores the need for extended practice and typically focuses on literal text meanings rather than sharing interpretations or critical readings.

13.   Kenneth S. Goodman, *What's Whole in Whole Language?* (Portsmouth, NH: Heinemann, 1986), 8.

14.   A short synthesis of early literacy research of the 1970s and 1980s is Nigel Hall, *The Emergence of Literacy* (Portsmouth, NH: Heinemann, 1987). See also Paulo Freire, *Pedagogy of the Oppressed* (New York: Herder and Herder, 1970); William Labov, *Language in the Inner City: Studies in the Black English Vernacular* (Philadelphia: University of Pennsylvania Press, 1973); Shirley Brice Heath, *Ways with Words: Language, Life, and Work in Communities and Classrooms* (Cambridge, England: Cambridge University Press, 1983); Geneva Smitherman, *Talkin and Testifyin: The Language of Black America* (Detroit: Wayne State University Press, 1986); Luis C. Moll, Cathy Amanti, Deborah Neff, and Norma Gonzalez, "Funds of Knowledge for Teaching: Using a Qualitative Approach to Connect Homes and Classrooms," *Theory into Practice* 31, no. 2 (1992): 132–41; and Kenneth S. Goodman and Yetta M. Goodman, *Making Sense of Learners Making Sense of Written Language: The Selected Works of Kenneth S. Goodman and Yetta M. Goodman* (New York: Routledge, 2013).

15.   Curt Dudley-Marling and Pat Paugh, *A Classroom Teacher's Guide to Struggling Readers* (Portsmouth, NH: Heinemann, 2004), xii. The two reports cited are National Reading Panel, *Report of the National Reading Panel: Teaching Children to Read* (Washington: National Institute of Child Health and Human Development, 2000); and Catherine

E. Snow, M. Susan Burnes, and Peg Griffen, eds., *Preventing Reading Difficulties in Young Children* (Washington, D.C.: National Academies Press,1998).

16. Dudley-Marling and Paugh, "The Rich Get Richer, the Poor Get Direct Instruction," in Altwerger, *Reading for Profit*, 156–71.

17. From a McGraw-Hill reading textbook sales prospectus cited in Shannon, *Reading Against Democracy*, 179.

18. Edelsky et al., *Whole Language: What's the Difference?*, 37.

19. A detailed discussion of the difference between whole language and "skills in context" is in ibid., 34–39.

20. Moll et al., "Funds of Knowledge."

21. Goodman, *What's Whole in Whole Language?*, 40. Goodman's book provides a parent- and teacher-friendly description of whole language theory and practice. A reissued and expanded edition is Ken Goodman, *What's Whole in Whole Language in the 21st Century?* (New York: Garn Press, 2014).

22. An overview—with many examples of teachers, classrooms, and schools working toward critical whole language—is Carole Edelsky, ed., *Making Justice Our Project: Teachers Working Toward Critical Whole Language Practice* (Urbana, IL: National Council of Teachers of English, 1999).

23. Now known as Toby Kahn Loftus.

24. This incinerator is still in the news. See Ryan Felton, "Detroit's Incinerator Has Folks Calling for Action," *Detroit MetroTimes*, July 8, 2014.

25. Freire, *Pedagogy of the Oppressed*. Toby Kahn Loftus, email correspondence with the author, December 19, 2015.

26. Bob Peterson, "Teaching for Social Justice: One Teacher's Journey," in *Rethinking Our Classrooms: Teaching for Equity and Justice*, ed. Linda Christensen, Stan Karp, and Bill Bigelow (Milwaukee, WI: Rethinking Schools, 1994), 30–38.

27. My own history as a whole language teacher from 1978 to 1994, described in "Growing Up Whole Language" (in Marek et al., *Reflections and Connections*, 187–210), parallels the history of whole language. See also my chapter, "The Whole Language Movement in Detroit," in Taylor, *Whole Language Teaching, Whole Hearted Practice*, 45–53.

28. Bess Altwerger and Elizabeth R. Saavedra, foreword to Edelsky, *Making Justice Our Project*, viii.

29. Constance Weaver, "Facts on the Nature of Whole Language Education" (1995); retrieved from the Heinemann website at http://heinemann.com.

30. Carolyn Burke, Rudine Sims-Bishop, Dorothy Menosky, and Dorothy Watson, doctoral students at Wayne State University, were honored in 1995 as "founding mothers of whole language," along with Yetta Goodman and Canadian educators Ethel Buchanan (Manitoba), Norma Michelson (British Columbia), and Margaret Stephenson (Alberta).

31. Carole Edelsky, "A Sorta the Same, Sorta Different Story of 'Ed Reform' Policies," speech at TAWL conference, Tucson, Arizona, 2012.

32. The songs are gathered in Yetta Goodman's "The Culture of the Culturally Deprived," originally published in 1971, and available in Ken Goodman and Yetta Goodman, *Making Sense of Learners*, 243–51.

33. The output from the Wayne State center included a comprehensive volume by Kenneth S. Goodman and E. Brooks Smith, *Language and Thinking in School: A Whole-Language Curriculum*, 3rd ed. (New York: R.C. Owen Publishers, 1987).

34. Jeannette Veatch discusses "Individualized Reading," first developed in the 1940s, in "Individualized Reading: A Personal Memoir," *Language Arts* 63, no. 6 (1986): 586-93. On the language experience approach, see Roach Van Allen, *Language Experiences in Communication* (Boston: Houghton-Mifflin, 1976).

35. Sylvia Ashton-Warner, *Teacher* (New York: Simon & Schuster, 1965). Among Vivian Gussin Paley's many works are *White Teacher* (Cambridge, MA: Harvard University Press, 1989); and *A Child's Work: The Importance of Fantasy Play* (Chicago: University of Chicago Press, 2005).

36. Patrick Shannon, *The Struggle to Continue: Progressive Reading Instruction in the United States* (Portsmouth, NH: Heinemann, 1990).

37. Yetta M. Goodman, Dorothy J. Watson, and Carolyn L. Burke, *Reading Miscue Inventory: From Evaluation to Instruction*, 2nd ed. (Katonah, NY: Richard C. Owen Publishers, 2005).

38. Yetta Goodman and Gretchen Owocki, *Kidwatching: Documenting Children's Literacy Development* (Portsmouth, NH: Heinemann, 2002). Denny Taylor describes ethnographic evaluation projects in *From the Child's Point of View* (Portsmouth, NH: Heinemann, 1993).

39. Mary Jo Regnier, interview with the author, 1994.

40. Altwerger and Saavedra, foreword to Edelsky, *Making Justice Our Project*, viii.

41. Sarah Costello quoted in Caryl Crowell, "Tucson TAWL—Past, Present, and Future," *Talking Points* 18, no 1 (2006); excerpted in "Our History," at http://tucsontawl.org/Tucson_TAWL/Our_History.html.

42. Lorraine Wilson, Australian teacher educator and past WLU board member, email correspondence with the author, 2014.

43. "North Dakota Study Group History and Purpose," retrieved from http://ndsg.org.

44. A group of teachers working with Kathy Short describe their experience in Clay Connor et al., *Teacher Study Groups: Building Community through Dialogue and Reflection* (Urbana, IL: National Council of Teachers of English, 1998). Myna Matlin and Bob Wortman, school principals in Tucson, Arizona, wrote *Leadership in Whole Language: The Principal's Role* (Portland, ME: Stenhouse Publishers, 1995).

45. Examples of publications by teachers are Bobbi Fisher's *Joyful Learning: A Whole Language Kindergarten* (Portsmouth, NH: Heinemann, 1991); and Kathryn F. Whitmore and Caryl G. Crowell, *Inventing a Classroom: Life in a Bilingual, Whole Language Learning Community* (Portland, ME: Stenhouse Publishers, 1994).

46. See Shelley Harwayne, *Going Public: Priorities and Practice at the Manhattan New School* (Portsmouth, NH: Heinemann, 1999). The Borton Primary School is described in Whitmore and Crowell, *Inventing a Classroom*.

47. The practice of offering small grants supporting innovative public school programs was later dropped when public funds were shifted to charter schools, siphoning students outside of the public system—ultimately decimating Detroit Public Schools. Dewey Center history is described in Debra Goodman, "The Whole Language Movement in Detroit."

48. Jerome C. Harste et al., "Practice Makes Practice, or Does It? The Relationship between Theory and Practice in Teacher Education," *International Journal of Educology* 16, no. 2 (2002): 116–91; retrieved from Education Resources Information Center at http://eric.ed.gov.

49. Heidi Mills, email correspondence with the author, April 26, 2015; and Richland School District website at http://richland2.org. The school history is described in Heidi Mills and Amy Donnelly, *From the Ground Up: Creating a Culture of Inquiry* (Portsmouth, NH: Heinemann, 2001).

50. Gloria Norton, "What Does It Take to Ride a Bike?" in *Becoming a Whole Language School: The Fair Oaks Story*, ed. Lois Bridges Bird (Portsmouth, NH: Heinemann, 1989), 114.

51. Typically these schools have had district support as citywide magnet schools, have a strong leadership team, or have an ongoing relationship with a university teacher education program.

52. Edelsky, "A Sorta the Same, Sorta Different Story of 'Ed Reform' Policies."

53. This is similar to today's scramble for Common Core–aligned materials.

54. Ken Goodman, *What's Whole in Whole Language*, 67.

55. This talk was included in a Whole Language Umbrella series of publications, a further example of the reflective work in the whole language community. Kathy Short and Carolyn Burke, "Curriculum as Inquiry," in *Critiquing Whole Language and Classroom Inquiry*, ed. Sibel Boran and Barbara Comber (Urbana, IL: National Council of Teachers of English, 2001), 18–41.

56. Ibid., 230.

57. Carole Edelsky, *With Literacy and Justice for All: Rethinking the Social in Language and Education*, 3rd ed. (Mahwah, NJ: Lawrence Erlbaum, 2006), 231.

58. Criticisms from traditionalists are understandable since whole language presents a direct challenge to deeply held traditional beliefs, such as a belief in one correct answer rather than the whole language belief in multiple interpretations influenced by readers' home discourses and personal histories, as well as a belief in the value of doing exercises on literacy skills rather than in authentic language use. Edelsky, *With Literacy and Justice for All*, 218–19.

59. Sharon L. Nichols and David C. Berliner, *Collateral Damage: How High-Stakes Testing Corrupts American Schools* (Cambridge, MA: Harvard Educational Press, 2007), 4.

60. The Business Roundtable's explicit campaign to "reform the entire system of public education" is documented by Bess Altwerger and Steven Strauss in "The Business Behind Testing," *Language Arts* 79, no. 3 (January 2002): 256–62; quote at 258.

61. Today's corollary aim can be seen in the "college- and career-readiness" touted by the Common Core State Standards and Race to the Top.

62. Edelsky, *With Literacy and Justice for All*, 214.

63. Heath, *Ways with Words*. U.S. achievement scores, literacy, and graduation rates have actually increased dramatically over the twentieth century, documented in Berliner and Biddle, *Manufactured Crisis*.

64. Quoted in Ronald Kessler, *A Matter of Character: Inside the White House of George W. Bush* (New York: Penguin Group, 2004), 92.

65. Gerald Coles reviewed the few comparison studies cited in the NRP report and found that whole language classrooms do as well as phonics classrooms, and are stronger in areas not examined by the report, such as writing proficiency. *Reading the Naked Truth: Literacy, Legislation and Lies* (Portsmouth, NH: Heinemann, 2003), 73–85.

66. Constance Weaver, *Reading Process: Brief Edition of Reading Process and Practice*, 3rd ed. (Portsmouth, NH: Heinemann, 2009), xv, xiv. In addition, Joanne Yatvin, an NRP panel member who provided a dissenting report, describes her experiences in "Babes in the Woods: The Wanderings of the National Reading Panel," *Phi Delta Kappan* 83, no. 5 (2002): 364–69.

67. Weaver, *Reading Process*, xiv.

68. Snow et al., *Preventing Reading Difficulties in Young Children*. The report is discussed in Coles, *Reading the Naked Truth*, 16–17.

69. Coles, *Reading the Naked Truth*, 11.

70. Weaver, *Reading Process*, xvii.

71. Quoted in Kessler, *A Matter of Character*, 103.

72. Carole Edelsky, "Relatively Speaking: McCarthyism and Teacher Resisters," in *Marketing Fear in America's Public Schools: The Real War on Literacy*, ed. Leslie Poynor and Paula Wolfe (Mahwah, NJ: Lawrence Erlbaum Associates, 2005), 11.

73. Coles, *Reading the Naked Truth*, 2.

74. Paul Crowley, Sonoma State University, California, email to author, January 26, 2016.

75. Quoted in Kessler, *A Matter of Character*, 102.

76. Early resistance to the corporate reform agenda include an edited collection by Ken Goodman, Patrick Shannon, and Roger Rapoport, *Saving Our Schools: The Case for Public Education, Saying No to "No Child Left Behind"* (Berkeley, CA: RDR Books, 2004); and Bess Altwerger's edited volume, *Reading for Profit*.

77. Altwerger, *Reading for Profit*.

78. Edelsky, *With Literacy and Justice for All*, 221.

79. Ibid., 220.

80. These critical discussions are documented in David Schaafsma, *Eating on the Street: Teaching Literacy in a Multicultural Society* (Pittsburgh: University of Pittsburgh Press, 1994).

81. Melinda Smith, from paper reflecting on her university education class, 2013. Used with permission.

82. Debra Goodman, "Wings to Read With: A Teacher's Perspective on Basal Readers," *Theory into Practice* 27, no. 4 (1989): 280.

83. Ken Goodman, "The Know-More and the Know-Nothing Movements in Reading: A Personal Response," *Language Arts* 56, no. 6 (September 1979): 657–63.

84. From Save Our Schools' "Guiding Principles" at http://saveourschoolsmarch.org.

85. Edelsky, *With Literacy and Justice for All*, 234.

86. Edelsky, *Making Justice Our Project*.

7. TEACHER SOLIDARITY BEATS SCRIPTED INSTRUCTION

1. This chapter draws from the author's interviews as follows: Libbi Swanson, May 15, 2012. Joint interview with Rodette Doreza and Iliana Panduro, October 21, 2011. Gabriela Spilman, July 26, 2012. Julie Cavanagh, February 23, 2012. Kate Beaudet, November 1 and December 28, 2011; July 23, 2012; and June 20, 2013. Except where otherwise indicated, all information on conditions and events at Soto Street Elementary School was obtained from my interviews with Kate Beaudet.

2. For critical perspectives, see Kenneth S. Goodman et al., *Report Card on Basal Readers* (Katonah, NY: Richard C. Owen Publishers, 1988); Patrick Shannon and Kenneth Goodman, eds., *Basal Readers: A Second Look* (Katona, NY: Richard C. Owen Publishers, 1994); and Nancy L. Jordan, "Basal Readers and Reading as Socialization: What Are Children Learning?" *Language Arts* 82, no. 3 (2005): 204–13.

3. For more on Reading First, see Richard L. Allington, *Big Brother and the National Reading Curriculum: How Ideology Trumped Evidence* (Portsmouth, NH: Heinemann, 2002); and Bess Altwerger, ed., *Reading for Profit: How the Bottom Line Leaves Kids Behind* (Portsmouth, NH: Heinemann, 2005).

4. National Center for Education Evaluation and Regional Assistance, *Reading First Impact Study: Final Report* (Washington: U.S. Department of Education, November 2008).

5. Selling to Schools, "Education Market Research Reveals Trends in the K-5 Reading Market," http://sellingtoschools.com/articles/education-market-research-reveals-trends -k-5-reading-market. The cited survey was conducted by Education Market Research, http://educationmarketresearch.com.

6. Robert Land and Margaret Moustafa, "Scripted Reading Instruction: Help or Hindrance?," in Altwerger, *Reading for Profit*, 67.

7. Duke Helfand, "Reading Taught the Scripted Way," *Los Angeles Times*, July 30, 2000.

8. The Coalition for Educational Justice website is at https://sites.google.com/site/cejinla.

9. Gary E. Bingham and Kendra M. Hall-Kenyon define balanced literacy as a perspective that "seeks to combine, or balance, skill-based and meaning-based instruction," adding

that it is "often conceptualised based on a view of scaffolded instruction, or gradual release of responsibility . . . where teachers provide varying levels of support based on children's needs. . . ." From "Examining Teachers' Beliefs about and Implementation of a Balanced Literacy Framework," *Journal of Research in Reading* 36, no. 1 (2013): 15, 16.

10. Diane Ravitch, *The Death and Life of the Great American School System: How Testing and Choice Are Undermining Education* (New York: Basic Books, 2010), 31–67.

11. On the scripting of balanced literacy in New York City—and teachers' creative resistance to this—see Marshall A. George, "Resisting Mandated Literacy Curricula in Urban Middle Schools," in *Critical Essays on Resistance in Education*, ed. David M. Moss and Terry A. Osborn (New York: Peter Lang, 2010), 105–24. George tells of a new eighth-grade teacher, well trained in balanced literacy at the university, who had innovative plans for teaching adolescent literature (which included the whole class reading the same novel) and for students to learn writing in multiple genres. She was disappointed to discover that her school's approach to balanced literacy forbade such innovations. Whole-class novels were not allowed in the school, and all students were expected to write a formula-driven five-paragraph essay each month during the school year (page 116).

12. Kath Glasswell and Michael Ford, "Let's Start Leveling About Leveling," *Language Arts* 88, no. 3 (2011): 208.

13. According to the RTI Action Network at http://rtinetwork.org.

14. The democratic tradition can be seen in Dixie Goswami and Peter R. Stillman, eds., *Reclaiming the Classroom: Teacher Research as an Agency for Change* (Portsmouth, NH: Boynton/Cook, 1987); and Gary L. Anderson, Kathryn Herr, and Ann Sigrid Nihlen, *Studying Your Own School: An Educator's Guide to Practitioner Action Research*, 2nd ed. (Thousand Oaks, CA: Corwin Press, 2007). Top-down and test-driven models are exemplified in Milbrey W. McLaughlin and Joan E. Talbert, *Building School-Based Teacher Learning Communities: Professional Strategies to Improve Student Achievement* (New York: Teachers College Press, 2006); and Kim Bailey, Chris Jakicic, and Jeanne Spiller, *Collaborating for Success with the Common Core: A Toolkit for Professional Learning Communities at Work* (Bloomington, IN: Solution Tree Press, 2014) . These progressive and regressive expressions in the field are helpfully delineated by Marilyn Cochran-Smith and Susan L. Lytle, *Inquiry as Stance: Practitioner Research for the Next Generation* (New York: Teachers College Press, 2009); and Andy Hargreaves, "Leading Professional Learning Communities: Moral Choices Amid Murky Realities," in *Sustaining Professional Learning Communities*, ed. Alan M. Blankstein, Paul D. Houston, and Robert W. Cole (Thousand Oaks, CA: Corwin Press, 2008), 175–98.

15. Richard L. Allington, *What Really Matters in Response to Intervention: Research-Based Designs* (New York: Pearson, 2008).

16. "Team Read: Teaching for Justice through Reading Workshop," https://centerx.gseis. ucla.edu/partnerships-grants/tiip/showcase/soto-project-portfolio.

17. Brian Cambourne, "Toward an Educationally Relevant Theory of Literacy Learning: Twenty Years of Inquiry," *The Reading Teacher* 49, no. 3 (1995): 182–90.

18. Cathy A. Coulter, "Literacy Instruction, First and Second Language," in *Encyclopedia of Bilingual Education*, vol. 1, ed. Josué M. González (Los Angeles: SAGE, 2008), 533–36.

19. Gloria Ladson-Billings, "The Pedagogy of Poverty: The Big Lies about Poor Children," in *The Big Lies of School Reform: Finding Better Solutions for the Future of Public Education*, ed. Paul C. Gorski and Kristien Zenkov (New York: Routledge, 2014), 7–10.

20. Carole Edelsky, *With Literacy and Justice for All: Rethinking the Social in Language and Education*, 3rd ed. (Mahwah, NJ: Lawrence Erlbaum Associates, 2006), 176–77.

8. A Transformational Curriculum in South L.A.

1. Lisa Delpit, "Lisa Delpit," in *Teaching for Social Justice: A Democracy and Education Reader*, ed. William Ayers, Jean Ann Hunt, and Therese Quinn (New York: New Press, 1998), 51.

2. This chapter draws from the authors' interviews as follows: Kahllid Al-Alim, July 31, 2012. Alex Caputo-Pearl, May 26 and July 28, 2012; and May 22, 2015. Joint interview with Alejandro Dias, Allen Harris, Fabiola Leyva, and Kateryn Salazar, May 23, 2012. Joint interview with Gwendolyn Flynn and Lark Galloway-Gilliam, April 30, 2012. Cathy Garcia, August 20 and 22, 2011; April 22, April 25, June 1, and July 24, 2012. Lewis King, November 2012. Fabiola Leyva, May 23, 2012. Breanna Morrison, May 8, 2012. Jeff Ponferrada, October 10, 2011; April 21, 2012; May 2, 17, and 30, 2012. Susana Rafael, May 24 and October 18, 2012.

3. See Richard R. Valencia, *Dismantling Contemporary Deficit Thinking: Educational Thought and Practice* (New York: Routledge, 2010).

4. Oscar Lewis, "The Culture of Poverty," *Scientific American* 215, no. 4 (October 1966): 23.

5. A. Wade Boykin, foreword to *Schooling Students Placed at Risk: Research, Policy, and Practice in the Education of Poor and Minority Adolescents*, ed. Mavis G. Sanders (New York: Routledge, 2000), xii.

6. See John Kretzmann and John P. McKnight, "Assets-Based Community Development," *National Civic Review* 85, no. 4 (1996): 25.

7. Deborah Meier, *The Power of Their Ideas: Lessons for America from a Small School in Harlem* (Boston: Beacon Press, 1995), Kindle Edition, chap. 8.

8. LeAlan Jones and Lloyd Newman, *Our America: Life and Death on the South Side of Chicago* (New York: Washington Square Press, 1997).

9. Meier, *Power of Their Ideas*, chap. 3; Arthur Costa and Bena Kallick, *Learning and Leading with Habits of Mind: 16 Essential Characteristics for Success* (Alexandria, VA: Association for Supervision and Curriculum Development, 2008).

10. This unit description is adapted from a workshop that Cathy Garcia presented at a "Social Justice Schools Conference" held at the UCLA Community School in Los Angeles on February 10, 2012.

11. Reflecting a Republican perspective were "Education Means a More Competitive America," in *2008 Republican Platform*, 43–46, retrieved from http://gop.com; Allison Sherry, "The 2012 Republican Candidates (So Far)," *Education Next* (Fall 2011), and "House GOP Spending Cuts: The List," *Washington Wire* / *Wall Street Journal*, February 9, 2011. From a "progressive caucus Democratic" perspective were "A Broader, Bolder Approach to Education" (Washington: Broader, Bolder Approach to Education, n.d.), retrieved from http://boldapproach.org.; California Budget Project, "A Decade of Disinvestment: California Education Spending Nears the Bottom," October 2011 (Sacramento, CA: California Budget Project), retrieved from http://cbp.org; and an excerpt from Linda Darling-Hammond, *The Flat World and Education: How America's Commitment to Equity Will Determine Our Future* (New York: Teachers College Press, 2010), 192–93.

12. The full rubric appears in *Reading for Understanding: How Reading Apprenticeship Improves Disciplinary Learning in Secondary and College Classrooms* (San Francisco: Jossey-Bass, 2012), 328–30. The rubric can also be accessed at the WestEd website at http://wested.org.

13. Testing data is based on California's Academic Performance Index Report, "School Report—API Growth and Targets Met, 2012 Growth," at http://api.cde.ca.gov.

14. Visiting Committee of the Western Association of Schools and Colleges, Letter to Los

Angeles Unified School District, March 27, 2012, excerpted in Alex Caputo-Pearl, email to "Ed-LA" listserv, December 2, 2012.

15. John Deasy, letter to Crenshaw High School staff, October 24, 2012; posted in Dana Goldstein, "In Los Angeles, a Promising and Progressive School Reform Plan Is Under Threat," November 12, 2012, at http://danagoldstein.net.

16. Visiting Committee, letter to LAUSD, March 2012.

17. See Kenneth Saltman, "The Rise of Venture Philanthropy and the Ongoing Neoliberal Assault on Public Education: The Case of the Eli and Edythe Broad Foundation," *Workplace* 16 (2009): 53–72; and Julian Vasquez Heilig, "Cloaking Inequity: The Broad Foundation and Broadies; Kings of "Disruptive" and "Unreasonable" Trickle-Down Reform," October 4, 2013, retrieved from the National Education Policy Center at http://nepc.colorado.edu.

18. Quoted in *Crenshaw*, a documentary film produced by Lena Jackson; website at http://crenshawfilm.com.

19. Jeannie Oakes, email to John Deasy and others, circa December 1, 2012; enclosed in Alex Caputo-Pearl, email to "Ed-LA" listserv, December 2, 2012.

20. Dalina Castellanos, "Most Crenshaw High Teachers Being Displaced in LAUSD Reorganization," *Los Angeles Times*, May 31, 2013.

21. An example is Manual Arts High School. See United Teachers Los Angeles, "Fighting the Manual Arts Reconstitution," 2012, retrieved from http://utla.net.

22. The coalition's website is http://youth4justice.org.

23. Jackson, *Crenshaw.*

24. Howard Blume, "Alex Caputo-Pearl Wins Runoff to Lead L.A. Teachers Union," *Los Angeles Times*, April 29, 2014.

25. United Teachers Los Angeles, "Contract Summary: We Won Round One in the Fight for the Schools LA Students Deserve," April 2015, retrieved from http://utla.net.

26. Annie Gilbertson, "The LA School iPad Scandal: What You Need to Know," National Public Radio/KPPC 89.3, August 27, 2014; retrieved from http://npr.org.

27. Abby Sewell, "LAUSD's Student Information System Becomes a Technological Disaster," *Los Angeles Times*, October 11, 2014.

28. Blume, "Alex Caputo-Pearl Wins Runoff."

AFTERWORD: WHERE DO WE GO FROM HERE?

1. Lewis F. Powell, "Attack on American Free Enterprise System," August 23, 1971, www.law.wlu.edu/powellarchives/page.asp?pageid=1251.

2. Denisha Jones, "5 Myths about Standardized Testing and the Opt Out Movement," *Empower*, June 3, 2015; retrieved from http://empowermagazine.com.

3. In fact, Stephen Krashen and others believe that corporate reformers are preparing a general shift away from year-end testing and toward daily testing integrated with instruction via "competency-based education." See Stephen Krashen, "The Testing Industrial Complex Is Not Giving Up Easily," January 14, 2016; and by the same author, "Pearson: Competency-Based Education Will Replace Standardized Testing," March 25, 2016; both available at Krashen's blog, http://skrashen.blogspot.com.

4. For fuller discussion, see Howard Ryan, "Beyond Opt Out: A Broader Challenge to Corporate School Reform," *Monthly Review*, June 2016; as well as the March 2016 issue of *Monthly Review*, which is focused on the opt-out movement.

5. See Rachel Cloues, "El Corazón de la Escuela: The Importance of Bilingual School Libraries/The Heart of the School," *Rethinking Schools* 30, no. 3 (spring 2016): 32–35.

Index